GUNNING FOR GREATNESS

MESUT ÖZIL

GUNNING FOR GREATNESS

My Life

with Kai Psotta

translated from the German by Jamie Bulloch

HODDER &
STOUGHTON

First published in Great Britain in 2017 by Hodder & Stoughton
An Hachette UK company

2

Copyright © Mesut Özil 2017

A CIP catalogue record for this title is available from the British Library

Hardback ISBN: 978 1 473 64992 7
Trade Paperback ISBN: 978 1 473 64993 4
Ebook ISBN: 978 1 473 64994 1

Typeset in Minion Pro by Hewer Text UK Ltd, Edinburgh
Printed and bound by Clays Ltd, St Ives plc

Hodder & Stoughton policy is to use papers that are natural, renewable
and recyclable products and made from wood grown in sustainable
forests. The logging and manufacturing processes are expected to
conform to the environmental regulations of the country of origin.

Hodder & Stoughton Ltd
Carmelite House
50 Victoria Embankment
London EC4Y 0DZ

www.hodder.co.uk

For my parents, without whom I wouldn't be the person I am today. Without whom I wouldn't be where I am today. Without whom I'd look at the world through different eyes.

For my parents, who always encouraged me to go my own way. I love you.

I'm a big fan of Mesut Özil and have great respect for him in every way. He's an absolute pillar of our national side and he's played in most of the games under me as manager. He's someone I can always rely on. With his style of play, Mesut's always creating special moments on the pitch. And in football these are often the key to winning games. Mesut is also very adaptable and has a high level of footballing intelligence. This is what makes him so valuable for me as a coach, because I can use him flexibly in different positions. He is an outstanding team player and we're all delighted to have such an exceptional sportsman in our ranks.

Joachim Löw

CONTENTS

FOREWORD

I'm always on the lookout for young players. And I found a wonderful one in Mesut at Bremen. An ambitious boy with a feeling for magic passes, a flair for dribbling, a player who could assist goals and score them himself.

But was he ready for a top team? Physically, not yet. Mentally, perhaps. Technically, certainly! In my head I put him on my golden list.

When I moved to Madrid I realised that I was missing someone capable of making the magic pass. Someone who could launch our attacks with brilliance. Then Mesut came to mind again.

When he proved at the 2010 World Cup that he was able to cope with high levels of pressure I decided to sign him. The transfer went through and a wonderful relationship was born. Özil behind Ronaldo and Di María, with Benzema or Higuaín.

I have many things to be pleased about, including those titles and records we achieved with Mesut. But what has particularly lingered in my memory are all those moments of exceptional footballing quality. The beauty of his passes and traps, as well as his goals.

The crowds in the special arena of the Bernabéu adored Mesut Özil. Large numbers of teammates have enjoyed playing alongside him. Even his opponents, I believe, have occasionally been astounded by the beauty of his dribbling.

Have I been able to give him anything as a coach? I do hope so. Although players like Mesut are not made by managers. They are born.

What else should I say about this boy? I miss him a lot. He's my friend. He's a star who never forgets where he came from, and never forgets the fun you get from the game.

Not only is he a world champion, he's a champion in life too, with all the challenges that brings – challenges he overcomes. I'm proud to have been part of his story.

José Mourinho

PROLOGUE

THE MOST IMPORTANT BOLLOCKING OF MY LIFE

If he says another word I'm going to explode. Just one more word. What does the guy want from me, anyway? Why's he picking on me? That's not normal. It's madness. Huh, what do *I* know what it is? Whatever, it's really unfair.

It's half-time and I'm sitting in the dressing room at Real Madrid. My club. The seat next to me is free. It's where Karim Benzema sits, but he's warming up as he's going on for the second half. Sami Khedira is absent-mindedly fiddling with his boots. Cristiano Ronaldo is staring into space. And José Mourinho, our manager, is ranting. And ranting. And ranting. Especially at me. In fact, his entire harangue up till now has been just about me.

But I ran my socks off. I played really well. Honestly. I'd admit it if I hadn't. We were leading 3–1 against Deportivo La Coruña. Our opponents took the lead after 16 minutes, but we turned the game around. Within 21 minutes Cristiano Ronaldo had scored twice and then Ángel Di María added a third.

The two of them are playing on the wing, with Gonzalo Higuaín up front. Behind me Khedira and Luka Modrić are in defensive midfield, keeping my back free. Everything's fine. But instead of praising us, me included, I'm getting another roasting. Mourinho's had it in for me over the past few weeks too. Against Rayo Vallecano he let me stew on the bench. In our defeat against Sevilla he took me off at half-time. Admittedly, I could understand his tactics that day. We were already behind after a Piotr Trochowski goal in the first few minutes and didn't exactly cover ourselves with glory.

But now? All of us had shown character. I was in control of my game. The passes were getting through.

OK, I admit, in the last few minutes before the half-time whistle I slacked off a little. A tiny bit. That's true. There I can't take issue with the coach who's criticising my commitment. Instead of going at full pelt, once or twice I just trotted as I ran backwards. I was only on it about 80 or 90 per cent. But I wasn't playing badly. Is it really a good reason to snap at me like that in front of the whole team?

I exchange a furtive glance with Sergio Ramos. My friend. I really like the guy. Then I lose myself in my thoughts again while Mourinho's dressing-room thunder continues.

I don't much like dressing rooms. No matter where they are. Whether they're old and revered or ultra-modern. Whether they're in the stadium or at the training ground. I know the allure of team dressing rooms for football fans around the world; they act like a magnet. Everyone wants a glimpse inside their club's shrine. Many are even prepared to spend good money to see

Cristiano Ronaldo's or Lionel Messi's locker on a tour of the stadium.

But there's nothing mythical about changing rooms for me. They don't radiate any magic. They're not special. Dressing rooms are control centres. They're like the towers at airports, with managers acting like air traffic controllers directing the flow of flights. But they're not sacred places. I find the changing room before the match or at half-time more like a cage. I want to get out of there. As fast as possible. Like a tiger longing for its freedom. But time passes more slowly in the dressing room. The quarter of an hour until the start of the second half always seems much longer to me. Because I'm desperate to get back out onto the pitch to continue the game.

The changing room is just for preparation. The pitch, the turf is my stage. It electrifies me. It's where I belong. For me it's liberating to step out onto the pitch. In your private life you can sometimes have problems, arguments, discussions, disagreements. But there aren't any problems for me on the football field. Those 90 minutes – sometimes more if there's extra time –signify peace for me. Pure pleasure. The grass doesn't even have to be perfectly cut. I don't need accurately marked-out chalk lines. I don't even have to be wearing the perfect boots to feel content. I just need a ball to kick around. It's the football field that makes me happy, not the dressing room, that cramped space, sometimes 60 square metres, occasionally 80. I want to get out of that cage. Especially now during this humiliation.

Mourinho is standing in the middle of the dressing room. He's talking and talking and talking. In fact, he's more like shouting: Mesut here, Mesut there, Mesut this. Mesut that.

I try to switch off. Allow the criticism to bounce off me. Because I can feel the anger beginning to bubble up inside.

'You think two passes are enough,' Mourinho screams. 'You're too refined to go in for the tackle. You think you're so good that fifty per cent is enough.'

He pauses. Stares at me with his dark brown eyes. I stare back. We are like two boxers eyeballing each other before the first round.

He's not showing any emotion, just waiting for my reaction. How I loathe him at this moment! Although in truth I love José Mourinho.

He alone is the reason why I went to Real Madrid from Werder Bremen in 2010. I didn't choose the club, I chose him. I chose the man, José Mourinho. I wanted to play for him and no one else.

I'd harboured this strong desire since 2008. Back then, at the beginning of October, I'd played for Werder Bremen against Inter Milan in the Giuseppe Meazza stadium. In goal for the Italians was Júlio César. The attack was Adriano, Zlatan Ibrahimović and Mario Balotelli. What names. What a team. Put together with the tactical brilliance of none other than José Mourinho. In the very first minute Adriano found himself in mid-air in our box and tried a sideways scissor-kick, which he fired just a few centimetres above Tim Wiese's goal. Soon afterwards Ibrahimović just missed too when he hit the side netting. After 14 minutes we were one down from a goal by Maicon.

Inter were strong. Doing everything right in this phase. During stoppages I'd occasionally look over at Mourinho, watching how he directed his team. The passion with which he motivated his side from the touchline. And how positive he always remained towards his players. It fascinated me.

In the sixty-second minute I broke through on the left wing, made a pretty perfect cross to Claudio Pizarro in the centre, who equalised. 1–1. Once more I hazarded a glance over at Mourinho, who seemed fairly impressed, or at least that's what I imagined. After the game he shook my hand and congratulated me with a firm slap on the shoulder. Now he had me. That night I told my then agent, Reza Fazeli, 'At some point I'm going to play for José Mourinho.'

What did I like about Mourinho so much? The way he spoke, the way he moved, his elegant dress sense. He always looked controlled and supremely confident. Back then it was a charisma I'd encountered in only a few managers.

Two years later, after the 2010 World Cup in South Africa, he actually wanted me in his team. Mourinho had just won the Champions League with Inter Milan, after which his move to Real Madrid was made public.

At the time there were five potential clubs in the mix. Arsenal had already shown their interest, as had Manchester United, Bayern Munich, Barcelona and Real Madrid.

My agent, Reza, met Bayern Munich. The bosses told him what their plans were for me, how they wanted to use me. He then had the same conversation with the other clubs. But in 2010 Bayern was quite a way behind Real Madrid and Barcelona. Under Louis van Gaal they'd just lost the Champions League final in Madrid against Mourinho's Inter. Viewed objectively, as well as from a global perspective, the two Spanish clubs were bigger, brighter, better. So for me these were the only two possibilities.

Not long after that I was enjoying a few days' holiday in a villa on Mallorca with my cousin Serdar, my brother Mutlu and some good friends, including Baris and Ramazan, when Reza came and said that José Mourinho was going to call us.

I still recall my head spinning when he told me about the impending telephone call. This wasn't any old conversation; it was *the* conversation.

I'm not someone who likes talking much, who enjoys being the centre of attention and having people hang on his every word, spellbound. And, more importantly, I couldn't speak Portuguese, Italian or fluent English. So I had no chance of speaking to Mourinho directly. Yet there were so many questions I wanted to ask him. The idea of him phoning today made me quite dizzy. I was as nervous as before my first call to a girl I'd fallen for as a boy.

My agent and I retired to a room at the back of the villa. Then the phone rang. Mourinho was calling Reza's mobile on a with-held number. When he said 'Hello' and then his name, I was unable to utter a sound at first. My heart was beating faster than after 20 interval runs in pre-season training.

Having put his mobile on the table in front of us and switched to speaker so I was able to hear every word, Reza began his discussion with Mourinho. I listened to the sound of Mourinho's voice. and tried to understand what he was saying, picking up words here and there without knowing what they really meant. From time to time Reza would interrupt the conversation to summarise and translate what they'd been discussing.

This telephone conversation drove me mad. Sometimes the two of them would say ten sentences at a time without any translation or I would hear both of them laugh. I kept nudging Reza, insisting he tell me what it was all about, but he just asked me to be patient.

After three-quarters of an hour the conversation was over. I prowled around the room in excitement. 'He really wants me. Did you hear? Mourhino wants me in his team!'

A few days later we were climbing aboard a private jet that Real Madrid had laid on for us. I felt like a Hollywood star. Until then I didn't know it was possible to travel in such luxury – I hadn't even seen a private jet from a distance. And now I was checking in at a separate terminal in Mallorca. Without any queues. Without having to wait to hand over my luggage. Until this August day in 2010 that world had been closed to me.

In Madrid there was a chauffeur waiting for us, who drove us in a limousine to the house of Jorge Valdano, who was then Real's director of football. A perfect gentleman, who'd already been involved in the signings of Zinédine Zidane, my absolute idol, Cristiano Ronaldo and David Beckham for Los Blancos. His shirt was the whitest I'd ever seen. His tie sat accurately in the middle. I barely remember anything more as my mind was focused on José Mourinho, who I was about to meet in person for the first time. And then he was there: the man who'd taken Porto to the championship and the Champions League. The man under whom Chelsea had won the Premier League and FA Cup. The man who, with Inter Milan, had cleaned up every national and international honour going.

As soon as he entered the room I immediately caught sight of the Real Madrid logo on the tracksuit that Mourinho seemed to be wearing with great pride. That golden crown. Those strong colours. Images started flashing in my mind. I dreamed of entering the Bernabéu, Real's stadium. These pictures were so overwhelming that I didn't take in what Mourinho was saying in the first minute or so.

But then reality caught up with me. I wrenched myself from my dreams, from that unreal world. Perhaps this legendary team was still too big for me? From Werder Bremen to Real Madrid? From a good Bundesliga side to the greatest club in the world? Who was I, anyway? In comparison to the Real stars, a nobody. A nobody on the great international footballing stage.

I'm neither naïve nor deluded. And, of course, I confront the issue of failure too. It would be reckless not to. But when you're a young player it's not enough to show you can play a good game. Because as soon as the whistle goes, what you've done in the past means nothing any more. These days ten good games are very quickly forgotten. As a footballer you don't have any credit – one or two bad games and you're out. Then you start back at square one. Would I actually get a real opportunity at Real Madrid? This question refused to stop plaguing me.

'Yes, that's what I'll give you,' Mourinho said. 'A very real opportunity! Train hard. Then play. Show me you want it and I'll have you in my team. If you want to get better, I'll make you better. Real Madrid isn't too big a move for you. Real Madrid is the only right move. Trust me. I'll turn you into a regular player. And then all the doors will be open to you. You'll be able to show the world what you're capable of. And, believe me, that's a huge amount.'

Mourinho swept all my doubts away. He gave me a good feeling, exactly what I needed to summon the courage for such a change.

After our discussion we all went to the Estadio Santiago Bernabéu, and Valdano took me through the sacred halls of Los Blancos. Past all the trophies that Real had won during its long history. Shining cups polished to a mirror finish; I could see my reflection in them. A magical sight. So alluring. With a clear message: welcome to a victorious club! A club of champions. Guaranteed trophy-winners.

From the corner of my eye I could see the Real bosses watching me. I'd have liked to have played cooler, looked more laid-back as I walked past the plates, cups and glass sculptures, but I couldn't disguise my enthusiasm. The trophies were glittering and I was beaming.

When I visited Barcelona shortly afterwards, all that was missing. No tour through the Camp Nou, the Catalans' stadium. No display of their victories, which had given me goose bumps in Madrid. Unlike Real Madrid, Barcelona had no emotional impact on me. They didn't show me their stadium. I wasn't taken to the training ground. The entire visit was less cordial, although I was inspired by their style of play.

But most disappointing of all was the fact that the manager of Real's great Spanish rival didn't take the time to meet me personally.

Even before I actually went to Barcelona I was convinced that was where I'd be transferring to. Or at least that was my preference.

At the time no team in the world played better football. It was a real pleasure to watch the magic of their combination play. They'd pass the ball amongst themselves 20 or 30 times, with the lightness and precision of a well-rehearsed piece of choreography.

But I was puzzled by the absence of Pep Guardiola. When Reza and I flew back from Barcelona I kept asking the question, 'Why wasn't the manager there?' His answer was always the same: 'He's on holiday.' Guardiola didn't ring me over the next few days either. Not even a text message. He gave no signal that he wanted me. And so my enthusiasm for Barcelona steadily declined.

After I'd been to see both major clubs I sat back down with my agent. 'Mesut,' he said, 'these are your options. These are the five doors you can go through.' Then we wrote a list of pros and cons. Classic, just like at school.

For example, on the pro-Barça side, it said 'great football'. Or: 'teammates: Xavi, Iniesta, Messi.' All in all I must have written down ten points in favour of the Catalans. But the single point that I jotted down on the con side was enough to eliminate Barça as a potential future club for me. 'Pep Guardiola – does he even want me? Am I his man?' My scepticism prevailed.

Ultimately I didn't want to go to Barcelona because of Guardiola's behaviour. But also because Mourinho was fighting so hard to get me. Was so convincing. So warm. So keen. He was the complete opposite of the Barcelona coach. So I plumped for José Mourinho and Real Madrid.

For the man who at this very moment is tearing strips off me. Ten minutes of the half-time break are over. And Mourinho still isn't finished with his bollocking. I've had enough now.

'What do you actually want from me?' I snap back at him. Then, more softly, I say to Ramos, 'He's making me mad. He ought to shut his trap. He's never content.'

'I want you to play as well as you can,' Mourinho yells. 'I want you to go into tackles like a man. Do you know what it looks like when you tackle? No? Let me show you.'

Mourinho stands on tiptoes, thrusts his arms down by his sides, purses his lips and minces around the dressing room. 'That's how you tackle. Ooh, I mustn't get hurt. And absolutely mustn't get dirty,' he shouts while repeating his Özil tackle parody.

He gets more and more fixated. His heart rate is probably 180. Mine's 200 for sure. Then I've really had enough. I can't hold back any longer. My southern temperament is overwhelming me. 'If you're so great, why don't you get out there and play yourself?' I scream now, ripping off my jersey and hurling it at his feet. 'Here. Put it on. Off you go.'

Mourinho just laughs spitefully. 'Oh, are you giving up now?' he asks. 'What a coward,' he says harshly, moving to within just a few centimetres of me. 'What do you want? To crawl under a nice, warm shower? Shampoo your hair? Be on your own? Or do you want to show your teammates, the fans out there and me what you're capable of?'

Now Mourinho's talking very calmly. He's no longer hot-tempered and loud, but controlled, which makes me even madder. How can he compose himself while I'm on the verge of losing it? I'm so pissed off. I'd love to chuck my boots at his head. I want him to stop. To leave me in peace finally.

'Do you know what, Mesut?' Mourinho says, louder now so

that everyone can hear. 'Cry if you like! Sob away! You're such a baby. Go and take a shower. We don't need you.'

Slowly I get up, slip out of my boots, grab my towel and walk silently past the manager to the showers, without dignifying him with so much as a glance. Instead he lobs one final provocation in my direction. 'You're not Zinédine Zidane, you know. No! Never! You're not even in the same league!'

I feel my throat constricting. Those last words of his are like a stab to the heart. Mourinho knows exactly what he's saying. He knows how much I admire that player. He knows the Frenchman is the only footballer I truly look up to.

'You're not Zidane!' Mourinho's words resound in my head for long afterwards. I'm now on my own in the dressing room. The team is back on the pitch. Kaká has been brought on for me. I don't find this out till later, but Sergio Ramos has nabbed my jersey and put it on underneath his. The black digits of my number 10 shimmer beneath his own shirt.

Pepe and Ronaldo both score in the second half to make it 5–1 against Deportivo, while I stand in the shower, lost in thought. I've never been bollocked like that by a coach before. I've never been so shaken in my conviction about what's right and wrong. What has happened here? Why did Mourinho, this great manager, make me look such a fool? What was he trying to tell me?

That evening, on 30 September 2012, just before 9 p.m., I started posing myself major questions like I'd never done before. The argument was on my mind for weeks. Who was I? And where did I want to go? To answer these questions I began to look back on my life.

1
MY EMBARRASSING HOME
WHAT FAMILY TIES CAN ACHIEVE

I'm standing on the top step of the staircase that leads down into the cellar, staring into the darkness. Ever since I can remember, the light switch above the banister has been broken. Like so much in this building on Bornstrasse in the Bulmke-Hüllen district of Gelsenkirchen – my home.

For example, the front door is so warped that we children, at least, have to launch our whole bodyweight against the thing to open it. Each time the metal strip at the bottom scrapes the floor, which is now full of scratches. The grey metal letterboxes are battered.

We don't even have a proper house number outside. Someone probably nicked the numbers at some point. Or, after decades of being exposed to the wind and rain, they just fell off and nobody bothered to put them up again. At any rate someone has sprayed 30 – our house number – in green on the white façade.

I want to go down into the cellar to get my bike. But I don't dare do it on my own. None of us children dares enter this spooky place alone. The stench is so bad you need to hold your breath, then go down and back up as quickly as you can. Most of all it smells of urine, although I don't know if some of our neighbours just pee down there or if the pong comes from the rats that live in their dozens in the cellar.

Yes, large, revolting rats have taken over the cellar and they're increasing in number by the year. The older children have told us of neighbours who've been badly injured by the rats. They've drummed it into us that the rodents will attack you and can give you nasty bites if you invade their territory.

But we can't leave our bicycles outside the house. They'd be stolen straight away. And my bike is like gold to me. I don't have many valuable things. My parents had to work very hard and save up for ages to buy the bike. So there's nothing for it but to charge into the scary cellar with the scary rats each time. Even when there's two of us we don't have the nerve to go down the steep, worn concrete steps. Only when my elder brother, Mutlu, accompanies us do we dare enter that cellar. But mostly it's five children going down there together, shouting at the tops of our voices and stamping our feet to frighten the rodents.

I live with my family on the fourth floor of the house, right at the top. It's a small flat. My sisters Nese and Dugyu share a bedroom. I sleep with my brother Mutlu in another. He's got a bed, but I just have a mattress that we move in the mornings so we've got a bit more room to play. There's no privacy here.

But in fact I like our flat. In spite of the scary cellar. My parents have tried to make it look as nice as possible.

When I later play for Rot-Weiss Essen, however, and there's a shuttle service that picks us kids up from the surrounding area, I feel ashamed of my home. Some of the other children live in unbelievably nice places; they have smart detached houses with their own garden. I'm so embarrassed by where I live that I give the club's shuttle service a different house number. Instead of being picked up from Bornstrasse 30, I walk a few metres down the road and stand on the opposite side of the street, in front of a building that at least doesn't have any broken windows.

But there's no way we could ever get a larger flat, where each child would have their own room and in a house that's not so run-down.

My mum's already working like mad. She's a cleaner in a school and does double shifts. The first is from 7 a.m. to 4 p.m., the second from 7 p.m. to 10 p.m. She's breaking her back for us children. Although I never hear her complain, I can see how exhausted she is. Sometimes, when she thinks no one is looking, she holds her overworked back, arches it and has a good stretch.

She's sacrificing herself for us. She cleans and cleans and cleans. Her life revolves around providing for her family and she doesn't seem to care that she's neglecting her own life in the process. Mum has no time for hobbies. And because she always has to work she's got no time for us either. When I get home from school there's no cooked lunch waiting on the table for me. I don't have a mum who opens the door with a smile, strokes my hair and asks me how my day was. She isn't there when I've got questions about my homework either.

My grandparents took my mother out of school after the ninth year. After that she had to work to earn money for the family. Neither my grandparents nor parents could afford the luxury of a good education, and we children suffered from the shortage of money too. That's why I didn't go to kindergarten. My parents simply couldn't afford a place for me. Just as, later on, they couldn't hire a private tutor for me or my siblings.

When I came home from school I was responsible for looking after myself. Nobody made sure I was doing my homework and there weren't any bedtime stories either. My father had to struggle for every cent too. To begin with he worked in a leather factory. Then he ran a tea-room for a while, and later a kiosk. After that he opened a billiard hall before going to work at the Opel factory. Time and again he reinvented himself to give his family a good life. He was unemployed several times between jobs, but he always fought to get back into working life.

A total of ten families lived in our house. Nine of them came from abroad. In the whole of Bornstrasse there were practically no Germans. We foreigners – that's how I saw myself as a child – lived pretty much amongst ourselves. It wasn't so much a case of us foreigners living together with the Germans as living separate lives.

Until I was four I spoke nothing but Turkish. At home we always spoke it anyway. But even outside our flat I didn't have any contact with the German language. Because I didn't go to kindergarten I was never in a position where I had to learn it.

So for me the cellar was called 'bodrum'. It wasn't dark, but 'karanlık'. And it filled me with 'korku' rather than fear. Especially because of the 'sıçan', the rats. Instead of 'Good morning' I'd say 'Günaydın' when I came into the kitchen in the mornings. The Lebanese kids we played football with on the rec integrated with

4

us Turks – we were in the majority – and learned our language too.

Before going to school I spent a year in pre-school, which is supposed to facilitate the transition from kindergarten to primary school. But first and foremost it helps those children who are not ready for school proper.

Ninety-nine per cent of the pupils there were foreigners. And although we were taught in German in the classroom, nobody of course spoke it at break time in the playground or on the way home. Which means I almost never had to speak German. Except when the teacher asked me to. I learned the language of my country of birth at a snail's pace. The four hours of German I had during a school day were counterbalanced by three times as many in Turkish.

Besides, this German sounded so funny, so coarse, so harsh. The inflection and intonation were very different from Turkish. I was also confused by the fact that certain letters were pronounced differently. For example, in Turkish the 'Z' is pronounced like an 'S'.

My grammar was appalling; in fact I'd go as far as to say that it was a disaster. For a long time I wrote my compositions without any punctuation. When my work came back corrected I always felt frustrated – red circles everywhere, so many words under-lined and endless marks in the margin referring to my mistakes. The same with dictation. It took me ages to work out what articles were. Only much later did I come to know whether the German word for dog was masculine, feminine or neuter.

Having to pick up a book and read out loud to the class was pure torture. I found books really hard going. These days I think that's such a shame. For now I know how essential education is. I've always impressed on my little sister Dugyu how important it is that she sits her school-leaving exams – the first member of our family to do so. And not only that. I've told her repeatedly, 'These days just doing your school exams isn't enough. You've got to be one of the best in your class. You have to study. You have to throw yourself into it.'

I sincerely hope that Dugyu will go on to college one day and of course I'll pay for her studies. That's why I've asked my current agent, Dr Erkut Sögüt, who represents me alongside my brother Mutlu, to talk to her seriously too and tell her how important it is to study. Explain how much fun student life can be. I can't rave about it to her myself. How can I appear as a credible advocate of university when I've never even seen the inside of a lecture theatre? But Erkut can. He worked his way up from a very modest background, studied law and is now a renowned lawyer. If he tries to persuade Dugyu it will have far more weight than if I just blather on.

I also regret now that my parents didn't speak German to us when we were little. I'm not criticising them for their decision to speak Turkish at home, because there was nothing malicious behind it. They weren't trying to disadvantage us. After all, Turkish has always been the language they've felt comfortable in. The one they use to chat to friends and neighbours. The one they can best express themselves in. But most of all Turkish was the language of their parents. They themselves grew up with Turkish.

Both of my grandfathers came to Germany in the mid-1960s. They were miners in Zonguldak, a town on the Turkish Black Sea coast. They worked for little money, and only when they were needed. Back then employment was hard to come by, especially in the more rural areas. When Germany sent out an appeal for guest workers and concluded an agreement with Turkey, by which several hundred thousand Turks were authorised to come over, my grandfathers too were enticed by the promise of a better life. Almanya. Land of work. Land of riches. Land of improvement. The Germans wanted my grandfathers and so they embarked on the journey into the unknown, leaving their wives and children behind, which was terribly hard for them. Work, save money, come back rich – that was the plan. They were even given a sort of instruction manual so that they wouldn't make mistakes in this country that was so alien to them. *Işçi olarak Almanya' ya nasıl gidilir?* (*How to be a worker in Germany*) was the title of the brochure published by the Turkish authorities. It said, 'Work hard and learn quickly anything you don't know. Strictly observe the regulations of your workplace. Arrive punctually. Never take days off sick unless it is absolutely unavoidable.'

My grandfathers took these guidelines to heart. They worked conscientiously. Industriously. Hard. Without complaining. They did contract work, often with colds and backaches. Every pfennig earned (the euro didn't exist back then) was saved. For the family and the dream of a better life. Although Germany was advertising for guest workers it didn't pay for them to have language tuition, at least not my grandfathers. To understand instructions within the business there were interpreters who explained the tasks to them. My grandfathers never saw the need to invest in a language course themselves. After all, it wasn't their plan to stay in Germany in the long term. For them what was most important was to earn money for a better life in Turkey and not spend any of it.

Later both grandfathers sent for their wives. And the wives brought their children: my mother and my father, who was two at the time.

My grandparents missed the sound of the sea outside their front door, the beaches of Kapuz and Uzunkum, their walks to the stalactite caves of Gökgöl Mağararsi. They missed the tooting of the ships' horns as they sailed into port. The screeching of the gulls. Fresh fish that my grandfather caught himself from the harbour wall. They missed their old friends. Their familiar life. But the security that their hard-earned marks offered was more important than giving in to their yearning.

So my grandparents remained in Germany with their children. And when my father and mother were old enough they married each other, as my grandfathers had once arranged. My parents weren't lucky enough to just meet each other in the normal way. They didn't have any first dates. My father didn't have to charm Mum to win her. They were designated for each other as was the tradition back then. Having said that, it seemed to me that my parents were always very loving and intimate with each other.

My mother and father had each other and their parents. They had Turkish friends and Turkish neighbours. Whenever they went out, they were with Turks. And so they needed almost no German to get by. For this reason they probably imagined that we – my brother Mutlu, my sisters Nese and Dugyu, and I – didn't need German either.

I think it was down to a lack of knowledge back then that lots of families made the mistake of not teaching their children the language of the host country properly from the start.

For a long time I found every German lesson at school a hurdle race – a race that I wasn't able to negotiate with confidence. Instead, at every hurdle I got stuck or lost my step. Often it wasn't just that I stumbled at the hurdles, but I felt as if I would never make it to the finish line.

And so to anyone who moves to another country, from no matter where, I'd like to offer the following words of encouragement. Make use of the opportunity to learn the language. Try to make friends with people from that country. Pay attention to your surroundings. Don't live separate lives in isolation. And most of all: read!

Nazan Eckes, the television presenter, wrote a book about her experiences as a woman born in Germany with Turkish roots. She interviewed me for the book, which is entitled *Good Morning Occident* and contains the wonderful sentence: 'My heart beats German and my heart also beats Turkish.' A great message that I can very much identify with, as I think like a German, but I feel Turkish.

How often in my young life have I been asked what I am. Turk? Or German? Do I feel more Turkish? Or do I have more German characteristics?

I don't like this exclusivity. I'm not just the one or the other. I've got fantastic Turkish friends, but equally I've got German friends who mean a lot to me. I met Fabian, my first German friend, when I was about seven and playing for Westfalia. He played mainly in goal and was captain of the team.

I grew up with boys from Lebanon, and over the course of my career I've lived in London and Madrid, and made friends from all over the world: Karim Benzema from France, Sergio Ramos from Spain, Cristiano Ronaldo from Portugal.

I consider myself fortunate to be able to adopt the best from both German and Turkish cultures. I've participated in Turkish customs and also tried out German ones.

Here's an example. When I was a child we had neither St Nicholas' Day nor Christmas – they aren't official religious festivals in Turkey. It wasn't until I got to school that I found out that in Germany you put your boots outside the door on 5 December and they're filled with sweets overnight. I'd never tried it.

We didn't celebrate 24 December either. Later on, however, in my mid-twenties, I did enjoy a classic Christmas with all the trimmings for the sake of my then girlfriend, Mandy. With a Christmas tree that we chose and decorated together, with presents and a large family meal. It was a lovely experience.

The family dinner as well as the conviviality and reflection on Christmas Eve are a little like the Turkish Sugar Feast – one of those religious customs we used to celebrate as children with our family. The Sugar Feast always takes place after the 30-day fast, and is a time when families spend several days together, celebrating the end of Ramadan.

These days I'm not able to fast. Personally, I find it's not compatible with my job as a sportsman. Especially in summer, it's difficult to cope with the exertions of top-flight sport if you're not supposed to eat between sunrise and sunset. We're not allowed to drink water or anything else either. This doesn't work for me. However, I admire and respect all other sportsmen and women who fast during Ramadan.

As Ramadan, which in Turkish is called Ramazan, always moves forwards by ten days, it occurs at a different time each year. So when I was 14 or 15 the fasting period was in winter. The sun didn't rise until around seven in the morning and had already set again by five in the afternoon. Obviously it's much easier to last these ten hours than the 16 in summer. Last year, for example, when the month of Ramadan was during the European Championship in France, sunrise at my parents' house in Gelsenkirchen was at half-past five. Sunset was after nine o'clock.

As a teenager I did fast occasionally. We children tried it out because we were curious. We wanted to know what it was like to eat nothing all day long. Of course, it also made us feel a bit more grown up. It was a mixture of several things. You wanted to be cool, because you were one of the adults if you fasted – children are excluded from fasting – and of course there was peer pressure too. In the afternoons we used to spend a lot of time with friends or relatives. You'd have looked silly if you were the only one in the group with a full tummy while everyone else was being good.

My parents never made us fast. They gave us the choice of observing Ramadan or not. I tried it two or three times. Once I lasted five days, and another year I even managed to hold out for ten days.

I remember the first time, dragging myself out of bed to the kitchen in a state of total exhaustion. The breakfast table was piled high with stuff. My parents had cooked like world champions so that we could really fill our tummies at 'sahur', which is the name of the meal before sunrise.

Fasting doesn't just mean that you can't eat; swearing and immoral behaviour are forbidden too. The time when the fast is broken is called 'iftar'. It's always the same procedure, beginning with a short prayer, then you eat a date and drink water.

I've never really had to justify myself for not fasting regularly. At any rate I can't ever recall having been criticised by Turks. And nor have I come across Germans who turn their noses up at fasting Muslims.

Looking back I can say that, with all the experiences I had between cultures, my childhood was decisive for my entire career. The awareness of being at home in different traditions has helped me to cope with all the unfamiliarity that's inevitable when you switch football clubs.

My mother has been particularly important for the path my life has taken. I was always impressed by how hard she worked. How she sacrificed everything to make a better life for us children in this country that was foreign to her, and how loving she was to us despite her arduous day-to-day existence. Most of all, however, my mum's devoted love for us children and the family inspired me to give something back to her. I wanted to achieve great things so she could be proud of me, and feel that her grafting hadn't been in vain.

2
MATTHIAS RATHER THAN MESUT

PEOPLE WHO RECOGNISE WHAT'S INSIDE YOU

My career as a footballer didn't take a straight path. This was partly down to my background. Although I've never been called explicitly racist names, Klaus Beier, spokesman of the far-right political party, Nationaldemokratische Partei (NPD), once referred to me as being German only 'on paper'. He was reported for his racist comments. I had another experience of xenophobia when I was a youth player, however, which had a more lasting influence. Between the ages of 10 and 12 I went to several trials to try to get into a Schalke 04 youth team. They have a much more substantial development programme than smaller clubs, which lack the money for advancing young talent to the same extent.

I first tried during my time with Teutonia Schalke, then when I was playing with DJK Falke Gelsenkirchen. I attended the trials four times, on each occasion driven with ambition.

I dribbled nimble-footed through the slalom poles. I shot the ball around the goalie's ears. And, as far as I could tell, did pretty much everything right in the games at the end. But I was never selected for any of Schalke's youth teams for those age groups. It seemed as if a Matthias or a Markus or Michael was always preferred to me, even if they weren't any better. Was it because of my first name that they hadn't taken me? Because they didn't want a Mesut? Because I was a foreigner? That's what it felt like, at least.

My father felt the same way. One day, when we were gloomily going back home after yet another rejection, I asked him what I could have done better. 'Dad, tell me what I did wrong.' All he said was, 'Nothing, my son. You can't do anything about the name you got from your mother and me.'

But it wasn't just my name that was an obstacle. Our financial situation didn't help either. Such as the time when I was playing for Rot-Weiss Essen, my youth club after Falke Gelsenkirchen. Before I changed clubs the boys always lost against local rivals Schwarz-Weiss Essen. It was usually a foregone conclusion: Rot-Weiss would go and get a pasting. But this changed when I moved there in 2000. In my first derby I scored seven goals against our rivals! Against all expectation Rot-Weiss beat Schwarz-Weiss 8–1. My first derby victory.

But for the next game I was on the bench. Rather than being rewarded for my achievement I was punished. All thanks to the parents of one of my teammates. Their boy was playing in my place because, as we later found out, his father was helping Rot-Weiss Essen financially. And this was clearly more important than goals that produced victories. The conflict did not last for too long, however. After a few weeks the coach became convinced that goals were more crucial than a set of jerseys for the team.

I was also given great support by the club legend, Werner Kik. Between 1960 and 1970 he played 293 games for Rot-Weiss Essen and was even selected in the club's team of the century. Kik bought me my first proper pair of football boots. Until then I'd always had to play in cheap ones. In worn-out trainers with holes in them, which gave me no grip. But now, at the age of 12, I had real Nike boots. They meant the world to me, supplanting my most valuable sporting possession up till then, a leather football that I'd been given on my eighth birthday. Every evening I used to rub it with leather protection cream and polish it for hours on end. Every single scratch on my ball pained me. And it got a lot of them because the 'Monkey Cage' – the name of the football pitch in Gelsenkirchen where we played – was a cinder pitch that badly damaged the old-fashioned coarse leather. When my ball became too scratched I carefully removed the individual leather panels and we just played with the inner bladder.

My experiences with Schalke and the supposed prejudice against foreign players affected me for a long time. But then, in my third year at Rot-Weiss Essen, I met Norbert Elgert. Rot-Weiss Essen had offered to make me a professional. At the age of just 15 I would get a contract and play for the second-division Essen side. For around 4,000 euros per month, if I remember rightly. That was a huge amount of money for me and my family; it would have changed our life overnight. Until then I was getting 'only'

150 euros a month, which still seemed quite a lot to me. In addition Werner Kik had managed to arrange for me to be picked up from home and driven the 20 kilometres to training when I was just 13. Normally this service was provided only to the age groups 16 and older. One of the drivers couldn't understand the exception the club had made for me and to begin with he would grumble, 'Do I now have to chauffeur kindergarten kids around?'

We declined this professional contract, however. Because of Norbert Elgert. At the time I was at Berger Feld school, which was right next to Schalke's stadium –you just had to cross the road to get to training. And this was the key thing. The school nurtured sporting talent. Three times a week those pupils gifted at football had extra training in the morning instead of maths, English or art. Thanks to a flexible timetable with substitute lessons we could catch up, usually with tutors in the afternoons.

Most of the good footballers at Berger Feld school were already playing for one of the Schalke youth sides. There were very few exceptions at the school, that is to say external players like me at Rot-Weiss Essen. The football training was run by Norbert Elgert. In one of the first sessions after the 2004 summer holidays he got us to play a three-a-side game against some Schalke boys on a small pitch.

I was playing with two other boys from my school whose names I'm afraid I can't recall. But I do remember exactly that the three of us beat the Schalke boys big time. When I was about to head back to school after training Elgert took me aside.

'Where are you playing?' he asked tersely.

'With Rot-Weiss Essen,' I replied.

'Where do you live?'

'In Gelsenkirchen.'

'Next year you're playing here!'

To begin with I didn't give much thought to what Elgert had said. It never occurred to me that I'd move to Schalke. They had rejected me four times already. Four times they'd preferred to go with a Matthias or a Martin or a Markus. Why should I now forgive them for this humiliation, seeing as things were going so well at Rot-Weiss Essen?

But Elgert spoke to me again after the next training session. 'I've got to talk to your father. You have to come to Schalke.' I mentioned Elgert's request to my father and we decided we'd give him a chance and hear him out. After all, this football coach seemed to be an honest and fair man. For our discussion Elgert invited us to Kronski, a pub in Buer Market in Gelsenkirchen. On our way there my father and I didn't say much. We didn't work out any kind of negotiation strategy, but decided just to listen to what Elgert had to say. In any case we couldn't imagine exactly what would crop up in the conversation. Besides, our past experiences with Schalke had left us disillusioned, so we didn't dare indulge in any dreams or fantasies.

After we'd ordered and were waiting for our food, Elgert turned to my father. 'Your son,' he said, 'is still terribly raw, but he's highly talented.' We just exchanged glances and let him continue. 'I can't promise that Mesut will become a regular player in his first season with us. I can't promise that he'll become a professional at Schalke. Nor can I promise that he'll become an international. There's only one thing I can promise the both of you. Mesut, I will give you the very best training in every aspect of the game: technique, tactics, footballing understanding and intelligence, athleticism, mental speed, emotional control as well team spirit and conduct. Apart from that I can't guarantee a thing. The only guarantee I'll give is that I'll always do everything I can for you. And that at Schalke we can improve your chances of fulfilling your ambitions.'

It all sounded good. It didn't sound like the usual blah blah blah, which you get from lots of agents and scouts, either. But we had huge reservations about Schalke. 'Schalke doesn't want a Mesut,' my father said curtly. And he told Elgert about the experiences we'd had. He listened to everything my father had to say, thought about it briefly and replied, 'OK, then. I'll give you another guarantee: Mesut will get a completely fair and genuine chance with me. Just like any player. All that counts for me is performance. Nothing else.'

After the meeting my father and I returned home in a thoughtful mood. Obviously a single conversation couldn't wipe out all the bad experiences we'd had at several trials – you couldn't just dismiss the way we'd been treated.

It's important to remember that I was 10, 11 and 12 when I had felt this form of rejection. I couldn't just swallow humiliation like that when I was so young. It's a hard enough lesson at that age to find out that you haven't been selected for something because you're not good enough. But if you are particularly good at something and yet have to face the reality that performance alone isn't good enough, and that a career depends on your background too, then that is really painful.

Elgert was very smart. After our conversation he didn't come running up and hassle me at each training session. It was a while before he invited us to another discussion, this time at the Marriot Courtyard Hotel, which is right next to the stadium.

'Let me tell you this,' he said to my father, without really addressing our reservations again. 'There's not much I'm good at. But I think I'm good with people and I know a bit about football.'

He proceeded to outline his philosophy. 'I see myself as someone who trains and nurtures young players. The primary reason for training footballers here at Schalke is not to win titles with our youth teams. Our chief aim is to produce as many professionals as possible.'

He turned back to my father and explained his position. 'Sure, players need to learn that professional football is about results. But at this age we mustn't ram into them that all that counts is winning, winning, winning. Otherwise we'll just make them mad, obsessed, neurotic. The goal of our training is to make them be better tomorrow than they were today. And the day after that to be better than tomorrow. If a player takes this to heart they'll automatically win a title some day.'

Then Elgert promised my father something else. 'I'm a circumspect man. I won't let your son become a professional too soon. Until my players are ready they stay with me. I don't let them go until they're fully equipped.'

We believed what Elgert was telling us. We liked his views. And so, putting aside his hostility towards the club, my father asked, 'Do you really think my son's good enough to play for Schalke?'

'I can't guarantee you a regular place. Mesut has physical shortcomings. He's really quite small. We also need to work on his right foot and heading. He must get better at winning the ball. But if we manage all this then he's got great potential.'

When we said goodbye we promised to consider Elgert's offer, even though a professional contract from Rot-Weiss Essen was already on the table. The money was tempting. For the first time I understood that you can actually get rich from football. But we were convinced that my career opportunities at Schalke were substantially higher.

When I played for Rot-Weiss Essen in the Lower Rhine Cup I saw Elgert on the touchline. Whenever I glanced at him he was watching me.

In the end I asked my coach at Rot-Weiss Essen, Michael Kulm, for advice. I wanted to know how he would respond to the Schalke offer if he were in my shoes. His honest answer was, 'Go for it. It'll be worth it.'

A few weeks later Elgert invited us to the boarding house for youth players to meet 'his' Schalke. After this we were finally convinced. This man really was fair. The efforts we could see him making to get me to come to Schalke meant he must have seen something in me. He wasn't interested in whether I was called Mesut or Markus. Elgert was interested only in my qualities as a player, not in my background. And so in 2005 I left Rot-Weiss Essen for Schalke.

3

THE WORLD OF FOOTBALL ISN'T A TALENT SHOW

THE MOST IMPORTANT THING IS A FIRM GROUNDING

At the start of my career I felt as if someone had pressed the double speed button on a DVD player. So many new impressions. So many new experiences. So many changes in such a short period of time. When I moved to the Schalke 04 youth team nothing was as it had been before. The first six months I spent there felt like a month.

In summer 2005 we went to a training camp in Billerbeck, 70 kilometres away, where we stayed in a hotel – I'd never seen anything like it. It was in the middle of a park, on top of a hill, with views over the town.

After we'd checked into our rooms, our coach Norbert Elgert had us assemble in one of the conference rooms. 'The truth is, a youth hostel would be good enough for you lot,' he began. The mumbling in the room stopped at once. 'You've really no business being here at all. No U-19 player needs luxury like this. But we took the conscious decision to bring you here. We're here to show you what's possible in your career. What you can achieve. How nicely you can live if you give it your all. My family has worked very hard and now we can afford to stay in hotels like this. As successful professionals you can have this too. But what's crucial to me is that you appreciate it. I want you to understand our gesture in the right way. Never take this for granted. Be friendly to the staff. I don't want to hear from any employee here that a single one of you has been snooty, arrogant or unfriendly. That you didn't say hello to the cleaners. Show some humility. The achievements of a professional footballer are never greater than those of a doctor, journalist or a cleaning lady. Have respect and be grateful that you've had the chance to stay here.'

After this Elgert gave us two other pieces of advice to remember: 'Your hands can be in the sky, reaching for the stars, but make sure both your feet remain on the ground,' and 'We at Schalke are firm in our belief that apprentices have to start by earning everything. You begin as an apprentice, then you're a craftsman and only right at the end, after lots and lots of hard work, are you a master craftsman.'

At Rot-Weiss Essen I'd sat in on lots of team meetings. But to be talked to like this was completely new. I liked it, just as I liked the idea that one day I might be able to afford to stay in hotels like this.

I'd never stayed in a hotel before. Up until then this world had been totally alien to me. We never went on holiday with the family in summer quite simply because we didn't have the money.

I'd practically never left Gelsenkirchen. The furthest I'd been was to visit my grandparents in Müllheim an der Ruhr. A 29-kilometre journey taking the fast road. I used to think that Gelsenkirchen was a world metropolis. The city seemed so big to me – I felt that there was no end to it. Today that's changed of course.

After the summer holidays I'd always sit in a semi-circle with the other children and all of us had to tell the class about the best thing that had happened over the summer. One after the other they all talked about their holidays. Someone had been in a hotel in Spain. Other children had stayed in villas in France or Turkey. There were even children who'd flown with their parents to countries I'd never heard of. Me, on the other hand, I never had anything to say. Or at least I couldn't talk about wonderful trips and hotel stays.

After the meeting Norbert Elgert assigned us a task. We had to come up with our own team credo, set out on a placard what we wanted to achieve together and how we imagined we would play. He also asked us to devise a list of 'penalties'. 'There are always rules in a community,' Elgert said. 'You must determine these yourselves, not me. You must stipulate the code of behaviour you think's important.'

When we'd finished he couldn't stop laughing. We had agreed on 15 or 20 points along with corresponding fines. Forgetting your shin pads was punished by a fine of 20 euros, arriving late – if I recall correctly – would cost you 100 euros. As a group we quickly agreed on the sums. But all Elgert said was, 'You can't be serious about the amounts of those fines. We pay you a few hundred euros pocket money per month so you can concentrate on your careers rather than having to get a job alongside school and football. This is the only opportunity you've got to save money so you can learn to drive. Do you really want to impose a fine of a hundred euros if someone turns up late? That's far too much. Your pocket money will soon be all gone. How about we halve the fines? They'll still hurt.'

A few days later he invited me for a one-on-one chat. Every player on the camp had conversations like this at some point. Elgert wanted to get to know me better as a person, find out about my dreams and ambitions. As he reminded me some time later, my answer back in summer 2005 was: 'I'm going to start by becoming a professional at Schalke. And later I'll play in Spain, for Barcelona or Real Madrid.'

Elgert replied that he approved of dreaming big. 'I like that,' he said. 'But can you imagine what I'm going to expect of you from now on? I'm going to keep a very close eye on someone who says they're going to play for Real Madrid or FC Barcelona. You've got talent. But talent alone will only get you to the threshold. To actually go through the door you need the right character, the right attitude – you have to be smart and work hard.' After that he added, 'Do you know what the problem is today? Everyone wants to be something, but nobody wants to make the effort to get there.'

Then he asked me if I knew about the TV reality show, *Deutschland sucht den Superstar (Germany Seeks a Superstar)*. At the time the programme was still quite new; there had only been two series. 'One good performance and these people are orbiting the earth,' Elgert said. 'Just because they've pulled it off once they suddenly think they're the greatest. But there's no firm grounding to their success. And that's the most important thing of all for a great career. Awaiting you up there in the firmament of your career are so many things you have to be prepared for. Only a firm grounding will bring you lasting success. That's why I advise every player to climb the ladder of success slowly. Of course, if you've got what it takes you can occasionally take two steps at a time. That's perfectly possible and I don't want to stop anyone from doing so. But you should not let yourself shoot from the bottom to the top rung. Because the quicker you get into orbit, the quicker you'll be plummeting back down.'

I nodded. I understood the core of what Elgert was trying to say. But I'd also been told often enough that it was important to have self-confidence if you wanted to be successful. How did these two things go together? I asked him. He replied, 'You need self-confidence or you don't have a chance. But with all the self-confidence you have, you must also have a realistic self-awareness. You should feel as strong as an ox, but I still expect you to estimate your abilities accurately rather than totally overestimate them. It's no contradiction to be humble and impatient at the same time. The key to success is to be patiently impatient.'

While I was still mulling over these words of Elgert's, he continued, 'If the world collapses for a budding professional footballer because he doesn't achieve his ambition immediately, that's crap. But it's also crap if a budding professional footballer doesn't care that he's not making progress and just thinks apathetically, "Oh well, I'll achieve my ambition some day".'

What Elgert said has meant a lot to me. Elgert was absolutely the key coach in my career. He saw something in me that others hadn't before. He always wanted the best for me and was always there for me too. I learnt so much from him. I was desperate to play – every time I wanted to know what I could do better. But often I ran around the pitch like a headless chicken. It was from Elgert that I first learned that something like tactics existed at all. Although many people will shake their heads at this comparison and refuse to accept it, Norbert Elgert was very similar to José Mourinho. He always said what he thought. He was never satisfied! He taught me the most valuable lessons and prepared me for my professional career. For example, in my first weeks in the Schalke U-19 side he kept grumbling that I wasn't running back enough. 'If I don't see more of that from you,' he threatened, 'you'll be on the bench.'

But Norbert Elgert wasn't the only one trying to further my career. Especially at the start, blokes I'd never met kept cropping up with grand plans. Telling me who should advise me in the complex business of football. Or advising me as to whether I should switch to another club. When you're young, in particular, you're forever meeting people who are ready to offer their help and promise you the earth. But if your rise is too rapid you can get burned before things have really taken off. Life isn't a Hollywood film, and nobody is gifted lasting success. Which means that as a young player you should always think very carefully about which offers you accept and which you turn down.

In January 2006 I went with Schalke 04 to Sindelfingen for the Mercedes Benz Junior Cup, a youth tournament that has taken place every year since 1991. We were being watched by Dunga,

Heiko Herrlich, Ralf Rangnick and Guido Buchwald.* Joachim (Jogi) Löw was there too, watching me whirl around the pitch. Teams from all across the world had come to Sindelfingen. There was even a team from Vietnam. Because those boys had never seen snow before, they didn't, at first, dare get out of the bus and into the mass of white flakes.

Before the tournament began all the teams went into the hall in turn. Like the parade of countries at the Olympic Games, we entered to the accompaniment of African musicians drumming and lasers flashing around the room.

I was wearing number 11 on my jersey. It looked more like a sack, however, as it drooped down from my narrow shoulders.

In the group stage we played Galatasaray of Istanbul, Porto Alegre, Werder Bremen and Borussia Dortmund, finishing top of our group without being defeated. In the quarter-finals we beat the U-19 South African national team 6–4 on penalties. In the semi-final we defeated Werder Bremen, again on penalties. In the final we won 3–0 against Basel and so were champions. My teammate Ralf Fährmann was chosen as the player of the tournament. I was the leading goal scorer with five, and afterwards I gave my first ever interview. 'It's a great feeling to be the top team,' I said. And: 'It's nice to have scored five goals. I'm very pleased.' Only a few words, but still.

* Carlos Caetano Bledorn Verri, commonly known as Dunga, is a former Brazilian international footballer and former manager of the Brazilian team; Heiko Herrlich is a football manager in Germany and a former player; Ralf Rangnick is also a football manager in Germany; Guido Buchwald is director of football at Stuttgarter Kickers and a former player and manager.

As well as catching the media's attention through the tournament, I caught the eye of other clubs too. For example, Thomas Strunz of the 1996 European Championship winning side and former Bayern Munich player, got in touch with my father. He had just been appointed manager at VfL Wolfsburg and was desperate to sign me. So my father went to Wolfsburg and listened to what Strunz had to offer. They sat in his office on the second floor of the VW stadium. You get a view from there of the stadium car park, the Mittelland Canal and the railway line to Berlin. It somehow wasn't a place for dreams and visions. It didn't inspire anything in my father, as he said when he got back. All very different from Real Madrid some years later. From the room where we signed the contract with Los Blancos you can look directly into the Santiago Bernabéu.

Strunz was a five-times champion with Bayern Munich. He had won the German Cup and the UEFA Cup and now wanted to bring that winning mentality to Wolfsburg. 'With talents like Mesut we want to create a new identity here,' Strunz said. 'Wolfsburg have only been in the Bundesliga for eight years and yet the club is already a brand, it stands for integrity and continuity. Wolfsburg has already been in the UEFA Cup once, four times in the UI Cup and has never been in danger of relegation.' It was an unbelievable development, he declared, and asked, 'How long did it take Leverkusen to get to this stage?'

My father listened, unimpressed, as he already knew all the facts. And yet he liked the confident way Strunz talked. 'Wolfsburg led the table eight times this year,' the manager continued. 'The team thrashed both Schalke and Stuttgart. No one has to feel humble here.' The club had enormous potential, he argued, 'and with Mesut on board there's lots we can achieve. Why should we be satisfied with fifth in the table or worse? We want more. And we can get more. Only if you aim high are you going to get anywhere.'

Strunz immediately offered us a professional contract, something I didn't yet have. He also promised my father a job at VfL Wolfsburg. And he suggested that our entire family should move to Wolfsburg – with the club covering the costs of our move, of course.

It was a flattering offer, which all of us gave some thought to. But at the time I didn't want to move away from Schalke. Norbert Elgert was such an important support for me. Gelsenkirchen was my home. It was where I was born and grew up, and where I wanted to take my first steps as a professional footballer. I loved Schalke; it was my absolute favourite club in Germany. So we declined.

The conversation with Thomas Strunz was one of many that my father would have over the coming weeks and months. Since my first few games in the Schalke U-19 side and my appearance in Sindelfingen, people offering advice were beating a path to my door. Football agents kept contacting my father and telling him what an exceptionally gifted footballing talent I was, and what a great future would be awaiting me with their help.

Whenever these strangers came into our flat and sat in our living room I found it very funny. Some wore suits and parked their big cars right outside the house. I hope it doesn't get touched, I'd sometimes think, expecting some neighbour to scratch the bodywork out of envy. It was a not uncommon dare amongst some of the kids in our area, though I was always too much of a coward to do it as I was scared of being arrested by the police.

'If I represent Mesut,' one of them said grandiosely, 'in three years' time he'll be playing for Bayern. Or for any other club you like. I can take you anywhere.' Somehow the agents' promises were all fairly similar. Each one of them claimed to have the best contacts to the greatest clubs in the worlds. They had impeccable rhetorical skills – these strangers in our living room we knew nothing about. Were they storytellers? Pied Pipers? Or were they really as influential and successful as they claimed to be?

I couldn't judge that. I saw the cars, the chunky watches that some of them displayed ostentatiously by rolling up their sleeves. And I kept hearing 'Manchester this', 'Arsenal that', 'Bayern Munich tomorrow', 'Real Madrid the day after that'.

This is why I left it up to my father to make the decision. We were desperate to have Norbert Elgert act as my agent, but he declined because, as he told us, it wasn't compatible with his job at Schalke. So unfortunately we had to look for someone else.

Once, in a state of excitement, my father gathered the family together. He'd met another agent, and this one, my father said, had offered us 50,000 euros to look after my career. An unethical offer, but one we couldn't turn down just like that. After all, we weren't big money earners. For us, 50,000 euros would have changed our lives on the spot. With that money my parents could have paid the rent on our flat for six years or bought a new car.

To earn 50,000 euros my mother would have had to work 12 hours a day for several years.

In spite of this we rejected the offer. My father thought the idea of 'selling me', if you want to call it that, strange somehow. Who knows what course my career might have taken if we'd placed ourselves in the hands of that man? I've no idea if he would have acted in my interests, or whether he would have encouraged only the transfers that were most lucrative to him.

For a short while Roger Wittmann was my agent. But I never had the feeling that I was really important to him. Then we let Dr Michael Becker look after my affairs. At the time he was representing the captain of the German national side, Michael Ballack, as well as Bernd Schneider and Oliver Neuville, both of whom were also playing for Germany. This lawyer's motto was 'mediocrity sucks', which appealed to us. Becker did not remain my agent for long, however. When he gave me a Michael Ballack jersey the same feeling crept over me as with Wittmann. I couldn't understand the gesture at all. What was I going to do with a Ballack jersey? I didn't want one. I wasn't a fan! I wanted Michael Becker to represent my interests, give me advice, help me carve out a great career. For that I needed a man who saw something in *me*, not a Ballack jersey.

I don't think it's bad to have switched agents several times over my career. You grow as a person. You grow as a personality and a footballer. You change, you mature. Perhaps after two, three or four meetings you get the impression that the agent sitting opposite is the right one. But after the fifth meeting you realise that, although you get along with him, you're not going to progress any further. As a footballer you have only one career and you mustn't ruin it with ill-considered decisions. That's why we terminated our relationship with Dr Michael Becker fairly quickly.

While negotiations about my future were going on in the background, I was trying to play as good football as possible. My first season with Schalke was almost over. In early summer 2006 we were in the semi-final of the German U-19 championship. Our next opponents were Hertha BSC Berlin, with a certain Jérôme Boateng. We were soundly defeated in the capital 2–0. The dream of a championship title was on the verge of being shattered. Only a 3–0 victory in the return game at home could save us. But after the hiding we'd had in Berlin, none of us players really believed we could do it.

When we'd changed, the dressing-room door flew open and Norbert Elgert burst in. In his hand was a golden dumbbell, which he flung to the floor in the middle of the room. 'Listen,' he said, and everyone turned their eyes to him. 'I'm going to tell you a story, a true story. I was a qualified fitness instructor and in this capacity I visited the FIBO, the trade fair for fitness and body-building. There was a competition – the unofficial German fitness championship – which I took part in. A fitness pentathlon with bench presses, bench jumps, sit-ups, pull-ups and three minutes' fast cycling. Fifty participants. The first ten made it through to the final round. I was eleventh, about to be eliminated. I was hanging on the bar, thinking, "I can't do another pull-up". My arms were burning and my head was saying, "Give up. You'll be out. The others are better." But I didn't listen. I fought my inner voice. And kept telling myself, "I'm not giving up. Never! Sod you!"' And then he did actually manage one more pull-up. And another, and another. 'I gave my inner bastard a kick up the arse,' Elgert said, as we listened with bated breath. 'Have a guess where I ended up coming?' He nudged one of our players and demanded an answer.

'Second?' the boy said timidly.

'Of course not! I won the thing! I whopped them all.'

All of a sudden there was a knock at the door. The referee came in and asked us to get on the pitch. 'The match is starting,' he said.

But Elgert couldn't care less. 'Not now,' he screamed, slamming the door in the referee's face.

'We've got him against us now too,' Elgert said, chuckling. Then he turned back to us. 'Do you know why I told you this story? To show you that everything's possible if you've got the belief. I was almost out of the competition and yet I did it. And you'll do it too. Losing 2–0 in Berlin is no reason to doubt yourselves. The defeat makes us stronger.' Then he picked up the golden dumbbell he'd brought with him, raised it above his head and shouted, 'This is our symbol for today. We're going to do it! Here's to the final! And now, out you go, boys!'

After this story there was no way we could lose. I felt as strong as an ox. As fast as a cheetah. As accomplished as Zinédine Zidane. Elgert had stoked such passion in us that we managed to beat Berlin 3–0 and made it into the championship final. Where Bayern Munich awaited us. The southern Germans had come out on top against Freiburg in their semi-final. Thomas Kraft was in goal for Bayern, Mats Hummels in defence and Sandro Wagner was up front. In my team we had Ralf Fährmann, Benedikt Höwedes and Sebastian Boenisch.

When Elgert saw the confidence with which the Bayern players were warming up he got us together and said, 'Let's do a sliding-tackle circle.' So we formed a 15-metre circle and tackled each other in turn. One of us stood in the middle, sprinted towards the players in the circle and launched a sliding tackle. At the very last moment they jumped over the tackler. As we performed this exercise we shouted our heads off and drew attention to ourselves. Anybody watching us apparently kicking each other's shins to bits – which, of course, we weren't doing – must have thought we'd lost the plot. Elgert's idea of the tackling circle was a brilliant one. It didn't just drive us on, it really intimidated Bayern too.

After 34 minutes we were already 2–0 up thanks to goals by Pisano and Boenisch. Bayern only managed to get one back. We were German U-19 champions.

My first title. Which was followed by my first real party. We began celebrating in the Courtyard hotel near the stadium. Then we moved on to a club. It was my first ever visit to a disco. Dad let me stay there till one in the morning. When I proudly told my teammates about my curfew they laughed in my face. 'It only really gets going at one,' they said. 'Nothing much happens before then.'

I felt like a complete idiot as I didn't know the rules of going out. When I begged Dad to let me stay longer he wouldn't relent. 'One o'clock's your limit,' he said. 'If you're not home by then, we're going to have a problem.' I nodded and set off. Of course, I didn't make any move to go when one o'clock came around. We partied, we danced, we drank. And totally forgot the time. When I checked and saw it was two, I realised that there was going to be big trouble the following morning. Oh well, I thought, it doesn't really matter if I get home at six now. My old man isn't going to be interested in whether I'm one hour late or three or four.

I've never been a big party animal. Because my friends were dreaming of becoming professional footballers too, we didn't tempt each other. All of us were addicted to football. We spent most of our time on the pitch. And when we weren't playing we were lifting weights or going running. I worked hard on the basics that Elgert had said were so important for our careers. Women and parties couldn't distract me from that. My father realised this too, which is why the telling-off I got the following morning wasn't so bad.

4

A BONE OF CONTENTION BETWEEN GERMANY AND TURKEY

THE ART OF MAKING THE RIGHT DECISION

Although I was born in Germany I had only ever had a Turkish passport. At the time dual nationality didn't exist. And, of course, as a child I didn't care about the difference either. What child scrutinises their passport and has lengthy discussions with their parents about their nationality? None, I bet. And understandably so. What normal child is interested in immigration policy? Or spends their spare time reading about citizenship law? Certainly not me!

But when I got older and it became apparent that I might have a great football career, I had to address the issue. I had to ask myself what I was, or what I wanted to be, on paper at least. German or Turkish? Who did I want to play for if the possibility ever came about? For the German national side or the Turkish one?

It wasn't a decision I made in a couple of minutes, just in passing. After all, we weren't talking about something trivial here, like whether you'd rather go with your friends to the zoo or the cinema. Whether you'd prefer to be Real Madrid or Barcelona on the PlayStation. Whether you'd rather have a margarita or a Hawaiian at the pizzeria. It was a decision that would fundamentally shape my whole career, and note I say *my* career.

All the same, I obviously discussed this difficult question with my family and listened to their different opinions. You can't make a decision like that all on your own, irrespective of whether you're 16, 17 or even 18. Everyone gave their honest view on the matter, and for that I'm especially grateful. The advice you receive isn't always objective, not even from family members. If a son asks his mother about whether he should take a better job at the other end of Germany, in most cases she will look for arguments against, because she doesn't want her son to move so far away, meaning she'll rarely see him. I completely understand that. Which is why I was so appreciative that everyone was very honest in what they said.

My mother, Gulizar, was in favour of me playing for Turkey. 'Remember,' she said, 'those are your roots. Your grandparents come from Turkey. That's where our origins are. If I were you,' she continued, 'I'd go for Turkey.' My uncle Erdogan was of the same opinion, He told me about Zonguldak and how he felt whenever he went back there. How he immediately felt at home there each time. I listened attentively to what he said as he was one of my most important advisers. But I didn't feel the same way as he did. After all, until I was 17 I'd only been to Zonguldak twice in the summer. I liked it there, but I never felt at home. When I stood by the sea there and took a deep breath I didn't get a real sense of having arrived.

My father disagreed with my uncle too. 'Mesut was born in Germany. He went to school in Germany. He's learnt his football with German clubs. And so he must play for Germany.' When my brother Mutlu spoke I laughed out loud. He'd spent the whole time up till then shifting around restlessly on the sofa, listening to the grown-ups. But now it all came out. 'Mesut has to play for Germany,' he cried. 'Do you know what Turkey's best performance ever is? Third place at the 2002 World Cup in South Korea and Japan. Germany, on the other hand: World Champions in 1954, 1974 and 1990.' I listened to everything and thought about it myself too. On the evening of our family summit my sister Nese also came to talk to me. She'd got wind of what we'd been discussing that afternoon, but without really understanding it. 'I prefer the shirts the Turkish team wear,' was all she said, with a big smile.

So, putting together all the family's opinions, it stood at 2–2, if you discounted Nese. What about me? From the start my thoughts had actually been the same as my father's, but I wasn't able to admit this to myself to begin with. For weeks I kept turning the decision over in my mind. I didn't want to rush into anything, make the wrong decision. Sometimes I'd lie in bed at night, imagining myself trotting into the stadium wearing the German strip. It was a wonderful image that put a smile on my face each time. The idea of it made me happy. Although this isn't to say that the idea of playing for the Turkish national side gave me a bad feeling.

There were also odd moments when I felt overwhelmed by the burden of having to commit myself once and for all. I didn't want to annoy or disappoint anyone. 'I'll decide tomorrow', I told myself almost as often as I abandoned the decision. I was playing for time against myself. Until I realised that this wasn't helping anybody. Least of all me. I was dodging a decision that I ought to have made long ago. Maybe because I was worried about the reaction from those I'd be rebuffing. But then I told myself: It's my life, my career, my decision.

In spring 2006 I finally let my family know my decision. That same year I went with my father to the Turkish Consulate General in Münster to surrender my passport – a necessary step for those wishing to acquire a German one.

Up till then my Turkish passport had simply been a document. Laminated paper with my name and photograph. Although I was very sorry that my mother and uncle were sad about it, I felt no emotion at having to surrender the passport. It just seemed a necessary step to get closer to my dream of being a top-flight footballer.

Upon entering the consulate we were on Turkish sovereign territory. And from the moment we told the official the reason for our visit, we were hated. He couldn't understand how a Turkish person could willingly surrender their passport. And not only was he unable to understand it, he didn't hide his anger at what he regarded as an outrage. 'Wait over there', he barked, pointing to a place in the waiting room, where we sat as instructed.

One after the other, the people waiting went into the official's room to sort out their business. It was the same procedure each time: a name was called out, someone got up from their seat, went into the office and came out again some time later to go home. The only name not to be called out was 'Özil'. People who'd arrived long after us were dealt with before us. After more than an hour my father had had enough, and he stormed into the official's room. 'When is it our turn? We ought to have been seen ages ago,' he grumbled. But in vain. In the official's eyes we were merely applicants with an outrageous request. 'I'll tell you when it's your turn,' the employee replied.

An hour or two later – in places like that you completely lose your sense of time – the Turkish civil servant came out of his office, with his coat on, and locked the door behind him.

'Excuse me, what's going on?' my father asked furiously. 'What about us?'

'Come back tomorrow. I really didn't have time to see you today.'

As exasperated as we were, it didn't change our situation. I hadn't been allowed to surrender my passport, which meant that we had to travel the 80 kilometres from Münster back to Gelsenkirchen empty-handed.

The next day, however, we were standing on the Turkish Consulate General doormat again. We waited. And waited. And waited. Until my father grabbed my hand, yanked open the official's door and blustered, 'We're not going away until my son's given up his passport.'

Things got loud. Very loud. My father demanded his right to be treated like everyone else here. 'Not everyone else here,' the official yelled back, 'wants to give up their Turkish passport.'

My brother Mutlu (left) and I were always close as kids, and now he acts as joint-agent for me with Erkut Sogut.

Mutlu and I – that's me looking a little sheepish with the dummy in my mouth! – were a vision in gold for this childhood snap.

My mother Gulizar gave all us children unconditional love, and both my parents encouraged me to go my own way.

That's me in the middle – the height of fashion – with my uncle Dogan and brother Mutlu out and about in Gelsenkirchen.

We may not have had the kit or the facilities but those impromptu boyhood games gave me (the one on the ball) a great grounding.

My first German friend, Fabian Maraun, is next to me on the right of the front row in the F-Youth team at Westfalia 04.

To this day, I often return to my favourite football pitch in Gelsenkirchen – it's all cinder, gravel and bumps but it's where it all began for me.

Left above: Norbert Elgert, my first real coaching mentor, presents me with the Laureus-Medien prize for social commitment in 2014.

Left below: My first significant honour as Schalke celebrate beating Bayern Munich to win the 2006 A-Youth championship.

Right: Black, red and gold: my heart beats German, yet it also beats Turkish, and I make no apologies for that.

Below: My goal for Germany against Turkey, of all teams, in a 2010 European qualifier in Berlin, but I felt it disrespectful to celebrate as I would normally have done.

The German Chancellor, Angela Merkel, catches me half-naked as she arrives to congratulate me on my goal and the victory over Turkey.

Happy days at Schalke as I join Fabian Ernst (8) in congratulating Halil Altintop (19) after a goal.

I still pray before every game as I've done since I was a boy, to ask for strength and guidance.

A 'spectator' at Schalke – a position I would find myself in too frequently for my liking.

Jubilation after my goal against Russia in the Under-19 World Cup in 2007, with Anis Ben-Hatira.

A new club, a fresh start: coach Thomas Schaaf (left) and general manager Klasus Allofs welcome me to Werder Bremen.

Old friends: the bond between (left to right) Jack, Serdar, myself and Erkut is solid and enduring.

He was taking our decision personally. Even though it was none of his business. He kept lambasting us with outrageous insinuations. For example, he ticked us off for not having 'an ounce of pride' and for not liking Turkey. Anybody leaving the Turkish community was a traitor. What nonsense! But eventually he complied with our request.

And that's where the matter ought to have rested. In September 2006, at the age of 17 years, 10 months and 21 days, I had my first international game for the German U-19 side. I played a further ten matches before I was moved up into the U-21 side by Dieter Eilts. According to FIFA statutes, junior international fixtures don't affect your eligibility for a national team. So although the question of Germany or Turkey was settled as far as I was concerned, for many others it wasn't.

Suddenly I was being pushed and pulled in all directions. Suddenly people were coming to tell me they knew what was good and bad for me. Dishing out advice for my life even though they barely knew me.

Metin Tekin, the chief scout of the Turkish football association's Europe office, who had been based in Dortmund and then in Cologne, had once swapped phone numbers with my father after spotting me at some trials. Now he tried to tempt me into going for the senior Turkish team. Out of the blue I was invited to a training camp for the Turkish national side. Later I had a call from the Turkish manager at the time, Fatih Terim, who promised that at the very least he'd give me a game against the Ivory Coast in February 2009. Hamit and Halil Altıntop, who'd both decided to play for Turkey, also tried to talk to me because the association had asked them to.

Suddenly everyone was discussing me and the decision I'd made. Not through any fault of mine, I publicly became a bone of contention between Germany and Turkey. And yet I'd done nothing wrong; I'd just made the decision I had to. I hadn't offended anyone. I hadn't snubbed anyone. I'd even listened to all sides, refusing to reject anything in haste, so no one could be cross with me. And yet for a while I felt like a pinball being knocked to and fro by both German and Turkish flippers.

At this turbulent time I was playing for Bremen, and Turkish journalists arrived at our training camp on the Turkish Black Sea coast to grill me. The Turkish assistant manager, Müfit Erkasap, also travelled from Istanbul, because he wanted to speak to me. I wouldn't talk to either him or the journalists as I felt I had nothing to explain and every word of mine would have been pored over at length. Which is exactly what I didn't want.

I didn't want even greater media focus on me. After Jogi Löw, with whom I'd had very friendly conversations beforehand, picked me for the international fixture between Germany and Norway, even German politicians started voicing their opinions. One said, 'I'm actively in favour of footballers with Turkish backgrounds who've grown up here opting for a sporting career in Germany. And so it's important to have players like Mesut Özil breaking the ice. In a few years' time there'll be no more discussion as to whether German Turks or other migrant groups belong in the German national team.'

But I never wanted to be an ice-breaker. I never wanted to become a bone of contention between Germans and Turks. I never expected the stir that would be created, especially in the media, by my decision to play for Germany. Mustafa Doğan, who played twice for the German national side in 1999, was asked what he thought I'd be feeling. He, too, was born in Turkey, but grew up in Germany and then, like me, chose to play for the German team. 'Before coming to his decision,' he speculated, 'Mesut must have spent sleepless nights.' Which was wrong. In general I'm not a bad sleeper. I rarely take my problems to bed with me. I'm not a brooder who spends hours staring at the ceiling instead of going to sleep. The only time I have trouble sleeping is after matches. When I come home after Champions League encounters, I find it hard to wind down. Irrespective of whether we've won or lost. I can't push my body to its limits for ninety minutes and then just go to bed and sleep. For hours after the game my body is still in power-mode. Usually I don't feel tired till three or four in the morning and only then can I think about sleeping.

But I had no problems sleeping because of the decision between Germany and Turkey. Nor did I feel personally torn. At most I had vague mixed feelings. Maybe it would have been different if I'd come to Germany after I'd been born. Maybe then I would have been more receptive to my uncle's arguments and would have felt the same as he did whenever I went back to Zonguldak.

Hakan Eseroglu, the director of the Turkish football association's Europe office, later accused me in *Bild* of slightly mucking the association around. 'Mesut's a good boy, a nice boy. But there are people influencing him.' Which was sheer nonsense.

In the days leading up to my first international game for Germany we had to shut down my website for a time as a few unsympathetic individuals had written the most offensive comments. Because they were able to hide behind pseudonyms their accusations were far stronger than those that had been made to my father and me by the official in the Turkish consulate.

After all, my decision in favour of Germany – and many people seemed to have forgotten this in the weeks that followed – was not an explicit rejection of Turkey. Just because I'd chosen to play for Germany didn't mean that Turkey wasn't close to my heart. I wasn't shutting myself off from Turkey and its people.

On 11 February 2009 the day had arrived. My first full international for Germany, at the age of 20 years, 3 months and 27 days. I started on the bench with Tim Wiese, Thomas Hitzlsperger and Simon Rolfes, amongst others. It was Germany's first friendly of the year, six weeks before the World Cup qualifiers were due to restart.

At half-time the German manager made some changes, taking off Per Mertesacker, Andreas Hinkel and Miroslav Klose, replacing them with Serdar Tasci, Andreas Beck and Patrick Helmes. It was a rather messy match – somehow we were confused and unable to build any pressure. Christian Grindheim scored from a corner to make it 1–0 to Norway.

The atmosphere in the Düsseldorf stadium had sunk to rock bottom. Joachim Löw made more changes, bringing Stefan Kiessling on for Mario Gómez and Marko Marin for Torsten Frings. Then, in the seventy-eighth minute, he took off Piotr Trochowski, and I was given 12 minutes on the pitch.

The whistling subsided briefly and when I sprinted on I even earned some gentle, but audible applause. I'm sorry to say, however, that no shiver ran down my spine as I cantered onto the pitch for the first time in full German colours. The conditions weren't right for that. The fans were disappointed, the team unable to find its rhythm, the result was 'wrong'. Of course, I was delighted that Jogi Löw was showing confidence in me. But it simply wasn't the right time for pure enjoyment.

Ever since a 2–0 defeat in the 1936 Olympic Games, Germany hadn't lost against Norway. And because the national side had also lost to England the previous November, after this defeat at the start of the year the press came down on us like a ton of bricks. Germany hadn't lost two home games in succession since 1956.

As I was leaving the stadium through the mixed zone a reporter asked me if I didn't regret my decision after this evening. Of course I didn't, but I refused to give an answer to such a stupid question. In any case, my 12-minute outing hadn't definitively committed me to Germany because the friendly against Norway didn't count according to FIFA statutes. It wasn't until I'd played a further six minutes in German colours, against Azerbaijan in August 2009, that the tug-of-war – which hadn't been anything of the sort – was over for good. Which was more than could be said about the debate over my decision.

This reached a climax in October 2010, when Germany were playing a qualifier in Berlin against Turkey for the European Championship. All the media were again full of discussion about my decision to play for Germany. Spiegel-TV filmed a report and called the match 'a celebration of football in the shadow of the debate about integration. The crescent moon against black-red-gold.' The journalists interviewed Germans and Turks. And of course they also found people who despised the decision I'd made. 'He's Turkish, not German. How can he be proud of Germany?' some asked. Others scoffed that I wasn't 'a proper Turk'. Their hostility was absurd.

Very soon it was no longer just about the game and the three points. After the match there was even some discussion about the colour of my boots. One newspaper, for example, wondered if with my choice of colours – a lot of red and a little white – I'd been trying to make a point and show the Turkish fans how close I felt to them, even thought I'd opted for the German national team and rejected the Turkish one. That wasn't my intention at all. To put it bluntly, I'd just worn any old boots. I hadn't thought about any kind of message; that would have been going too far.

The media, on the other hand, thought long and hard about the matter. Christof Kneer of the *Süddeutsche Zeitung*, for example, was worried about my narrow shoulders, on which the whole debate was apparently resting, and wrote, 'The issue has been so prominent that soon it's likely someone will ask Philipp Lahm why he decided to play for Germany.'

Nobody did ask Philipp Lahm, of course. But he played a pivotal role in this volatile encounter. In the seventy-ninth minute he passed the ball to me. All of a sudden I was approaching the Turkish goalie, almost unchallenged. With my left foot I shot it through his legs. 2–0 to Germany. But I didn't celebrate. Because, to cite Nazan Eckes again, 'my heart beats German and my heart also beats Turkish.'

After the match I headed straight for the shower and then had a bit of treatment. Having felt a little twinge in my thigh during the game, I grabbed one of our physios and asked him to massage my muscles. In the Berlin Olympic stadium the massage tables are in a separate treatment room, which meant I had no idea what was happening in the changing room. It wasn't until I shuffled back slightly wearily in my flip-flops and with a bare torso that I found out.

Chancellor Angela Merkel was standing in the middle of our dressing room. Her government spokesman, Steffen Seibert, and President Christian Wulff with his daughter Annalena were there too. I was so embarrassed I just wanted to turn around and leave again. After all, I wasn't on the beach on some club holiday where you can easily stroll up to a woman or a girl without a top on – quite apart from the fact that this woman was the most important and powerful person in the country. I hastily looked for something nearby to slip on. You can't stand face to face with Mrs Merkel half-naked, I told myself. But as she turned to me, smiling, I couldn't find anything apart from a towel, which I made a quick grab for. But before I could throw it around my shoulders, she was already holding her hand out to me.

'Well done for that victory, Mesut,' she said. 'And for your goal, of course.' She called me by my first name. 'I imagine it wasn't an easy game. But all that whistling whenever you got the ball didn't seem to trouble you.'

She spoke calmly and was very friendly. She looked me in the eye. 'I've had more difficult games,' I replied, before adding, 'I deliberately didn't celebrate after my goal because I didn't want to provoke anyone.'

'You handled it well,' the chancellor said.

We went on chatting a while longer. I told her that I'd been particularly impressed by the conduct of our opponents. 'After the game the Turkish captain came up to me and wanted to exchange shirts. I was thrilled. I didn't feel any resentment amongst the opposition that I've decided to play for Germany.'

Because a photographer from the chancellor's office was present the image rapidly went around the world. Before publishing it he'd secured the OK from the German Football Federation. When my friends saw it they texted me in jest: 'You and the chancellor? Have you got something going?'

Of course, the picture caused a great stir in the media again. *Die Zeit* described me as a 'model immigrant'. My name kept cropping up in discussions about immigration. For example, Joachim Herrmann, the Bavarian minister of the interior, referred to me as 'someone who brings his fantastic skills to our society, who gets every opportunity in this country.' During a debate on immigration on the TV programme *Hart aber fair*, there was a discussion about how German I actually was. The American writer, Heather De Lisle, argued that I wasn't an example of successful integration because I was German.

Virtually everybody voiced their opinion. Sometimes it was positive. Sometimes people sneered that I couldn't be taken as a role model as I was unable to say a single German sentence without making grammatical errors. In fact, I couldn't do anything except play football, they said.

I never took part in these debates. I never elevated myself above others or felt superior. After careful consideration I chose to play for Germany. I did my job well. And I feel comfortable and at home in the country of my birth. But I feel comfortable in Turkey too. And I've also had great times in Madrid and London. The media often tries to force you to tie yourself down to one thing. Along the lines of: 'Come on, tell us. What are you? German? Or Turkish? Where do you prefer to be? Germany or Turkey? You have to choose one. Come on, commit yourself. You can't be both. There's only black and white. There's only Turkish or German.'

I had to make the decision about whether I wanted to play for Germany or Turkey. Logically I had to opt for one or the other; there was no way around it. But I don't like being hustled in that sort of way.

You can definitely belong to two cultures. And you can certainly be proud of two cultures. A heart can beat Turkish and German at the same time. You can think like a German and feel Turkish. That's how integration works. With mutual respect, like in a great football club.

I'm proud to have chosen the German national team, in spite of the pressure. And I'm happy that I've never turned my back on Turkey.

5
RUNNER-UP
WITH SCHALKE

DON'T BE AFRAID TO MAKE MISTAKES

By now I'd also signed my first professional contract with Schalke. After winning the U-19 championship I moved up to the first team. As I've already said, everything that happened in these 12 months felt as if it had occurred in a few weeks. And the madness continued. Suddenly head coach Mirko Slomka put me in the German League Cup match against Bayer Leverkusen. Because I'd never thought this a possibility I couldn't alert anyone in my family. My brother Mutlu was on holiday with his family in Turkey, where he watched me play my first minutes in an official match for Schalke on television. When I returned to the dressing room after the match, which we won, I saw on my mobile that he'd already texted me. 'Wow! You nutmegged Carsten Ramelow,' and 'I'm proud of you!'

Shortly afterwards the 2006–07 Bundesliga season began. Before our opening fixture against Eintracht Frankfurt, we were on our way to the team hotel in Münster when

Lincoln* spoke to me. 'Mesut,' he said, 'go to bed early tonight, close your eyes straightaway and get some sleep.' To begin with I had no idea what he was trying to say. When I looked at him in astonishment, he smiled, placed his hand on my shoulder in a paternal fashion and explained, 'Let me tell you a secret. But you didn't hear it from me. This is an insider tip-off: you're playing tomorrow. You won't be in the starting line-up, but I know the manager's going to bring you on.'

I wanted to jump for joy. Shout out loud. Cheer. Hug him. Hug the manager. The entire world. I was going to get my first appearance on the pitch in a real Bundesliga match.

I bet no player in the world has ever forgotten his first minute in a league match. It's the milestone on the way to the top. I've played with so many talented players in youth teams. So many I was sure were going to become great footballers. But then one's girlfriend became more important than a potential career while another enjoyed partying long and hard, and was fed up with self-denial and discipline.

Millions of children around the world dream of playing in the Bundesliga at some point in their life. And now it was going to happen to me. Or, at least, that's what Lincoln was saying. But I wondered where he'd got his information from. Or was he just winding me up and playing a terribly bad joke?

'Are you sure? I thought the coach wasn't going to reveal the line-up until tomorrow. Come on. How do you know that? Please tell me. Please.'

* Lincoln Cássio de Souza Soares, commonly known as Lincoln, is a former Brazilian footballer who played for Schalke 04 between 2004–07.

But Lincoln just smiled and went away with the words, 'Don't say anything to anyone. And make sure you're prepared tomorrow.'

Instead of going to bed early for a relaxing sleep. I tossed and turned that night. I switched from lying on my stomach to my back. Put the pillow over my head. But nothing worked. I was so restless that even my roommate, Halil Altıntop, couldn't sleep.

'What's wrong?' he said. 'Why are you so worried? Is it because of tomorrow?'

Altıntop seemed to know too. So I opened up to him.

'What if I make a mistake?' I asked. 'If I don't play as the manager thinks I will?'

In truth I've never been the type of person to be plagued by self-doubt. I've always had a good deal of confidence. But that night, at least, things were different.

I found it a big help that Halil told me about his first Bundesliga match. Three years earlier, the same thoughts had churned around in his head when he found out he was going to play for Kaiserslautern against Cologne. 'I asked myself the same questions, Mesut. But do you know what? You can make mistakes. We're behind you. We'll get the ball back if you lose it. Play as normal. Trust yourself. Whatever you do, don't start passing sideways just to avoid making bad passes. That's not your game. Take your natural risks. And don't hide behind safe passes. Now go to sleep. You need your energy.'

Halil's words were of some comfort. But I didn't fall into a deep sleep. Not for a second. When I looked at the radio alarm on the bedside table between Halil and me, it said three o'clock. After what felt like another 20 minutes, only five had actually passed. Thirty glances later it was still only four o'clock. This night was simply refusing to pass.

When Mirko Slomka showed us the team sheet after breakfast I wasn't in the starting line-up. But Lincoln had said I wouldn't be. However, Slomka didn't mention anything about me being brought on during the game. So I took my place on the bench with Manuel Neuer, Rafinha and Sebastian Boenisch, amongst others, still uncertain as to whether or not my dream would come true today.

The game got underway. Halil scored with Kevin Kurányi assisting to make it 1–0. An hour had gone – no: only half that. This darned sense of time. We played well. Our tactics were working. The passes landed accurately at players' feet. Only the score didn't reflect the run of play. It wasn't happening for Frankfurt, as they say. We were playing in a manner that was in keeping with the ambition we'd set ourselves for the season. 'We want the title. Our team is now considerably stronger. It would be implausible to set out any other objective,' our coach Mirko Slomka had clearly stated.

In the half-time chat I was still hoping he'd mention my name. He didn't.

We began the second half by continuing to dominate as we had in the first. Until the fifty-first minute. After a foul on Kevin Kurányi we were awarded a penalty. Levan Kobiashvili was going to take it, but Lincoln grabbed the ball because he claimed he had a good feeling about it. His strike landed in the arms of Frankfurt's keeper, Markus Pröll. And all of a sudden the game turned on its head. Our dominance was gone.

While I was finally warming up I had to watch Ioannis Amanatidis take advantage of Eintracht's second chance and head the ball into our net. The equaliser. Followed by unmistakable whistling from our fans. Then, shortly after five o'clock, I was called over to the manager and told to get ready. Just a few seconds remained before I'd be making my first appearance as a professional in the Bundesliga.

Mirko Slomka put a reassuring arm around me as the fans kept whistling. He didn't say much, nothing monumental anyway. He just gave me a few tactical tips. He was going to bring me on for Hamit Altıntop. Then he said, 'Just enjoy it!'

In the weeks leading up to this game he'd fielded many questions about me from journalists. As had Andreas Müller, our director of football. 'We know what a great talent he is,' Müller had once said about me. 'He's a smart and carefree player, instinctively he always does the right thing. His footballing intelligence is incredible.' I found it almost uncomfortable to listen to, even though it obviously felt good too.

Gerald Asamoah had the ball. He played it to Kevin Kurányi. Via Løvenkrands it came to Lincoln. I watched the ball go from one to the other, while 79 minutes had already ticked by on the clock. With each pass I was being robbed of more seconds. A pass to the left, to the right, forwards, back again. 'For goodness' sake,' I heard my inner voice shout, 'just kick the bloody ball into touch.'

The desire to get my first taste of the Bundesliga was driving me mad with impatience. I was virtually unrestrainable; I was desperate to get running at once. Even though I'd be entering a forlorn match situation. Joining an uncertain team that which had squandered all its dominance. That which had inexplicably lost the flow of play. In which nobody wanted to take responsibility.

And yet I was as excited as a little child. How often had I discussed with my friends what it must be like to play in the Bundesliga? Up till then my biggest match had been the League Cup game against Leverkusen. It was only back in June that I'd won the German U-19 championship at the Lüttinghof stadium in Gelsenkirchen-Hassel in front of 6,528 spectators. Now I was a few seconds away from playing in a real Bundesliga game in front of ten times as many people. I'd invested every minute of training for this moment. Every shot at goal, every dribble had been in preparation for now.

As I stood on the wrong side of the touchline, waiting for the substitution, I allowed my gaze to wander around the stadium. In our goal was Frank Rost.

How that man had bugged me. Rost was a real grump. In 1999 he'd won the German Cup with Werder Bremen. In the penalty shootout in the final against Bayern Munich, he saved Lothar Matthäus's strike and then converted one himself to make it 6–5 for Werder. Rost had also played in the UEFA Cup against teams like Arsenal and he'd stood in goal for Germany.

I would always give Rost a wide berth wherever possible. To escape his snarling. He let us young players know what he thought of us – absolutely nothing! Whenever you got close to him he'd bare his teeth, and each time I fancied I could hear a menacing 'Grrrr'.

Once, when I was getting a massage after training, Rost, then 33, came in and shooed me away. Back then there weren't as many treatment tables and physiotherapists as there are today.

'How old are you?' he snapped.

'Seventeen.'

'Are you playing this weekend?'

'No!'

'Get down then.'

This is what it was like back in 2005. The hierarchy was stricter. The older players called the shots. The younger ones had to work their way up submissively. That's just how it was. And I didn't find it perverse or bad.

In retrospect it was good for us young players. Who were we to contradict someone like Frank Rost? To work your way up by finding favour with the elder players was an incentive.

When later I was with Werder Bremen – to fast-forward briefly – things hadn't changed. Thomas Schaaf and his assistant manager Wolfgang Rolff often joined in our piggy-in-the-middle game. It had been 18 since Rolff had won the UEFA Cup and so not only were his ball skills a little rusty, but his reactions weren't as quick as they had once been. And yet he never wanted to be in the middle, not even when one of his passes had been intercepted. Thomas Schaaf also turned out to be rather reluctant when it came to chasing the ball. Sometimes, just on a whim, he'd fire passes to us younger players, especially Sebastian Boenisch, that were impossible to bring under control. If he saw the ball bounce off our feet or thighs like off a concrete wall, he'd laugh and order, 'You're in the middle. It was your mistake.'

Back when I was younger you still needed a lot of discipline. We'd lug the balls, we'd fetch the jerseys, we'd carry the cones – and we didn't dare answer back when the Frank Rosts of this world said something. Today it's much more common to see young players in their first season as professionals parading around like spoilt brats and seasoned stars who've already got 300 top-flight league games under their belt. They answer back arrogantly as if they've already been champions several times and experienced everything on the pitch . . .

The ball is still in play. Gustavo Varela makes a sliding tackle on Patrick Ochs. Then the time has come. In the eightieth minute I'm brought on for Hamit Altıntop. My first minute in the Bundesliga has begun.

These days, after more than 570 hours as a professional footballer on pitches all over the world, 70 of which have been in the Champions League, I'm barely aware of the crowd during the game, apart from when there are corners and throw-ins. As soon as the whistle has gone, it's as if the mute button has been pressed on the remote control. The moment I'm on the pitch I blank out the background noise. No more voices. No cheering. No whistling from opposition fans. I've only got ears for my teammates. I hear the warnings from these 11 men if an opposition player's getting close to my back. I hear the calls to play the ball to them. Or their criticism if I'm hanging on to it for too long. Nothing else.

In my first game, however, it was very different. I heard the whistles of the Schalke fans, who couldn't understand the drop in our team's performance. I even picked out individual faces whenever I looked at the stands.

I had to think of Altıntop and his advice to play courageously, rather than hiding behind safe football. Not to worry about making mistakes. I ran, called for the ball, got the ball, played it on. Ran. Ran. Passed. Whistle! What? Already? How could that happen? I'd only been on the pitch for 20 seconds. It wasn't possible! Wolfgang Stark, the referee, must be mistaken. Or perhaps not. No, he wasn't. The match was indeed over.

And unfortunately I hadn't been able to change the scoreline. It stayed 1–1. Not good enough for a team with our lofty ambitions. I wasn't really satisfied with my debut either. Although it felt good finally to be part of the team, we – title contenders – had dropped two points in the very first game of the season.

In the next league match in Aachen I started on the bench again. Not a problem. But of course the cinema in my mind was playing the whole time. I saw a film in which I came on as substitute and played my second Bundesliga game. I couldn't think of anything else. I was totally excited. Shifting restlessly on the bench. But after 45 minutes Mirko Slomka wasn't thinking of making a substitution. Nor after 50 minutes. Once more, time didn't seem to be passing. Sixty minutes had gone by without the manager thinking of bringing me on.

As a young Bundesliga player you're always on a knife edge. On the one hand, footballers are dreadfully impatient, or at least I was. Not a bad quality to have, really, because anybody who sits back patiently and gives the impression of being satisfied isn't going to get far in this bear pit. Football is a hard and highly competitive business. You can't just be technically and tactically brilliant. You need nerve too. Occasionally you also need to make demands on your coach. He needs to feel how determined you are, and part of this is that you won't ever accept a 'No' from him.

On the other hand, you mustn't allow yourself to be devoured by your impatience, especially not at the beginning. Good managers usually know how to slowly acquaint young players with the Bundesliga. When they need match time and how much. They also know how to protect young players from burning out or immediately losing control in the media whirlpool.

Some journalists are prepared to give a really poor rating to a player who makes a few errors due to nerves in his first Bundesliga appearance, and will claim that he's not 'top league material'. Of course, you get wind of this as a young player. Your parents read it. As do your siblings. Your grandparents. Friends from school. And because you're not experienced enough you can't just brush off a rating like that. The joy at having made your debut dissipates. You feel insecure, and put yourself under pressure in the next game, in which you mustn't make a single mistake. You start to think about things too much. And then make the next mistake.

I bet every employee makes mistakes when they start a job, whether they're working in a travel agency or as a roofer. A trainee in the hotel industry who is unable to cope with the computer system has to call for help while a guest is waiting impatiently at reception. A young assistant doctor doesn't manage to take blood at the first attempt, making a wild stab with the needle. All rather messy. But all, ultimately, perfectly normal. Just not in football, where perfection is demanded of young players from the outset. If a journalist isn't happy with what they've just written, they can delete the sentence and rewrite it. But once made, a pass can't be taken back. In the worst-case scenario it lands at an opponent's feet and leads to an opposition goal. Then it's easy to bandy words around such as 'catastrophe', 'bad', 'disastrous' or 'embarrassing'. And yet, as they're typing these harsh judgements most journalists probably don't consider the effect these words are going to have.

Mirko Slomka didn't bring me on in the Aachen match. Nor did I play against Werder Bremen. My ten minutes as a Bundesliga player could be set against 260 as a reserve. The next time I came on as substitute, against Hertha BSC Berlin, we were already 2–0 down. Christian Giménez had scored twice. Løvenkrands had to come off, I went on, but there was no change to the scoreline.

Another game that didn't go as I would have liked. We dropped to sixth in the table. Slomka wasn't happy, the fans weren't happy and nor was I.

Our next match was against Wolfsburg. The atmosphere in the stadium was poor. The fans mercilessly booed our performance in the first half. No goal. Somehow that wasn't right. After we changed ends Slomka brought me on and I swore that today I'd finally be celebrating a victory with my team. I was desperate to find out what it felt like to experience the ecstasy of a great game with 60,000 spectators.

I stepped onto the pitch with my right foot. As I've always done. When I get out of bed I also put my right foot on the floor. I eat with my right hand, even though I'm left-handed. There are religious reasons for all of this. The right hand is the pure one,

the left hand is for removing dirt. For example, I brush my teeth
with my left hand. If I were to put my left foot on the pitch first I
wouldn't be able to play.

I pray just before kick-off. That's also a tradition of mine. It's
always the same text that I recite to myself on the pitch before the
whistle goes. In Turkish, the prayer goes:

*'Allahım bugünkü maçımız için bizlere güç ver ve özellikle beni ve
takım arkadaşlarımı sakatlıklardan koru. Allahım sen bu rızıkı hem
veren hem de alansın. Bizleri doğru yoldan şaşırtma. Amin.'*

Which, translated, means:

'Allah, give us strength for today's game and protect me and my
teammates from injury. Allah, you can open up the path (success)
to us or close it. Do not lead us away from the right path. Amen.'

This is my third prayer. Earlier, when we're warming up, I say
a few more sentences in Arabic:

Bismil-lahir-rahmanir-rahim.
alhamdu lillahi rabbil-a'lamin.
ar-rahmanir-rahim.
maliki yawmid-din.
Iyyaka na'budu wa iyyaka nasta'in
ihdinas-Siratal-mustaqim.
Siratal-ladhina an 'amta alayhim
gayril-magdubi alayhim walad-dalin.

Which means:

'In the name of God the gracious and merciful!

Praise be to God, Lord of all the worlds, the gracious and merciful, the ruler on the Day of Judgement.

We serve you alone and you alone we ask for help! Lead us on the straight path, the path of those to whom you are merciful, not of those with whom you are angry, and not of the errant!'

And finally, there is another prayer I say in the dressing room just before we go out onto the pitch. In Arabic again:

'Bismillahir-rahmanir-rahim.
Qul Huwallahu ahad. allahus Samad.lam yalid walam youlad.
walam yakun lahu kufuwan ahad.'

Translated, this means:

'In the name of God, the gracious and merciful!
He is Allah, the One, the eternally besought of all.
He begetteth not, nor was begotten.'

I learned this prayer from my parents when I was a child. I also say it when I get up and after eating. It's such a part of our lives that I've adopted it into my day-to-day routine. Even as a young boy I prayed on the football field before a game. And I've kept this up till today, because I derive a lot of strength and confidence from prayer.

So Slomka brought me on at half-time. Eleven minutes later a Kevin Kurányi goal put us ahead, while just before the full-time whistle Lincoln made it 2–0. The conclusion of the *Süddeutsche Zeitung* was:

> By the end of the first half the atmosphere was faintly apocalyptic. Those in the stands were suffering miserably. In the second half the manager was able to lift the crowd's low spirits with a substitution and by changing the formation. Coming on for Peter Løvenkrands, seventeen-year-old Mesut Özil animated the midfield and also inspired Lincoln to substantially up his game. Eventually the combination started to flow and Schalke looked almost serene. Now the fans were singing and dancing in the stands and love was in the air everywhere, as if this were a musical.

That was the feeling I wanted to experience. Sixty thousand people singing. People cheering. People bursting with joy, delighted at our performance. As I walked across the turf and applauded them, I felt as if I'd grown a few centimetres. As if I'd become taller and stronger. The celebrations of our fans were so loud my ears were droning when I vanished into the underground dressing rooms.

After two more games where I came on as sub, I spent four matches in a row on the bench. I had 14 minutes in our 4–0 win over Mainz, then two fixtures – against Cottbus and Bochum – where I didn't play an active role. And 23 minutes against Bielefeld were followed by 360 more in the worst place in the entire stadium: the substitute bench.

Spending time as a reserve is part and parcel of football, of course. It's the fate of every player that they can't be on the pitch permanently. Obviously the manager has to rotate players, make tactical changes and respond to fluctuating performances. I understand that and accept it. But I'll never sit on the bench, smile contentedly and look forward to an afternoon of good football, even if I have a spectacular view of proceedings from the bench – and all free. I want to play. I want to help. On the bench you feel like only half a footballer. Even a trainee chef wants to conjure up dishes rather than merely peel potatoes. Several more months passed, in which I had to exercise patience, before my first appearance in the starting line-up. On 10 March 2007 the day came when Mirko Slomka entrusted me with this responsibility in the game against Hannover.

Probably only because Gustavo Varela, Peter Løvenkrands, Christian Pander and Gerald Asamoah were injured. Rodríguez and Lincoln were also missing because of bans. I was going to play as the third striker alongside Kevin Kurányi and Halil Altıntop.

Our team was lacking in confidence. Although we'd topped the table since our victory against Werder Bremen in our twentieth match, in the three games since, against Wolfsburg, Leverkusen and Hamburg, we'd managed only one wretched point, thus forfeiting valuable ones on the way to the championship.

We had a tense relationship with our fans. But they seemed to be in a conciliatory mood before the Hannover game and accompanied us along the A2 motorway to Lower Saxony.

After 92 seconds a corner from me went to Halil Altıntop, who put us in the lead.

My first start in a league game and a beginning like that! But the joy at my first assist wasn't to last long. Because 108 seconds later Hannover got an equaliser. Jan Rosenthal disrupted Manuel Neuer after a corner and then Michael Tarnat pushed the ball over the line with his outstretched leg.

A jittery game followed with plenty of poor passes on both sides. Midfield skirmishes mostly, interrupted by lots of minor fouls. There were no more goals.

The fourth game in a row without a win. Afterwards we argued as to whether their goal had been legitimate. 'Rosenthal touched me with his hand; I wouldn't have let go of the ball otherwise,' Neuer protested. Slomka described it as 'a clear foul'. But Andreas Müller said, 'There's no way the ref would have blown his whistle for that in the Champions League or in England.'

Ultimately it was completely irrelevant whether the goal ought to have counted or not. In referee Knut Kircher's eyes it was legitimate and we didn't manage more than one point. All the discussions were a result of the frustration we felt at our own performance. And so I was in a bad mood on the journey home.

With 50 points we were heading the table. Werder Bremen were in second place with 47, ahead of Stuttgart. In fourth were Bayern Munich with 44 points.

Slomka put me in the starting line-up again for the next match – the top-of-the-table clash with VfB Stuttgart. I was desperate to show him that he'd made the right decision. I began like a wild bull. In the fourth minute I broke through on the left. All alone I was running towards Stuttgart's goalie, Timo Hildebrand. Ten more metres. Eight. Six. Four. Shoot. But my shot went just over the bar. 'Siktir lan,' I cursed (a general expression of frustration in Turkish, which is always appropriate when you're annoyed at yourself, someone else or the whole world). I ought to have taken advantage of the chance. Opportunities like that don't come around frequently. 'Siktir lan.'

I often talk to myself on the football field. Especially when I'm angry at myself and have made mistakes. But I also do it for encouragement. I didn't realise it at first. But my friends certainly did. When they followed my games on Sky they noticed that I was always chuntering away. Particularly before a free kick or a corner.

As in the seventy-sixth minute against Stuttgart. The ball had been released. I was four paces away. 'Go on, cross it,' I told myself. 'Right onto Kurányi's head.' I took a deep breath, kept the air in for a second, blew it all out again, ran and crossed the ball into the box. Not completely onto Kurányi's head. It bounced off him towards Hildebrand, who couldn't take it cleanly. Mladen Krstajić swooped in and put it in the back of the net. 1–0. Which was how the match ended.

This meant we were now seven points ahead of the team from Swabia. But thanks to a 2–0 victory over Mainz, Bremen were still breathing down our necks. We won four of our next six games, although we lost to Bayern and Vfl Bochum, and then again in our penultimate game against Borussia Dortmund. We'd gone into the encounter just one point ahead, and following our 2–0 defeat, Stuttgart now overtook us in the championship. We'd all flopped. None of us was even approaching our normal form.

For so long we'd been on course to be champions in my first Bundesliga season. We had led the table uninterruptedly for 13 rounds. At times we were ahead by six points. But now, if VfB Stuttgart won their home match they'd take the title. If the Swabians drew, we'd have to win our game by four goals. When we were leading Bielefeld 2–0 after early goals by Lincoln and Altıntop, a glimmer of hope sparked again. Especially when the video cube showed the scoreline in the match between Stuttgart and Energie Cottbus. Sergiu Radu had put the visitors in front and, all of a sudden, it looked as if we could be champions after all. But our hope lasted for all of eight minutes. First Thomas Hitzlsperger scored the equaliser and then our dreams were shattered when Sami Khedira's goal took Stuttgart into the lead.

While they celebrated the title in Stuttgart, an aeroplane paid for by some Dortmund supporters circled above our stadium, trailing a banner that read: 'A lifetime without a title'.

6

A DIRTY
SMEAR CAMPAIGN

SUCCESS REQUIRES A GOOD NETWORK

In my first season as a professional in the Bundesliga I made 19 appearances. Twelve of these were when I came on as substitute. I played the full 90 minutes on three occasions. So all in all I was on the field for only 28 per cent of the total playing time.

I'd been patiently impatient, as Norbert Elgert had advised me. But now I wanted more out of my second season. And I let Schalke know this too. Since late summer 2007 the club had been wanting an early renewal of my contract, which was due to expire in 2009. They offered me a basic monthly salary of 35,000 euros. If I played more than 30 competitive games in the season, this would increase to 60,000 per month and be retroactive. In addition to the basic salary there was a bonus of 5,000 euros per point. And if I were to play my first senior international fixture there would be a special payment of 100,000 euros.

In the best-case scenario I could have earned 1.52 million euros gross – an unbelievable sum that made me proud. Nobody in our family had ever seen such an amount of money. The idea that any one of us would ever have a salary like that was unimaginable to all of us. Even the 4,000 euros I earned per month as a young professional was a vast sum of money for me – and had improved the life of our entire family in a flash.

As I mentioned earlier, I never got pocket money as a child. I used to deliver papers, although I have to admit that my brother Mutlu ripped me off. It was actually he who'd been employed by the firm as a paper boy and he'd been given three districts to do, for which he earned 50 euros. I had no idea of this and was delighted when he gave me one of the districts, for which he paid me 5 euros.

I spent years wearing second-hand clothes that my mother was given by friends. It was irrelevant whether they were nice, stylish or a particular brand. All that mattered was that I had something to put on. There are childhood photos of me wearing pink jumpers – girls' clothes. I had to wear them because they'd been given to my mother by friends and it would never have occurred to her to throw them away unused just because they weren't blue or grey.

My favourite food as a boy, which I had to make myself after school, was white toast with curry ketchup. A packet of toasted bread cost about 55 cents. You could get the ketchup at Aldi for less than 1 euro too. I could easily fill myself up with that for days on end.

Compared to the misery I saw years later in a refugee camp in Jordan, mine was a carefree life. But we never had it easy. We knew exactly what it meant to have little. Not to be able to afford anything. And I knew exactly what it was to work hard for your money.

But when we negotiated my new contract with Andreas Müller, the money wasn't important. For my father and agent it was all about securing the best prospects for me from the deal. At the forefront of negotiations was not whether I'd be earning half a million or two million – we wanted a salary in line with what was normal – but how I could get as much match practice as possible.

The director of football assured us that I would get more playing time because Lincoln, Schalke's playmaker, was about to leave. The club anticipated that I'd be able to grow into this role. But no sooner had Lincoln gone to Galatasaray than Schalke announced the signing of Ivan Rakitić.

The Croat is a wonderful guy and a great footballer. I would go so far as to say that he's a friend. But when Schalke shoved him ahead of me, I was flummoxed. In our discussions with the Schalke bosses, which we'd felt had gone really well and been full of trust, there had been no talk of getting a replacement for Lincoln.

I had thought that Andreas Müller and Mirko Slomka would trust me and rely on me. From the club's viewpoint it may well have been a legitimate move to find another player for Lincoln's position after his departure – he'd been in control of Schalke's midfield for three years, scoring 31 goals in 113 games and assisting a further 34 – in case I wasn't up to the job. But they should have been fair and honest about it, and told me beforehand. How could they express their trust in me while suddenly signing a rival in secret? That's not how you deal with people.

Unable to understand Schalke's behaviour, we decided not to sign the contract that we'd agreed verbally straight away. We wanted to wait to see how the season developed and especially what role I'd play in the team – a perfectly reasonable course of action. We just wanted the certainty that Andreas Müller and Mirko Slomka would keep to their word and that in my second season at Schalke I'd be able to make significant progress, i.e. play much more. We weren't asking for more money or an amendment to the contract.

I was in the starting line-up against Stuttgart and set up Levan Kobiashvili's goal that put us ahead 1–0. At half-time I was substituted. Against Dortmund I was on the bench until a few minutes before the end, whereas Rakitić played from the start. I only had brief outings in the Wolfsburg and Bayern fixtures too, but I was on the field for 87 minutes against Leverkusen. Next, against Arminia Bielefeld and MSV Duisburg, I was in the squad but remained on the bench both times. So, after eight matches I had played only 185 minutes of football, even though I didn't think I'd been poor in training. Over the same period of time Rakitić had played 615 minutes – more than three times as much – in part, possibly, because the club had paid Basel about 5 million euros for him. I was free.

Because of a torn and sprained ligament I missed the games against Rostock, Bremen and Hamburg, but then I assisted two goals against Hannover and one against Frankfurt. On 15 December I played 61 minutes against Nuremberg – my last outing in a Schalke jersey.

I still hadn't signed the contract. I didn't have a great feeling about it and the promises that Slomka and Müller had made weren't reflected in the time I was spending on the field. Given these circumstances, I wanted some time to myself to consider whether Schalke was still the right club for me. But while I was hesitating, my contract renewal was a done deal as far as Schalke were concerned. When I looked at my bank statement I could see that they were already paying me more money. As if everything had already been signed and sealed. I rang my father and agent straight away and told them about it. 'Don't touch the money,' they advised me. 'We'll sort this out.'

When they contacted Schalke and asked what was happening they were told that we'd had a handshake agreement on the extension to my contract. Surely we'd been happy with the offer? But we had never accepted it. We regarded the financial offer as more than fair; all we wanted was time to weigh up whether the contract was right from a footballing perspective.

In the assumption that everything was fine – apart from the different interpretation of our discussions – I went to Istanbul on holiday during the season break. But nothing was fine. All of a sudden mudslinging began in the press, and I've never experienced anything like it since in my career.

On 30 December the German Sunday newspaper *Bild am Sonntag* revealed the contract that Schalke had offered me, even reprinting four pages from it. 'Schalke talent (19) turns down 1.52 million contract,' went the headline. There was a definite negative undertone to the text: 'An inconceivable offer for a footballer who's only played 30 Bundesliga games in his career and hasn't scored a goal.' Later, it said, 'A crazy offer that was only made to Özil because manager Mirko Slomka has a high regard for him.'

I hadn't noticed much of this high regard. But what I wanted to know most of all was how and why these documents had ended up in the paper. The only logical explanation that we could come up with was that Schalke themselves had wanted them published. It certainly wasn't in our interest.

The mudslinging continued the following day. This time *Bild* took up the story, and this article wasn't neutral either, but clearly targeted me: 'Money-grabbing young star playing games with Schalke.' There was another article to the side with the headline, 'When stars just can't get enough'. It began, 'Unfortunately, Özil's attempt to rip his club off is not an isolated case.'

I was at a total loss. I was 19 years old and being paraded in public. I had to learn the hard way that a football career was dependent on more than just talent, hard work and training. That you needed a network and people inside the club supporting you, who would leap to your defence in a power struggle like that. I had none of this. We were inexperienced and powerless, and didn't know what was happening.

When I turned up for training at Schalke at the beginning of January, Andreas Müller came stomping into the changing room. This wasn't unusual; he often paid a visit, especially when he wanted to put a bomb under the team before an important match. I was expecting him to say a few words about our preparation for the second half of the season. But I was wrong.

'Mesut Özil,' he said, without looking at me, 'is no longer going to play for Schalke. Not for the first team. Not for the seconds.

Not even for the youth team. And he won't be training with us either.'

I thought I couldn't be hearing him right. Why wasn't I going to play for Schalke any more? Just because I hadn't yet agreed to renew my contract? Just because I had been thinking about my future? Just because I'd dared to say 'No'?

As long as I nodded amiably and said 'Yes' to everything, they were nice to me and promised me everything under the sun. But now, from one moment to the next, they had turned into monsters who wanted to destroy my career. All of a sudden I was facing a pile of rubble. Facing the end. At the age of 19 I had to realise that as a footballer you're just a commodity and at a stroke you can become the plaything of directors and managers.

I looked around the dressing room helplessly. I was afraid for my future. I thought I was losing the opportunity of a lifetime. But nobody came to my assistance, even though there were so many seasoned players in the room. Our places were arranged according to the numbers on our backs. To my left sat Rafinha, with number 16, who would go on to play for Bayern. To my right was Darío Rodríguez, who wore number 18. Why were none of the old warriors siding with me? No Marcelo Bordon? No Mladen Krstajić? No Jermaine Jones? Nobody said a thing. Nobody defended me, even though I hadn't done anything wrong. I didn't even know who I should be angry with. My teammates, who were keeping silent? Or Müller, because he was embarrassing me so deviously in front of all my friends and colleagues?

What I really wanted to do was to shout at Bordon, 'Come on, defend me. Tell him that it's not on what he's saying, all that crap.'

Bordon was 32 at the time. He'd seen a lot in his life and what he said carried weight in our dressing room. I thought he really ought to have come to my aid. Now I know that the boys were obviously thinking of their own futures. Now I can understand their reticence. In this hard and uncompromising professional business they couldn't risk their own careers just because another player had a problem with the coach and the director. But at the time I was terribly disappointed in them. And furious.

Especially with Andreas Müller. While he stood in the changing room grinning after his speech, I had to cling onto my locker and stop myself from flying at him. The way he'd made me look like a fool was so unfair, so mean, so ugly. I didn't have the words to hit back at him, especially not since I'd been taken off guard and unprepared. I was desperate to let my fists do the talking. But I wasn't a thug, nor was I so stupid as to do him this favour.

When I went home I was a different boy from the one I'd been that morning. Pure chaos reigned inside my head. One minute I wanted to cry, the next run away – away from this bloody town with its bloody football club. At another point I swore I would become the best footballer in the world, and straight after that considered never playing professional football again.

But I didn't have a whole range of options in my life. I couldn't switch from one thing to another just like that, as in , 'If it doesn't work out with your medical studies, just become an architect or a pilot.' The only chance I had to make something of my life, to escape our very basic existence, was to become a footballer.

And now it felt like Mirko Slomka and Andreas Müller were trying to take this very opportunity away from me, ruining my chance of a better life. Just because I wouldn't submit to their rules. I feared I was going to lose the thing that gave me the most pleasure. And they knew that I didn't have the slightest chance of defending myself. Because who was I? A nobody. A talented no one! In this game I was powerless.

Baris Ciftci, one of my best friends, often lent me his ear at this time. He didn't mind me going over the same old stuff almost every day. 'I don't want to leave Gelsenkirchen,' I would say. 'This is where my friends are. You're all here. I want to stay with my family. It might be normal for other people to change clubs. But not for me. What should I do?'

Because we didn't want anything said against us, I turned up at Schalke every day despite my training and playing ban. That's what my father and manager had advised. 'We mustn't make ourselves vulnerable,' they explained. So I went to the weights room, the only place I was tolerated. I was pumping iron in a place where I was being treated like a leper. I wasn't even allowed to be treated by the physios.

On one occasion Bordon came up to me and said, 'Mesut, why don't you just renew your contract? Everything will be fine again. All they want is the certainty that you'll stay at Schalke. Things will get better for you at once.' But since Müller's little speech things weren't that simple any more. Although I loved Gelsenkirchen and Schalke was the club dearest to my heart, I couldn't just pretend that nothing had happened and happily stay with an employer who'd treated me so lousily.

I kept myself fit half-heartedly. I pumped iron without any enthusiasm. Did a bit of running. I was keeping myself busy rather than doing any serious training. And my evenings got longer; I'd hang around with my mates until late at night. We played PlayStation. We chatted. Sometimes we went to a different house. I needed the distraction – it prevented me from going crazy.

Was I living like a pro? No! Did I feel like a pro? No! Was I worried about my future? Yes, very much so.

While I just hung out and went through hell, Andreas Müller made sure that the public pressure on me increased. He went to a New Year's reception, one of the regular events that Schalke organised for its fans, in Letmathe in the Sauerland. Usually you don't get more than small talk there – harmless stuff – but the fans are thrilled to be able to see their stars up close. Policy statements aren't made at such events, nor will a manager announce any transfer news. But Müller used his visit to the Haus Lennestein pub to make the fans hostile towards me. 'Mesut Özil,' he said, 'won't play another game for Schalke 04.'

Over the following days the press was full of stories about me. I was described as 'scandalous' and 'a problem player'. *Sport Bild* took Schalke's side, too – or at any rate its chief football writer, Jochen Coenen, wrote a piece that said, 'Thank you, Schalke. Finally a club is cracking down and refusing to let players do as they please. Sure, Mesut Özil is one of the most talented footballers in Germany and has a great future ahead of him. But he hasn't achieved great things yet. From now on he's going to be seen as a money-grabber. And he should brace himself for the fact that this will hound him for the rest of his career. It's his own fault.'

At least the *Frankfurter Allegemeine* uncovered the club's behaviour as a campaign against me – a political issue in which I didn't stand a chance:

> Özil is now looked upon as a young professional who, after roughly thirty Bundesliga games, has lost all sense of moderation, has gone back on his word and is playing games with Schalke, as *Bild* puts it [. . .] The details of the contract were used as the basis for a campaign against the young player. No footballer of this age has ever been put under so much public pressure for this long. If this serves anyone besides the paper, it's FC Schalke. Any club that cannot or will not hold on to a money-hungry player looks better in such circumstances.

Every time I left the flat over the next few days to have a stroll through town I had to run the gauntlet. The people of Gelsenkirchen believed what the media and the club were saying. I can understand that they were annoyed. After all, they didn't know what was going on behind the scenes. It got to the stage where I even received threats. People would ring our doorbell to insult us. Hate mail arrived in our letter box – but I can even sympathise with that today.

People saw in me a young lad for whom an annual salary of 1.52 million euros was not enough. A young lad who, wanting more money, had gone back on his word. For someone living in Gelsenkirchen who's a stranger to luxury, who continually has to struggle for survival and who has to save every cent to be able to afford a ticket to the stadium, that's shameless behaviour. But of course this wasn't how it really was.

'Get me away from here,' I told my agent one day. 'I can't take it any more.' The club closest to my heart was causing me heartache. The sudden loss of affection was like your first girlfriend unexpectedly chucking you without any warning. In this winter of 2007–08 Schalke robbed me of my smile.

As I lay in bed at night I prayed that this wouldn't be the end of my career. But part of me thought it might be. On several occasions I said dejectedly to my brother Mutlu, 'Perhaps God doesn't want me to become a footballer. Perhaps I just have to come to terms with that. Maybe it's my destiny.'

Fortunately, however, alternatives to Schalke 04 soon emerged. Manchester United showed a keen interest in having me on loan. At the time they were the team to beat in England. In 2006–07 they'd won the Premier League by six points over Chelsea. Cristiano Ronaldo had scored 17 goals for Man United and Wayne Rooney 14. The title-winning squad also included Patrice Evra, Rio Ferdinand, Ryan Giggs and Paul Scholes.

In his 2013 autobiography, Alex Ferguson revealed that Wayne Rooney had once criticised him for not having tried to sign me. In the book, Ferguson wrote, 'Wayne said that we should have pursued Mesut Özil, who had joined Real Madrid from Werder Bremen. My reply was that it was none of his business who we should have gone for. I told him it was his job to play and perform. My job was to pick the correct teams.'

Ferguson didn't let on that he had actually tried to sign me earlier. And it hadn't just been a half-hearted effort either. But somehow the thought of living in Manchester had frightened me. Ten hours by car, eight by train or two by plane from

Gelsenkirchen. At any rate, 900 kilometres from my family, from all the people I loved. With whom I'd lived for the past 19 years in such cramped quarters.

I wasn't mature enough to make this big move. Not mature enough for the UK. I didn't feel I was sufficiently independent yet, especially not for a country where I didn't speak the language. I'd hardly ever been abroad. I'd once played for Schalke in Valencia. I'd been to Nancy, where we lost a UEFA Cup match 3–1. The U-19 European Championship had been held in Austria. But that was pretty much it as far as my trips abroad were concerned. At the time I only really felt comfortable in North Rhine-Westphalia. Manchester was too big for me. Too foreign. Too far away. Perhaps the spat with Schalke had also robbed me of a little of my self-confidence. In any case I soon told my agent he could say 'No' to Manchester United.

While in the background we were trying to save my career, Schalke kept up its attack against me. Mirko Slomka, still my coach, said, 'The player has to come to me or Andreas Müller and admit he was wrong.' And he claimed, 'If Mesut could make the decision himself, he'd certainly choose Schalke straight away. But he's clearly not allowed to have his own opinion. He's being controlled remotely.'

In an interview, Schalke's president, Josef Schnusenberg, also denied that I had my own will in these matters: 'I don't want to judge Mesut. The situation is clearly too much for him. He doesn't realise the opportunities he could have had at Schalke 04. He would have had the support of the fans, received a solid training and not a bad sum of money. I think it's a shame because he's a super guy. I can only hope that he'll find the right club now, for otherwise that will be the end for one of the most talented footballers in Germany today.' Schnusenberg described the bond of trust as 'completely broken' and said – probably to score some points with the fans and make me out as the bogeyman – 'It's about what you're prepared to put up with as a club and where the line has to be drawn. It's also a signal to anyone looking to sign a contract with Schalke 04.'

In the meantime I'd called Yıldıray Baştürk, who'd now gone to Stuttgart after stays at Bochum, Leverkusen and Berlin. He told me a bit about the club, the city and the manager, Armin Veh. I didn't meet Veh in person, but my agent spoke with him. I did, on the other hand, have contact with Dieter Hecking, whose Hannover 96 team was in fifth place in the Bundesliga after the first half of the season. Hecking really went for it. 'Do you know why you absolutely must come here?' he asked me, looking deep into my eyes. 'Because with me you'll play thirty games a season. I'll back you. I'll let you play. I'm convinced you need to be allowed to play. And that's what I'll do. Believe me: at Hannover you'll get more time on the pitch than at any other club.'

I liked the way Hecking talked. These weren't half-hearted promises, but concrete statements. All the same, for a long time I was leaning towards Stuttgart just because of Baştürk. I felt it would do me good to know I had a back-up in him. That he'd give me a feeling of home, when I was so far away from my family.

Armin Veh fought for me publicly, too, by letting everyone know his high opinion of me: 'He's one of the biggest talents in Germany and so far advanced for his age. But I mustn't praise

Özil too much or other clubs will start showing an interest in him.' Martin Kind, the boss of 96, also confirmed publicly that Hannover were trying to sign me. 'Yes, we're interested. We've been talking about it.'

It felt good to read and hear these words. Slowly I started to regain some confidence. As there was clearly some interest in me I didn't have to fret about my career. There would be some solution. The longer the discussions continued in January, the less frustrated I felt. The more I found myself slipping back into the role of a professional.

While I prepared myself mentally for a move to Stuttgart, Werder Bremen came knocking out of the blue. At the time they were a top club in German football.

In 2004 Bremen had won the double, that's to say both the Bundesliga and the German Cup. This was many years before the Brazilian striker Ailton hit the jungle in the German version of *I'm a Celebrity*. With 28 goals he was the leading goal-scorer above Bayern's Roy Makaay. Bremen was a team that, in the three-and-a-half years that followed their double success, would also go on to beat opponents like Ajax and Chelsea, while in the Champions League they even took Barcelona to the brink of defeat in September 2006, thwarted only by an eighty-ninth-minute equaliser from Lionel Messi.

Werder played exciting football with a clear plan. Week in, week out, the club showcased fun football, their only flaw being that they were sometimes a bit naïve in defence. But they played a direct, purposeful and elegant game, and at great speed too. Watching Werder was sheer pleasure.

Whenever the then manager Klaus Allofs was interviewed, it went without saying that he'd be asked if Werder Bremen wanted to be champions. And it went without saying that his answer was, 'Yes, we're aiming for the title.' If a Bremen player said, 'We can compete on equal terms with Chelsea and Barcelona,' nobody was surprised and it wasn't regarded as arrogance. It simply reflected their realistic aspirations.

When Werder's playmaker, Johan Micoud, went to Bordeaux after almost four years at the club, the Bremen team didn't fall apart. Instead they signed the 21-year-old Brazilian Diego Ribas da Cunha from FC Porto. His career had stalled at Porto; he'd had a falling out with coach Co Adriaanse and was banished to the stands. His career in the national side suffered too. After his debut for Brazil under Carlos Alberto Parreira, Diego played until the Copa América in 2004, but then wasn't considered for any World Cup qualifiers, nor for the Confed-Cup and then not for the 2006 World Cup itself in Germany.

But no sooner did he arrive at Werder than things started to go well again. Thanks to the support he got from Thomas Schaaf and managing director Klaus Allofs he also managed to regain his place in the Brazilian side. All these things were obviously important criteria for me. If Thomas Schaaf could bring Diego back to form after his problems at Porto and turn him back into an international player, why shouldn't he be able to do the same with me?

When I later sat down with Thomas Schaaf he explained his idea of football. We met at the Jürgenshof, one of Bremen's most traditional pubs – as Klaus Allofs, who was also there, told me.

The half-timbered building was only 15 minutes away from Bremen's stadium. We had our discussion in a private room – I think it was called the 'Friesenstube'. Full of excitement, I spent the whole time clutching my glass without taking a sip.

This meeting was very different from the discussions I'd had with Norbert Elgert. Back when I was making my move from Rot-Weiss Essen to Schalke, there was no time pressure; I was still a youth player. But now the clock was ticking and we had to come to an agreement that would give some direction to the future of my career. Besides, I was sitting here with a championship-winning manager and director. Between them, Allofs and Schaaf in their playing and management careers had won eight European titles, four Bundesliga titles, eight German Cups and one European Cup-Winners' Cup. An impressive collection. So I listened to the two men in awe and admiration.

I already knew, of course, that Bremen played the long ball and combination passes. I'd seen it a dozen times on television. But now my potential new manager explained the Schaaf principle in a few clear sentences: 'I want the team to be pro-active. We don't react to the opposition. They react to us. We set the tempo. I want us to play with fast and tight combinations, yet remain focused on getting the results.'

'Tim Borowski has progressed so far with us,' Schaaf continued, 'that Munich's going to buy him off us this summer. Miro Klose, too, took great strides here in Bremen. We helped him become the leading goal-scorer in the Bundesliga and German Footballer of the Year. So we know exactly how to nurture young players.'

We also discussed my problems at Schalke and my image in the wake of the smear campaign against me. 'I'm not interested in what's in the papers,' Schaaf said, before giving me his unequivocal assurance: 'If you come here to make trouble, we'll have problems. If you come here to play football, we'll have a lot of fun together.'

His expression was serious and purposeful. After a brief pause, he continued, 'I like exceptional players. I like people with distinctive, special personalities. If you send eleven carbon copies onto the pitch you're never going to have any success. I expect something specific from each of my players.' Then he explained, 'I value Per Mertesacker's calmness and lucidity. I love Torsten Frings's wild determination. From Naldo I want the power of his tackles. And I want your lightness of touch, your nimble foot, your dream passes.'

At the end Klaus Allofs reinforced what he and Schaaf had already said: 'You've got a great future ahead of you. Let us help you develop this. We want you to progress with us. We'll give you all the help, and especially all the time, you need for this.'

After the conversation with Allofs and Schaaf I was very keen on Werder. All the same I rang Sebastian Boenisch. My former teammate had already been with Bremen for six months. Although he'd missed lots of games since October because of a knee problem, he raved about Werder. Just like Baştürk in Stuttgart, he became an important advocate for the club.

It didn't take long for me to realise what I wanted – to go to Bremen! I wanted to join Thomas Schaaf and finally leave the Schalke episode behind.

On 30 January Schalke 04, still officially my employers, were playing Wolfsburg in the German Cup. Until a few seconds before the final whistle we were leading thanks to a goal from Lövenkrands. But in the last play of the game Wolfsburg equalised. From a Marcelinho corner Karimov scored to make it 1–1. There were no more goals in extra time so it went to penalties. Everyone scored except for Mladen Krstajić. Schalke were out.

Just before 11 p.m., when the team were on their way back, Andreas Müller's mobile rang. It was Klaus Allofs, telling him that he wanted to sign me for Bremen. Obviously I don't know the exact content of the conversation between the two club bosses. All I know is that my name appeared on the transfer list the following day. Alphabetically I was in-between Sanibal Orahovac, a centre-forward from Karlsruher SC, and Đorđe Pantić, a goalkeeper from TuS Koblenz.

That same day I signed my release from Schalke. There were no goodbyes. No presents. No flowers. No thanks. Nothing! In a short text message I let both Altıntop twins know that I'd signed for Bremen and was now gone. That was it. After 43 appearances, one goal and five assists. I'd worn the blue-and-white jersey for 37 hours.

In all honesty I wasn't sad that they didn't give me a send-off. It wouldn't have been appropriate given the situation. And at the time I had only a handful of friends in the team. So why should anyone have made a big fuss about my departure? It would have looked hypocritical and rather strange.

In spite of the difficult ending, my time at Schalke was a useful lesson in life. It taught me that a career doesn't always depend on ability alone. That power struggles and political intrigues can sometimes be decisive. And so you need people within the club to support and look after you.

If I were to meet Andreas Müller or Mirko Slomka today I'd shake the hand of both of them. I'd be friendly and can even imagine chatting about superficial, harmless things. But not about personal matters or in-depth topics, as I don't trust them any more.

I've never been a rebel or a hustler. I've never courted scandal or been greedy. I never went behind anyone's back at Schalke. I was a 19-year-old boy fulfilling his dream of a great footballing career. In retrospect I've often wondered whether I ought to have reacted differently, whether there might have been any way of preventing this dreadful conflict. Perhaps we should have been clearer in impressing on Müller and Slomka that the whole thing had been about my sporting prospects, nothing more. Perhaps we ought to have sought another conversation, in spite of what Müller said in the dressing room. But would they have granted us one? I don't know. At any rate, it was unfair for them to have thrown a spanner in the works.

At the time Andreas Müller was already 45 years old and had a great deal of experience. He'd been a professional himself for almost two decades. I wish he could now understand that he almost destroyed me. That you can't treat a young player like that. He and Slomka were responsible for me. But instead of shielding me they allowed me to be thrown to the media sharks.

7

MESUT AT HOME ALONE
YOU CAN'T BUY GOOD FRIENDS

On my first day of training in Bremen it was freezing cold. At no point in the day did the thermometer climb above four degrees. In truth I hate the cold. I'm the sort of guy who's drawn towards the heat. Who needs heat. And sun. Who hunches his shoulders when it rains and would rather crawl indoors. But not on that day, 2 February 2008. On that day everything was fantastic in spite of the cold.

As I was getting changed for training in the Bremen dressing room I relished every moment. I looked at my new colleagues, and enjoyed all the familiar sights and sounds that had been denied me for a month. The ripping of bandaging that some had around their bruised joints for stabilisation. The clacking of the boots on the hard floor. When I saw the balls, cones and bibs I really felt warm all over.

While Thomas Schaaf briefly introduced me to my new team-mates before going on to explain what he was expecting from us in training, I could feel my legs tingling. I didn't want to talk. Or stand still. Or listen. I wanted to kick, run, tackle, pass and score goals. To finally feel like a normal footballer again.

We got going. The ground was still heavy from the rain over the past few days. Even as we were warming up I realised that this was going to be an arduous session. But I didn't care. It was so liberating to feel the grass beneath my feet again. I felt like a foal that had been locked in a small, dark stable for weeks and suddenly set free again. I raced after every ball. I even went for passes I knew I had no chance of reaching. I expect I spent the entire session grinning like a young boy who's found and plundered the secret place his parents hide the sweets. Finally I had a fixed, defined daily schedule that I could stick to again. Finally some rhythm had returned to my life.

My desire to play was boundless. My energy, on the other hand, was limited. After a month of minimal training and spending most of the time just hanging around worrying about my future, my stamina was a bit of a disaster. I felt liberated, but worn out. In my head it was carnival time, but my legs were on strike. Nonetheless I ran as hard as I could.

After the first training session I went back to the hotel. Werder had organised a room for me until I found somewhere to live. They put me up in the Park Hotel, one of the best in Bremen. It was in the middle of the Bürgerpark. During the football World Cup of 2006 the Swedish squad stayed here. In the lobby hung an autographed photo of the actor Bud Spencer, who was once a guest here. Absolutely everything you could want was on hand. Except what I really needed – my family.

Because of the rotten headlines that were still very much in people's minds I had no desire to wander through Bremen or sit in the hotel restaurant and suffer looks from other people. So I dialled room service and had food brought to me. Every day I would order a club sandwich – it reminded me a little of my beloved curry ketchup toast from my childhood – then I'd phone my parents, my siblings and my friends from Gelsenkirchen.

I blossomed in training, while in the hotel I went stir-crazy. Even today I'm not a fan of hotels. Of course, we footballers have the privilege of being able to stay in the most upmarket places in the world and for that I'm very grateful. But every season I get increasingly tired of hotel life. I don't have any sense of freedom in a hotel. Life there is terribly boring. For me it has meant long periods of just watching films and series.

When I was younger I devoured one film after the other. Later I switched to watching TV series, as the tension builds more slowly and lasts longer. Or I watched American sitcoms such as *Two and a Half Men*. Now I understand that you can use your time more wisely and so I learn languages. For example, now I work on my English in the hours before a match, in order to speak it more accurately and fluently. But in the past, during my time at Bremen, I would spend almost all my free time looking at my laptop.

The only other entertainment I had was looking around apartments. In the first few weeks I might spend up to three hours viewing apartments and houses, just for something to do. With each property I'd pick out something I didn't like so I could see more the following day. Until I finally found somewhere. After nine-and-a-half months in a hotel I rented a lovely maisonette apartment, where access to the bedroom was via a spiral staircase.

One of the first nights I was there I suddenly heard strange noises. As children, my brother and I had always slept with the door closed. The knowledge that he was lying only a few metres away gave me a sense of security. But now I was all alone and, hearing the stairs creak, I held my breath and listened in the darkness. Nothing. But no sooner had I taken another breath than I heard the next sound. Someone's there, I thought, pulling the duvet over my head. But what good's that? I thought. What on earth was I to do now? My mobile was downstairs, where I'd plugged it in to charge. I certainly didn't want to turn on the light; the burglars would immediately know I was here.

Something had fallen over. Or at least that's what it sounded like. The noise was now slightly more distant again. I decided to creep into the bathroom, which was also upstairs, right beside my bedroom, and barricaded myself in there. I turned the key very carefully. Then I searched the room for something I could use against the intruders if it came to it. I armed myself with a mop I found in a cupboard.

I stood behind the door, clutching the red handle. Because I didn't have a radio alarm in the bathroom, nor was I wearing a watch – as I said, I'd only just moved in – I didn't know how much time had passed. My breathing was awfully loud; surely they could hear me? It was just a question of time before they'd find me. For some reason I was convinced that at least two people were sneaking through my apartment. I really didn't stand a chance. Two against one. Unscrupulous intruders against me. A 19-year-old against experienced burglars. With a mop as a weapon? I felt that my only chance was to take them by surprise.

So I took a deep breath, said a short prayer, then threw open the door, switched the light on and charged through my apartment, screaming. I rushed down the stairs, leapt into the sitting room, tore open the kitchen door and searched every room. *Aaaaaaagh!!!!* Nothing! The front door was locked. No smashed or open window. Where were they hiding?

Still holding my mop at the ready, I did another patrol of the house. But I didn't discover anybody on my second round either. Because nobody *was* there. What had scared me were a few branches being blown by the wind outside against the outside wall and gutter. My mind had been playing tricks on me.

Over the next few days and weeks I spent a lot of time on the motorway. Even though I liked the mentality of the people of Bremen and their kind, open manner – not like the gruff inhabitants of the Ruhr area – I escaped as often as I could. However much I enjoyed all the friendly greetings, I couldn't warm to the city at first. I missed my family too much – my parents, siblings and friends.

Most of my teammates at Bremen were in firm relationships. Many were already married with children. Whenever I was with them I felt like the odd one out, a fish out of water. I couldn't join in conversations about changing nappies, day care or first teeth. Although they took me with them and were happy to admit me into their community, I felt out of my depth. On the pitch I was happy, but away from it I found things tough early on.

After training I'd get into my car and head straight for Gelsenkirchen. Along the Osterdeich to Arsten and from there onto the A1 motorway. Past Osnabrück and Münster to home. A total of 248 kilometres, which would take between two and three hours, depending on traffic.

With every kilometre further from Bremen I felt better. At home my parents joked that I might as well give up my flat in Bremen, seeing as I was driving to Gelsenkirchen every day. I didn't find the driving a strain. Nor did I mind getting less sleep because I had to drive back early the next morning to make it to training on time. The key thing was that I was with my friends and could enjoy a few hours in my familiar surroundings.

After a few weeks, however, we all realised that things couldn't go on as they were. Sometimes I was driving 1,500 kilometres per week. Something had to change, we decided, even if we couldn't immediately work out what. Then one day, when I got back to my apartment after an away game, I found the front door open. This time my mind wasn't playing tricks on me; it really was open. The lock was broken. Someone had forced their way into my flat. I carefully poked my head around the door and peeked inside. 'Hello? Is there anybody there?' No answer. Again I called out tentatively into the darkness of my apartment. Then I notified the police.

This time burglars had indeed broken in. They'd rummaged through everything and stolen three or four watches to the value of 40,000 euros. I'd treated myself to them from my first higher monthly wages. For most of my childhood I didn't have a watch. In summer I used to go back home when the streetlights came on – that was my guide. But even as a boy I loved cool watches. To be honest I didn't think about how much money I was spending

– I simply wanted them. But they didn't give me much pleasure, because they were stolen soon afterwards.

The valuable watches had looked beautiful. I loved seeing them on my wrist. But that evening I learnt that it's not expensive watches that make you happy, but having friends around you who are a support and can even calm your anxiety at staying on your own in a large, lonely apartment that's just been broken into. I'm talking about real friends, mind you. Like my mates from Gelsenkirchen who I'd known since early childhood.

You can't take proper friends for granted. Nobody can. But it's especially true for people in the public eye like me. Over the course of my career I've met many people, including some who only wanted to be my friend because my name's Mesut Özil. For them I'm the professional footballer with the big salary. They haven't wanted to spend time with me because they think I'm a nice chap or because they value who I am as a person. They've wanted to be near me because they've been hoping for fame and money.

That's the other side of the coin. We professionals always run the risk of having friends who aren't genuine. We have to develop a sense of who is honest and who is phony and deceitful. Which is also true as far as women are concerned. There are so many girls who pretend to have strong feelings for a celebrity, but are targeting their money rather than their heart. For them love only works by credit card. Terrible. And awfully sad, in fact.

This is why I'm very cautious when it comes to women. I'm not someone who's quick to introduce my partner to my parents. I'm of the belief that it's a special moment – I'd be ashamed to keep on presenting new girlfriends to my parents. It's a question of respect. I also find it crazy how young many footballers are when they get married and have children. Barely is the career over and the husband no longer permanently in the limelight, than love dies.

It's all very different from my idea of a relationship. One day I'd like to marry a woman who I'm absolutely sure is the right one for me. I only want to bring children into the world when I'm convinced that they'll grow up in a caring and loving home. For me marriage is a special promise, not something you easily give up for a new partner.

In theory it might sound simple to fulfil one's dreams of the perfect friends and partner. In reality, however – especially in a situation like mine – you need very good insight into human nature.

And you need to be happy in yourself too. There are phases in life where you're more susceptible to charlatans, whether female or male. Such as when you've been alone and feeling lonely for some time. Fortunately I hadn't been. Or at least not for long. For soon after the burglary my friends Baris, Erkan and Ramazan, my cousin Serdar and brother Mutlu started paying regular visits. This spared me the endless drives from Bremen to Gelsenkirchen and made me feel much happier in my apartment. My familiar surroundings came to me and also protected me from false friends.

From that point on we virtually lived together, like in the US TV series *Entourage*, one of my favourite programmes. It charts the life of young actor, Vincent Chase, whose friends and acquaintances help him find his way in the unfamiliar world of Hollywood.

I got to know Bremen with my friends. I ventured out more often. In the afternoons I trained. In the evenings we went out to eat, our favourite haunts being Vapiano and Subway. On the phone my mother also taught me how to cook. Sometimes we spoke via Skype so that she could show me some techniques live. Over the course of several weeks she turned me into an almost perfect cook. To start with she explained how I should hold my fingers when cutting and chopping, then showed me the simplest hand movements. Later she sent me recipes that I learned to cook. She made me go shopping and then together we'd make baklava – a Turkish dessert made with filo pastry– and other delicacies. After a patchy start, I was feeling increasingly comfortable in Bremen.

8
FOOTBALLERS AREN'T POLITICIANS

ACTION IS BETTER THAN TALKING NONSENSE

I had a patchy start with Werder on the sporting front too. It took a while for me to establish myself in Bremen. Once my transfer to north Germany had been finalised, Schalke's director of football, Andreas Müller, couldn't refrain from taking one last swipe at me. In a public statement he sneered, 'He wanted to play more, and now in Bremen he's got the best ten in the Bundesliga ahead of him. Let's see whether he gets more time on the pitch than he did with us.'

To be honest, things didn't immediately look great. I was given short outings and was praised for what I delivered. For example, Jürgen Born, the Bremen chairman, said of my 30 minutes against Bayern Munich, 'He did a few back-heels that really put his opponents in a spin.' But I wasn't playing regularly. One day Thomas Schaaf came to see me and said he was considering putting me in the seconds that Saturday. The alarm bells immediately started ringing. I hadn't moved to Werder Bremen to play for the second team.

I thought of Norbert Elgert and his lesson of patient impatience. 'If the world collapses for a budding professional footballer because he doesn't achieve his ambition immediately, that's crap. But it's also crap if a budding professional footballer doesn't care that he's not making progress and just thinks apathetically, "Oh well, I'll achieve my ambition some day".'

So I rang my agent and vented my anger. 'If you allow me to play for the seconds, then we've got a problem. Stop that happening. I came to Bremen to play football. I'm working my balls off. I'm doing well in training. I'm doing everything I can here to make progress. But if I have to turn out for the second team at the weekend then I'm going to look for another agent.'

I was so frustrated. My outburst had nothing to do with arrogance – or impatience. I was convinced my career would stall if I went along with the suggestion. 'If I allow this to happen,' I told my agent, 'I'll have difficulties. They'll keep asking me to play for the seconds. Then the exception will become the rule. I've got to stop that. I want to become established in the Bundesliga. My teammates say that I've got what it takes. They're always encouraging me. Just make sure this doesn't happen.'

My agent promised to take care of matters. 'Calm down, I'll sort it out.' An hour later he rang back and said, 'You won't be playing for the seconds this weekend. And you won't be playing for the seconds next weekend either. You're a first-team player. Now go and visit your parents for a couple of days. Relax. Forget the whole discussion and then come back.'

My anger didn't just dissipate at once, of course. I drove back home with my friends. We played cards. Went to the cinema. But didn't talk about football.

It's often said that we footballers are immature and can't think for ourselves. That we're too slick, emotionless, superficial and unwilling to say anything critical. We're only interested, it's said, in showcasing the club's brand as well as our own, without levelling criticism at anything. Another complaint is that we only speak in rehearsed phrases and refuse to give our opinions on important and topical subjects.

I see things differently. If we're talking about me and my career, I am perfectly capable of speaking very plainly, as the case of my planned demotion to the second team shows. I gave both my agent and Bremen a very clear idea of how I felt. I warned them of the consequences and let them know my standpoint in no uncertain terms. I also remained firm in my dealings with Schalke and refused to give in to the pressure that was being placed on me from many sides. Does that smack of immaturity? I don't think so!

But I didn't have to make this episode public. If I'd started a quarrel with Bremen in the media would I have achieved the result I was looking for? Would I have been regarded as a more self-assured footballer? Certainly not.

And anyway, why do we footballers need to take a stance on every political or social question, as is so often asked of us?

Of course, I have opinions on many issues. There are things in the world that disappoint me greatly. That make me sad. And angry. But does that mean I have to run around and express my opinion to every camera? Especially seeing as some of the media these days regrettably feel the need to blow even a few words out of all proportion. A minor remark becomes big trouble, even though none of those involved were thinking in that way. Such turmoil often poses a threat to sporting success. So why do we have to reply to every question journalists put to us?

During his time as manager at Munich, Louis van Gaal was often very honest with his answers. He admitted that he made his daughters speak to him using the more respectful polite, rather than the familiar, form in Dutch. 'It used to be the custom in Holland. And I want my daughters to continue with it. I find it good to have some distance. I'm my children's friend and they love me. But they need to know that we're different generations. My younger daughter has never had a problem using the polite form, although my elder one has.'

After these comments he was described by some sections of the media as 'cranky'. But why? If he wants to live life that way it's his business. But, most importantly, it says nothing about his professional qualities. If he willingly reveals this detail from his private life, he should not be derided for it. It's not surprising that, after the reaction he got, his responses in subsequent interviews were superficial and monosyllabic.

Sometimes answering certain questions only makes you look stupid. I'm not an expert on politics and I don't have a detailed knowledge of the history of all the countries that have hosted World Cups or European Championships. But that's got nothing to do with any lack of interest. I'm a footballer and I'm paid to be one. I earn my money by dribbling, one-twos, tackles, assists and goals. Not by trumpeting political statements to the world, which wouldn't change things anyway.

Before the 2012 European Championship in Poland and Ukraine, the German Football Federation drafted some possible answers for we national players, in case the media quizzed us about the political situation in Ukraine and Yulia Tymoshenko. Its press release said, 'We don't want to muzzle our squad over the Ukraine situation, but given the current [!] situation we don't think it's a good idea for a player to voice his opinion. Joachim Löw and Oliver Bierhoff have also declined all media questions up till now.' To help us answer possible questions that might be fired at us the Federation therefore prepared three statements that, as it said, 'everyone could choose from'.

I think it's responsible of the German Football Federation to provide such assistance these days. It's a good thing that we national players are made aware of situations rather than being left to our own devices. It's also presumptuous to say that internal memos such as these go beyond the duty of care and prevent players from forming their own opinions. However, it's also important that no player gets the impression they're being persuaded to abandon their convictions. These communications are meant purely as suggestions and advice, and should not stop us from having our own views. For fundamentally, I am in charge of my own mind. Nobody dictates what I can say where and when. Nobody drafts an opinion for me, not even the German Football Federation.

Béla Réthy, the long-time commentator for the German channel ZDF, once complained, 'Many professional footballers in

Germany these days are like those children that go to British private schools; they're given twenty-four-hour care. The only thing that might not be checked is their fingernails. Young sportspeople are told they're jewels. They're told that the world outside is a bad place and that everyone's got it in for them.'

But he's forgetting that we sportspeople are also under scrutiny 24 hours a day. That we're forced to grow up earlier and can't secretly make mistakes like any normal young person. You certainly can have strong opinions as a sportsperson, but you don't have to blurt your opinion into every camera and voice recorder.

Réthy also said, 'Stars who've been given media training can't actually be interviewed any more.' I'd disagree with that too. You can't generalise about this and make it applicable to everyone. For example, I've had media training too. It was made clear to me that 'these days, what with all the social media, unfortunate comments can have disastrous consequences.' I've been made aware of how easily you can say something in all innocence, and then have it used against you. In fact, I learnt many important things during this training. But in some of the interviews that followed I couldn't recognise myself, and I didn't like it. Which made me realise that I'd rather go through my football career without this kind of support. That I don't want to mince my words, or be over-cautious and permanently worried that the wrong words might spill from my lips. That I want to say what comes into my head. That I don't want to hide.

There are many players who need this media training, but it's not my thing. And if reporters like Béla Réthy don't like my answers then it's not my problem. It's crucial to me that if I can personally change something, that's what I'll do. But with actions, not by talking big. Who would have benefited if I'd given my opinion on the Ukraine conflict during the European Championship? Nobody! All the same it was important that the competition took place in Ukraine. Why? Because, apart from anything else, it allowed some children to benefit from the BigShoe Project, which I also give money to.

BigShoe was born back in 2006, when football fans from Lake Constance, where the Togo national squad was staying during the World Cup, decided to collect money to pay for an operation for a young African girl called Nourrisson. That one good deed led to more. The organisation grew and grew, and in the following years started helping children in the host countries of subsequent international competitions, such as South Africa, Poland, Ukraine and Brazil. BigShoe supports a team of doctors that mainly undertake operations to correct cleft lips and palates. Heart defects are also corrected, and foot, hand and facial disorders operated on, as well as burns, which are a big problem in developing and emerging countries where people sit around fires and rely on kerosene lamps for light.

When we became World Champions in 2014 I gave part of my prize money to BigShoe. This allowed 23 operations to be performed on children in a makeshift jungle hospital in Coroatá, north-eastern Brazil. That's how I make my social contribution, not by gabbing away. And this was precisely the reason behind my trip to the Middle East in 2016, which was so widely reported on.

In truth I'm reluctant, even in this book, to talk publicly about this tour. After all, I didn't go to the Middle East to be hailed as a good person. It wasn't a PR stunt – not something to help polish my image. So why am I writing about it now? Because of Alexander Gauland – the deputy leader of the far-right political party, Alternative für Deutschland (AfD), who made the most shocking comments about my trip just before the European Championship, talking most disparagingly about me and my actions, even though he'd never met me and quite clearly had no idea about how I think and what makes me tick.

Because I'd gone to Mecca in my free time and from there had tweeted a photo of me in front of the Kaaba, the most sacred site for Muslims, he and some of his party colleagues thought they had the right to criticise me. First the Saxony branch of the AfD called it an 'antipatriotic signal', then, in *Der Spiegel*, Gauland described my trip as 'something that would require a lot of getting used to for a party that doesn't regard Islam as a part of Germany.' He also said things like, 'As I'm not interested in football I don't really care where Mr Özil takes himself off to. But for civil servants, teachers, politicians and decision-makers I would definitely ask the question: Is democratic Germany the right place for someone who goes to Mecca?' As far as he was concerned, 'Islam didn't belong in Germany.'

All I can do in response to such comments is shake my head. And I don't want to sound off about the man as it would make him more important than he is. Most important, I'm a footballer rather than a politician. And I'm a person. Someone who wants to help when he can. With deeds rather than words. And it was

I join the children of the huge Zaatari refugee camp in Jordan, a haunting and humbling experience, and a far cry from the world in which sportsmen normally move.

A pilgrimage to Mecca – and a photo which I tweeted with the hashtags #HolyCity #Islam #Pray.

This small boy never left my side during the visit to Zaatari. 'I am you, but smaller,' he said.

With his superb skill and work ethic the Brazilian playmaker Diego was a great role model for me at Bremen.

We became known as 'the kicking club' after Tim Wiese's boot caught Iva Olic in the face in one of Bremen's fierce derbies with Hamburg.

Joy unconfined after my winning goal for Bremen in the 2009 German Cup final against Leverkusen.

Bremen supporters mischievously recreated an over-sized version of the ball of waste-paper which bizarrely help us beat Hamburg en route to the 2009 UEFA Cup final.

Bremen coach Thomas Schaaf offers me encouragement and instructions before extra time against Shakhtar Donetsk in the UEFA Cup final

A euphoric Bremen squad after the 2009 German Cup final in Berlin, when I was fortunate enough to score the decisive goal.

In the media spotlight – where I seldom feel comfortable – after becoming a Real Madrid player following my move from Bremen.

To wear the legendary all-white strip of Real Madrid is a privilege for any player – and I was no exception – from any football culture in the world.

Togetherness personified as Sami Khedira, myself, Lukas Podolski and Bastian Schweinsteiger savour a goal for Germany against Australia in the South Africa World Cup.

My delight after scoring against Ghana in the 2010 World Cup is plain for all to see.

I adore lions, and the World Cup in South Africa gave me a chance to get up close and personal with one along with fellow big-cat admirer Lukas Podolski.

A beautiful sight at the Bernabeu Stadium as the Real fans make a colourful show of their passion during my time there.

precisely for this reason – to help – that in spring 2016, not long before our preparations for the European Championship, I first went to visit a refugee camp in Jordan and then, because I was already in the region, visited Mecca.

The idea for my trip came about six months earlier. In November 2015 I met the Jordanian prince, Ali bin al-Hussein, who, that same year, challenged Sepp Blatter for the post of FIFA president. A true gentleman, he was educated in both the UK and USA. His sister, Haya, was, for a while, president of the International Federation for Equestrian Sports, and he has been the head of the Jordanian Football Association since the age of 23. During this time one of his achievements has been that women with headscarves can now play football too. And Prince Ali is also a big Arsenal fan!

When we went for dinner together one gloomy November evening – it was pouring so hard that the rain was flooding out of the drains – we started with small talk. About Leicester City, who at the time were the surprise leaders of the Premier League after 13 matches, ahead of Manchester United, Manchester City and us. We'd won eight games and it was tight at the top of the table; we were just two points off the lead.

'Who's going to win?' Prince Ali asked.

As quick as a shot I obviously answered, 'Arsenal!'

Over the course of the evening we got on well and started to discuss more interesting matters. And our discussion gave birth to an idea. Prince Ali told me about children in a refugee camp in Jordan who had experienced the war in Syria at first hand, and had had to leave their home country in fear of their lives. Small children, who might never have a real chance in life, just because they had the misfortune to be born at the wrong time in the wrong part of the world. 'For many people life really isn't fair,' Prince Ali said. Together with his foundation he had set up children's football pitches so that they could entertain themselves for a few hours a day by playing football.

That evening we hatched our plan to visit the refugee camp together. Arsenal had already asked me once to fly out to Dubai with our club sponsor Emirates. The previous year I'd had to decline. But next year, I told Prince Ali, I could fly to Dubai and then on to Jordan, thereby linking both events. And so we gradually planned a week-long tour of the Middle East, which would take place at the end of the 2015–16 season.

I'd have preferred to undertake the trip privately without any press. But that was impossible because Arsenal were on board and Prince Ali was firmly of the belief that my visit to the refugee camp was giving out an important message. He was right, of course. So I allowed myself to be persuaded to have some photos taken, but declined all interview questions about the matter. After it had come out that I'd visited a refugee camp in Jordan, some members of the media wanted statements from me. 'You could say something like, all European countries must look after refugees,' was a suggestion from one journalist. But that's exactly what I didn't want. I didn't want to create any headlines; I just wanted to help those young children through their difficult times. It was perfectly fine, I thought, to draw attention to the issue with photos.

I went to Jordan via Dubai and Abu Dhabi with my team

– that's to say Serdar, Ramazan, Erjan, Erdal and Erkut – and we spent a day in the camp. A bumpy road leads to Zaatari, the biggest refugee camp in the Arab world. Around 85,000 people live here. Every day children are born as refugees in this gigantic temporary home with its seemingly endless rows of white tents and containers.

The camp was opened in 2012. Fenced in behind barbed wire, it's just a few kilometres from the Syrian border crossing at Jaber. 'Zaatari,' one of the workers for the refugee aid organisation UNHCR told me, 'is deliberately meant not to look like a city, so there are no proper houses here. The idea mustn't take root that this is here for ever. We don't want to create the impression that this is a final destination.'

Fifty per cent of the inhabitants of Zaatari are minors. The children are, at least, able to go to school, but many of them sleep badly. At night time they try to avoid falling asleep for fear that there'll be another explosion the minute they close their eyes. 'There's very little that's beautiful in Zaatari,' the man from the aid organisation told me. 'But there's food and most of all there's security,' the most important thing for children.

When I got out of the car a young boy came running up to me straight away. He looked about ten. And he was wearing a football shirt that was very familiar – a Real Madrid one with the number 10 and my name on the back. 'I'm a mini you,' the boy said proudly, and from then on he wouldn't leave my side. When I put my arm around him he pressed himself close to me and smiled. 'Come on, I'll show you where we play football,' he said, tugging my hand.

It was a moment I'll never forget. I know that this is a well-worn phrase, a cliché that people just come out with. But I mean it in all seriousness, even though I find it hard to describe the emotion of this moment with real words. I know that this little boy had experienced things in his life that would stay with him for ever. That images of war, which many adults would have trouble coming to terms with, were burned in his mind. Up till now this mini-Mesut hadn't had much to laugh about in life. But on this day there was a broad grin across his face. As we walked over to the pitch his eyes were beaming and radiating an incredible and infectious joie de vivre. He didn't want to let me go.

I didn't have much when I was small. But compared to these children I can look back on a golden childhood. I never had to fear for my life. I never had to hide from soldiers. I was able to play football and, unlike these poor things, I had a real chance to make something of my life.

When we got to the pitch I suddenly saw the children laugh. I heard cheerful cries, giggles of happiness. I saw how carefree they were when they played with or against me. I know that my visit didn't make the world a better place, and it would be naïve to think so. But I'm proud to have given those children a brief moment of happiness. And I'm pleased to have seen with my own eyes how hard other people in the world have to struggle. Anybody who's been to Zaatari knows how minuscule and insignificant their own problems are.

The next and final stop on our Middle Eastern trip was the aforementioned visit to the Kaaba in Mecca, the most important building in the world for we Muslims. It's in the inner courtyard of al-Haram Mosque (the Great Mosque), and in our faith it is the first house of God on earth. In my childhood I kept hearing about Mecca and the Kaaba. From my parents at home and especially when we went to the mosque. Once in a lifetime every Muslim who is able to should make the pilgrimage there as a reminder of God, his commandments and his love for mankind. I'd already heard and read so much about Mecca – I simply felt the need to visit this place once in my life. To experience it myself. To see it and soak up all the impressions. My going to Mecca is comparable to devout Catholics visiting the Vatican.

More than two million people liked my photo in front of the Kaaba, which I'd intentionally accompanied only with the hashtags #Mecca #HolyCity #SaudiArabia #Islam #Pray. People there were queueing to have photos taken with me. Young people from Indonesia, in particular, were completely ecstatic to meet me there.

Stefan Kuzmany in *Der Spiegel* gave its opinion on my trip and my tweet, as follows:

Mesut Özil has never made a secret of his faith; he spoke about it publicly years ago. And yet the picture from Mecca gives a stronger message than the earlier interviews. It's a proud acknowledgement. Because it's so casual Özil's photo is a powerful statement in the German debate about Islam. Because anyone who cheers him on – the key player, popular figure and World Champion of 2014 – is just as casually answering the question of whether Islam belongs as Özil does with his pilgrimage photo. Of course it belongs. It would be sad otherwise. If the World Champion Mesut Özil, a religious man, didn't belong to Germany we wouldn't be World Champions.

I was delighted to read this assessment, especially in *Der Spiegel*. The news magazine hadn't been one of my greatest fans. During the 2014 World Cup it published a story about me that said I was a less than impressive public figure.

Der Tagesspiegel, for its part, called my tweet from Mecca 'shocking in the best sense of the word' and wrote: 'Few people can be unmoved by the picture. It's fascinating in a foreign, almost exotic way. Mesut Özil is posing as a pious, devout individual. This is unusual, bewildering, particularly in Germany and Europe, the religiously illiterate old continent [. . .] A picture like Özil's just reminds us that, from a global perspective, faith is the norm and the lack of it a deviation.'

To be frank, I hadn't meant to spark a debate with this picture. Nor did I ever ask myself whether my faith corresponded to a norm or not. It's just part of my life. It gives me strength and direction. And it's taught me to treat other people with respect and brotherly love, especially when they have less than I do. If my visit contributed to some sort of understanding then, of course, I'm delighted. For if there's one thing I've learned, both in the Monkey Cage in Gelsenkirchen and on my trip to Jordan, it's that most people are basically very similar, irrespective of what they believe in. They want a good life and the opportunity to make their dreams come true.

9

KUNG FU GOALIE

TEAM SOLIDARITY IN STORMY WATERS

After my involuntary hiatus at Werder, there were only more short outings to begin with. In one game, as I was about to take a free kick, the referee even came up to me and said, 'Why doesn't Schaaf play you more often?' I thought I'd misheard him at first. Was the referee, an independent arbiter, expressing his surprise at the brevity of my appearances? Did he really ask that? When I looked at him, baffled, he expanded on what he said and now I realised I hadn't misheard him: 'Bremen plays differently with you in the side – better!'

This praise reinforced my conviction that I was correct to resist any demotion to the second team. I was on the right path. And although I was desperate to be in the starting line-up for every Werder game, I remained patient and from then on trusted all of Schaaf's decisions. It would have been inappropriate for me to complain or bring more unrest into the team. The situation was difficult enough as it was.

After the first half of the season at the end of 2007, Bremen and Bayern Munich were equal on points at the top of the table, with 36 apiece. But Werder had scored 11 more goals. Arminia Bielefeld had been blown away in our 8–1 home victory. We'd put five past Bayer Leverkusen too. However, Schaaf's squad had also conceded 16 more goals than the German championship record-holders.

The squad had suffered a number of injuries in the first half of the season. Patrick Owomoyela was missing from mid-September to the end of January because of thigh problems, and was unable to play in 19 games. In the second half of the season the injury woes got even worse. Torsten Frings missed 12 games because of a torn ligament in the knee, and didn't rejoin the squad until mid-March. A subsequent capsular injury then ruled him out of another game in April. Ivan Klasnić struggled with muscular problems, missing three weeks and four games in March. Diego missed two games, one because of a pubic bone stress injury and the other due to thigh discomfort. Per Mertesacker was absent for two games in mid-March after being sent off in the previous fixture against Stuttgart for a professional foul in the eighty-ninth minute. Our plague of injuries didn't spare Daniel Jensen or Tim Borowski either.

Consequently we had a shaky start to the second half of the season. We lost against Bochum. Drew against Bayern. At the beginning of March we were hammered 6–3 by Stuttgart, lost 1–0 to Wolfsburg, drew 1–1 with Bielefeld, then were beaten 1–2 by Duisburg. After 17 weeks at second in the table, and breathing down Bayern's neck, we suddenly plummeted to fifth.

'Werder in ruins,' was *Bild*'s accurate headline. The paper thought we lacked determination and discipline, which wasn't altogether incorrect. When we were knocked out in the UEFA Cup last 16 by Glasgow Rangers, Diego and Aaron Hunt clashed in the dressing room. Personally I don't find that such a bad thing. Players must be able to disagree at times – it shows that a team still has life and passion to it.

I would find it worse if players merely accepted defeats or poor performances without any discussion. If they happily came to terms with failure and were able to shuffle it off without any frustration. It's important to shout sometimes, voice your dissatisfaction, argue about bad passes or stubbornness on the pitch. It can be liberating as long as such discussions don't cross the line. It's fine to hurl criticism at others, air your grievances, as long as you don't say anything personal or insulting. The following day, when you next see that person, you need to be able to look them in the eye and still have mutual respect.

Completely out of order, however, are physical attacks on teammates. But that's exactly what happened when I started with Bremen. In a practice match, while trying to bring the ball under control, Naldo kicked Boubacar Sanogo in the stomach. He crumpled to the ground in pain. I'm pretty sure the kick was unintentional, and all Naldo said was, 'I didn't see you.' But he didn't apologise.

Shortly afterwards it was Naldo who was on the ground. Just a few tackles later Sanogo had given him a rather nasty whack in the calf.

Just what the media had been waiting for. At the time I was impressed by how Thomas Schaaf and Klaus Allofs dealt with the situation. In public the manager defended his team. 'I'm always combative. If anybody wants to pick a fight with me then be my guest. I'm here,' Schaaf said, countering his critics and defending his work and players. He wasn't going to give any of his players a public bollocking just so journalists had something to write about, he said, playing down Sanogo's attack on Naldo.

He was given the same backing by the club that the manager had given us. Allofs said, 'I don't see the coach doing anything wrong, and I'm at training almost every day.'

Internally, however, there was a different take on matters. Schaaf got rid of our free Sundays and sometimes scheduled two training sessions per day. He made us sprint and do press-ups until our arms burned. He also impressed on us that 'without team solidarity we don't have a hope in future.'

The table football we used to amuse ourselves with in the dressing room disappeared too. In all honesty I have to say that I find this sort of punishment a bad idea. You don't win and lose matches because of table football. It's good for your mind without being physically strenuous. Playing two against two for 20 minutes doesn't leave you exhausted. You might be able to punish kindergarten children by taking toys away, but not professional footballers.

Thomas Schaaf is an exceptional manager. A very good coach with an unbelievably high level of tactical understanding who was also very clear, like José Mourinho. He doesn't laugh much. In fact, he doesn't laugh at all, apart from when he's nutmegged Sebastian Boenisch or me in the circle. You just have to accept that Schaaf's not a smiley-face who runs around the field in an irresistibly good mood. But that's not his job.

Ever since the beginning of my career I've tried to pick up and soak up the best qualities from each manager. What I certainly didn't take from Schaaf was his way of punishing players. In this respect Mourinho is an outstanding coach. When I was at Real Madrid he never stopped us from going out to celebrate. He really didn't have the slightest interest in what players got up to privately. Under Mourinho nothing was prohibited. He didn't get irritated if we used our mobiles in the dressing room. We were allowed to text and even if we were called a minute before the start of training, he didn't mind. I don't know of any manager who is as relaxed as him. The only thing he demanded of us was 100 per cent commitment on the pitch. He wanted us to focus only on football and not get distracted by anything else.

If there was something he didn't like, he'd let us know in a different way. His criticism was more subtle. For example, once I was tempted to smoke on holiday. A completely stupid idea, and not worthy of a football player. There's no discussion needed. But somehow I just felt like it. We were on a yacht with friends. All season I had led an ascetic life, forgoing alcohol, sweets and unhealthy food. And all of a sudden there was this packet of cigarettes, the sun was shining and I fancied one.

Of course, a paparazzo caught me from his dinghy 100 metres away and took a photo of Özil puffing away. When we returned to Madrid ready for the first training sessions, Mourinho gave a brief speech beforehand. He welcomed us back and said what he expected of us. Then he took out a photo collage and held it up. One picture showed me looking cool on the yacht with a cigarette out of the corner of my mouth. Bare torso, sunglasses, blue sky and sea. In the other photo was my teammate, Fábio Coentrão, our left-back. He'd pulled his cap right down and was standing in a dark corner, puffing on a cigarette too. 'There are two types of footballers,' Mourinho said, still holding up the photos. 'Footballers with class, like Mesut here. And footballers who have no class.'

Everybody laughed. But of course we'd all understood the actual message. Mourinho wanted us to know that if we behaved unprofessionally on holiday he'd get wind of it and wouldn't be impressed. But for him it was enough to tell us in this way. He could have easily had a fit and expressed his disgust at our lapse more directly, but he relied on our personal sense of responsibility.

In Bremen we gradually got back on track. We halted the plunge down the table and won against Berlin, Schalke and Rostock, scoring nine goals in total. Then came 26 April. We were playing Karlsruher SC in the Wildpark stadium. Sebastian Freis put the home side into the lead. Diego equalised. In the twenty-ninth minute Tim Borowski passed to me and I shot with my left foot. I didn't strike the ball cleanly at all. From 20 metres it lolloped towards the goal. A really embarrassing strike that could at best be described as a back pass. I was waiting for their keeper to gather the ball with a smile and put it back into play. But all of a sudden the ball was in. In the goal. My limp shot put us into the lead because a small bump had made the ball change direction, giving Markus Miller a nasty surprise. My first goal in the Bundesliga! That made me Werder's nineteenth scorer in the season – a record, as in the history of the competition to date no single club had had so many different players on the scoresheet.

I watched the goal countless times online on YouTube – I kept pressing Replay, to start the thirty- or forty-second clip yet again. Your first goal in the Bundesliga is just as exhilarating as your first Bundesliga appearance. It's just that the feeling of happiness comes as a greater surprise. Before my first appearance I was ecstatic the night before. I felt the strongest emotions on the touchline just before the fourth official signalled I was coming on. Obviously, you can't have these same feelings before a goal because, logically, you don't know you're about to score.

I saw the ball leave my foot and hobble towards Miller. How embarrassing, I thought. Then, when it was in the goal, I couldn't take it in at first. And while I was pondering how the ball could have found its way into the back of the net I was already haring around the pitch in celebration. Without properly realising it. It wasn't until I felt all those hands on my body, pulling me this way and that, ruffling my hair and slapping my shoulder, that I regained my senses. 'I've scored a goal, I've scored a goal,' I heard an inner voice say. I was grinning so broadly that my cheekbones were aching.

But the joy didn't last long, because Sebastian Freis scored for the second time that afternoon. And after a goal from Edmond Kapllani we were even behind for a long time before Sanogo scored the equaliser.

We won the next game against Energie Cottbus. After that our next match was the northern derby against Hamburger SV – one of the most heated games I've ever witnessed, if only from the bench. Everyone was fired up. Nobody ducked out of any tackle. As a Bremen player you couldn't lose against Hamburg. It's not allowed. And everyone on the team performed with this in mind – an impressive sight. Our physical presence on the pitch was just right. Everyone was running around as if to say to the opposition: 'Nobody's getting past me. What do you little Hamburgers want anyway?' Everyone pursued the ball. Nobody rested even for a second. No run back was too strenuous.

Whenever our ball play wasn't enough, there was pushing, barging and a bit of provocation. Daniel Jensen swore. Tim Borowski jostled. Hugo Almeida mouthed off at his opponent. Attempts at intimidation! But the Hamburgers put up resistance. Paolo Guerrero elbowed Tim Wiese. Vincent Kompany went hard at Diego in the same way.

At the start of the second half Frank Baumann was shown the red card for holding on to Rafael van der Vaart's shirt. Soon after Jurica Vranješ was also sent off after his hand found its way into Timothée Atouba's face. In addition we got five yellow cards and Hamburg three. 'There were scenes straight out of a wrestling bout,' Ivan Klasnić said afterwards.

We'd been leading 1–0 since the fiftieth minute, thanks to a dream goal by Hugo Almeida. On the ground, Daniel Jensen had poked the ball towards Almeida, who stepped back, surrounded by five Hamburg players, struck the ball perfectly from 17 metres and saw it disappear into the corner of the net.

Tim Wiese was responsible for the biggest talking-point of the day, however. In the forty-second minute a high ball flew towards his box. Because Naldo didn't challenge the advancing Iva Olić,

Wiese had to intervene. He rushed out of his goal to the edge of the box and leaped with his right foot in the air – at the same level as Olić's head. With his studs pointing outwards he went for the ball and did hit it, but in the process crashed into the HSV attacker's shoulder.

The Hamburg team and the media went for Tim Wiese afterwards, accusing him of watching bad karate films the night before. The foul was judged to be 'attempted grievous bodily harm'. He'd charged out of his goal like a madman and committed the 'most brutal foul of the season'. After the game Wiese explained that he'd hit the ball first and that Olić 'didn't have to go for it. He ran straight into me.' *Bild* thought his statement was 'twaddle'.

To begin with Klaus Allofs tried to defend Wiese's challenge, for which he was only yellow-carded, by saying, 'A yellow card is absolutely right. I mean, Tim was going for the ball.' But after hearing the general opinion on the kung fu kick, he backpedalled. 'We couldn't have complained if the ref had sent him off.'

When Franz Beckenbauer, in his role as TV pundit, claimed that Wiese's challenge was 'almost attempted murder', the hostility escalated. Comparisons were made with Harald (Toni) Schumacher's attack in 1982 against France's Patrick Battiston, who'd lost several teeth in the process. And also with Eric Cantona's kick when he attacked Crystal Palace fan Matthew Simmons off the pitch.

Referee Lutz Wagner, whose yellow card was wrong – as a teammate I'm prepared to say that – admitted the next day, 'I slept badly. It won't leave me in peace. Having seen the TV pictures I have to say I ought to have sent him off.' And yet Tim Wiese was defended by Toni Schumacher, who, as a goalkeeper, was voted Germany's Footballer of the Year in 1984 and 1986. 'In the heat of the moment all you see is the ball and you don't have any time to think about injuring people. If someone accuses him of attempted murder, that's bullshit!'

From then on we were known as the 'kicking squad'. Also because we'd had seven red cards so far that season. People even spoke of Werder's image being tarnished.

There are teams that will be unsettled by things like this. Teams that lose their focus on the essentials, wasting energy that's urgently needed elsewhere on re-evaluating and justifying the incident. But not Werder. In their calm way Klaus Allofs and Thomas Schaaf prepared us for the final sprint of the season. We were in second place, on course to qualify automatically for the Champions League, two points ahead of my ex-club Schalke 04. My former teammates were no longer being coached by Mirko Slomka, however. In the wake of our 5–1 victory over Schalke, Slomka was sacked. Mike Büskens and Youri Mulder took over.

In the first game after Wiese's kung fu performance we showed that we weren't a kicking or fighting squad, but that the long-standing admiration for our combination football was justified. Against Hannover, who'd also wanted to sign me, we produced an incredible spectacle. Hugo Almeida, Tim Borowski, Ivan Klasnić, Markus Rosenberg and Aaron Hunt all scored in our 6–1 victory. Everything was all right again with the media; we were praised and flattered for our performance. Because Schalke defeated Frankfurt 1–0, they were still on our tail and theoretically had the chance to overtake us in the last round of matches. Even a draw, however, would automatically qualify us for the Champions League.

In the end we managed a victory, Rosenberg scoring ten minutes before the end. Another goal close to the final whistle. No other team in the Bundesliga had scored more goals – 18 – in the last 15 minutes of matches. This was down to Schaaf, who taught us always to maintain our concentration until the whistle went.

When referee Michael Kempter blew the final whistle, Ivan Klasnić was on the pitch. Half an hour before the end, Schaaf had brought him on for Hugo Almeida. This quite individual man. Ivan, the warrior. The bold. The indestructible! A man you simply have to marvel at.

Ivan didn't play football for almost the entire year of 2007 due to illness. His kidneys had stopped functioning and he was fearful for his career and his life. Compared to kidney disease any other football injury is a joke. His body was no longer able to rid itself of toxins. Klasnić's body rejected the kidney donated by his mother, after which he received one from his father and this time the transplant worked. And then he actually returned to playing – the first professional footballer to do so after such a procedure. I played with him on seven occasions and was able to see how this impressive man never lost his cheerfulness or bottle.

As a footballer you rarely have serious doubts about your body. You toil every day to turn it into a high-performance machine, to strengthen the muscles, ensure that your motor functions are working smoothly and keep the tendons and ligaments stable. When you take a shower in the mornings you see a well-trained body, tailor-made for the exertions of training that will follow. When you return home in the afternoon you might be tired, but you've proved that your body is functioning well.

Because you feel so strong you don't think about injuries or hazards; you go for every tackle in both training and matches. You trust in the fact that your body's going to hold up. But Klasnić's example shows that even a well-trained body can have its weaknesses that you can do nothing about. It doesn't matter how many kilometres you run, or sit-ups and press-ups you do.

I love playing football. For me it's the best thing in the world. If I could I'd keep playing for all eternity. But that's not going to happen. At some point my body will start to show weaknesses. And I dread it. I'd love to remain at the level I'm playing at now, but I know that's impossible.

Together with Ivan Klasnić I was a runner-up in my first season with Werder. Which meant that in my first two years as a professional my team had come second in the Bundesliga. Contrary to Andreas Müller's predictions, I'd actually spent more time on the pitch in my first six months with Werder than I had in the first half of the season with Schalke 04. Thomas Schaaf gave me 615 minutes in the Bundesliga, whereas at Schalke I'd played for 558.

These two years had seemed as if they'd been on permanent fast-forward. At Schalke I was part of the turmoil there – the plaything, the object of hostility. I learned to suppress stuff, swallow it, ignore it and to deal with slurs. In Bremen I learnt how things can be different. How much backing a club can give its players.

Thomas Schaaf and Klaus Allofs never let the injuries, the squabbles inside the squad or transfer rumours, which were permanent companions of the season, get to them. They had an impressively calm manner, which meant that Werder didn't suffer any long-lasting damage.

I can't imagine any other club managing to get through a season with such fluctuations. It might sound corny, but we really did veer between genius and insanity. This period included an 8–1 win against Bielefeld as well as a 6–3 defeat against Stuttgart. On good days we beat Real Madrid; on bad ones we couldn't muster a chance against Olympiakos Piräus. We scored 75 goals but also received seven red cards. And at the end Werder qualified for the Champions League for the fifth season in succession.

It was my great fortune to be able to mature for two years in Diego's slipstream. Diego has this relaxed interaction with the ball. It doesn't bounce off his foot. It sticks to his thigh, even to his head if he so wishes. Even at top speed he keeps the ball incredibly close to him. He's a magician who's unbelievably effective. And, most of all, in spite of this he's a real team player, without vanity, and never regards himself as too important to help out in defence either.

I had some incredibly frustrating training sessions when I performed textbook tackles on Diego yet was still unable to win the ball. I'd be on his right foot and he'd flick the ball to his left. I'd try to attack there and he'd dodge out of the way. As a teammate, he was often sheer pleasure to watch. As an opponent, he could do your head in with his close ball control and cheeky dribbling. But that was so important for me. In every session I not only had to keep up but also play at his tempo. He demanded double passes. He demanded you make runs. If you didn't do what he wanted, he'd roll his eyes in disdain. Sometimes in the evenings I'd watch his tricks in slow motion, to try to make sense of them.

After training I'd often stay out on the pitch with him and Naldo, and we'd have free-kick competitions. Naldo used pure power, whereas Diego bent his unbelievably. He regularly stroked the ball over the wall.

The longer I was at Bremen, the more I became part of the 'Werder midfield diamond'. This ingenious creation, the lynchpin of the team. With wonderful players such as the precision passing machine Diego, the strategist Frank Baumann or the ringleader Torsten Frings.

10
VICTORY IN THE GERMAN CUP
HOW TO SWALLOW DEFEAT

In my second year at Werder they even started calling me Messi. 'Diego's important for us, but Messi plays really well too,' Frings once said publicly in an interview.

The Argentinian Lionel Messi is almost a year and a half older than me. At the age of 24 he became the record goal scorer at Barcelona. Twelve months later he'd already scored more than 200 goals in the Spanish league. Between 2009 and 2012 he was International Footballer of the Year four times in a row.

In Bremen, of course, I was miles away from this. Although I must admit that it's my goal to win this accolade one day. Jumping ahead, when I later joined Real Madrid, my coach José Mourinho said very clearly to me, 'If you don't become international footballer of the year one day that would be disappointing.' And that's how I see it too. I've set myself the ambition of being awarded this distinction. It's a real incentive. But more about that later.

Because before I actually began with Real Madrid there were more lessons to learn at Bremen – some minor and some major.

In the summer of 2008, Patrick Owomoyela, Ivan Klasnić, Pierre Womé and Tim Borowski left us. Claudio Pizarro came from Chelsea and we signed Sebastian Prödl too. I also went on my first pre-season training trip with Bremen, sharing a room with Sebastian Mielitz. Up till then he'd been playing for Werder's U-19 team and had now made it into the professional squad. The older players – stars like Frings, Pizarro or Wiese – had their own single rooms. We younger players didn't enjoy such privileges. On the first evening I lay down on my bed. We'd trained hard, I'd eaten and already had my massage. The television was on and I was watching one TV series after the other, as I usually did to combat the boredom in the hotel. Sebastian Mielitz didn't have his massage till later, then came into the room at around 9 p.m. and watched a bit of telly with me. After no more than half an hour he asked me to turn the television off. 'I have to sleep. We've got important training tomorrow,' he said. I waited for him to burst out laughing or pull some other face. But, no, he was being deadly serious. 'Look, mate,' I said, 'I haven't got a laptop with me. It's half-past nine; I can't kip for twelve hours.' But Mielitz didn't care. He was a big sleeper. And he really wanted to go to bed at half-past nine.

It was a trivial matter, of course. Completely insignificant. But you have to get over such petty things together. Most young professionals in the Bundesliga share a room. Which means you have to engage with each other and be tolerant, even when someone wants to go to bed at a ridiculous hour. I gave Mielitz my headphones and asked him whether they blanked out the noise. With that the matter was sorted.

Although we were all satisfied with our pre-season preparation, we had a poor start to the season. We only managed draws against Bielefeld and Schalke. In Gladbach we were 3–0 down in the middle of the second half, and finished up just 3–2. A beginning unworthy of last season's runners-up.

I set up a goal against Cottbus as I had in our 1–1 draw against Schalke. Then, in our fifth match, we beat Bayern 5–2 in Munich, with me assisting the first two goals of the game, by Markus Rosenberg and Naldo. I scored the third myself, to make it 3–0, hammering it into the corner from 15 metres. It was a very special day for me. Not many players put five past the German record-holders at their home ground. Many teams are happy enough to come away from the Allianz Arena with a draw, but we dictated the rhythm and determined what happened on the pitch. Against world-class players such as Philipp Lahm, Bastien Schweinsteiger, Zé Roberto and Luca Toni.

So I'd had a pretty good start to the season, in which I'd be in the starting line-up for 20 games. By the end of it I'd managed three goals and 15 assists. I would have been pleased with this, had it not been for our disastrous performance in the league. Only once did we get as high as third in the table, then finished in an unacceptable tenth place. But instead of beating ourselves up about our poor showing in the league, we salvaged the season in a different way. We forgot the many bad weeks through some good ones.

We masked our problems by shining at key moments. When it counted we were on it. In the aforementioned Champions League game against Inter Milan, for example. This was the match after which I told my agent that at some point in my career I would play under Mourinho.

Following the game, Inter's coach got a bit of a roasting from the German media. 'Werder shuts up big mouth Mourinho,' *Bild* said. The Portuguese star manager had been bragging at the pre-match press conference, saying, for example, 'There's none better than me.' He also snapped at a reporter because he didn't like his question. 'I expect you wanted to become a football manager, but only made it as far as a journalist.' And he spoke provocatively about the media speculation over his salary at Inter: 'They're always talking about nine million euros. It's not that little. I get eleven. With sponsorship money it goes up to fourteen million.'

Once again Mourinho had bagged the headlines for himself over the next few days. And I'm pretty sure that this was his plan. Given the experience I've had of him at Real, I suspect he wanted to distract attention away from other things – there could have been problems within the Inter Milan team – injuries, discussions about the formation or something else. At any rate, when we worked together in Madrid he often behaved like that. Mourinho would already know in the evening if the two big Spanish daily sports papers were going to lay into the team the following morning. He knew if *Marca* or *As* were going to turn against us, which would have unsettled the team. So he would attempt a diversionary tactic. He didn't care if the counter-attack ended up being at his own expense and his image suffered as a result of supposedly provocative comments. He was an interceptor, without whom the team would never have escaped unscathed, nor could we have gone about our work in peace.

Another occasion where Bremen shone was in January 2009. In the last 16 of the German Cup we were up against Borussia Dortmund, the previous year's runners-up. For Dortmund the game against us was the prelude to celebrations to mark the club's 100-year anniversary. But we had no intention of turning up like good guests and handing out presents.

At the start of the match, however, that's exactly what it looked like we'd come to do. Alex Frei put Dortmund into the lead with an early goal, and then we gave him and Mohamed Zidan five other major opportunities to score. Only after that did we rally and play with a confidence that didn't match our position in the table. First Hugo Almeida scored, followed by Claudio Pizarro. Which clinched our quarter-final spot.

There we faced VfL Wolfsburg, who had enjoyed the best start to the second half of the season, winning four games and drawing one. They'd scored ten goals and conceded only three. By contrast, we hadn't won a single league game since the turn of the year, bagging only two miserable points and scoring three goals, even though we'd had 103 attempts. Our accuracy was diabolical; we were just shooting wildly and indiscriminately.

The game against Wolfsburg ought to have been a pretty clear-cut affair, especially as we were seriously weakened in goal. Both Tim Wiese and his deputy, Christian Vander, were out through injury, which meant that Nico Pellatz played his first competitive fixture for Bremen. Until then he'd been in goal for our second team against other third-division sides like Unterhaching, Sandhausen and Kickers Emden.

But we managed to have another Werder moment. Diego put us in front with a strike from the edge of the box. I made it 2–0 after dribbling into the area. Edin Džeko got one back for Wolfsburg with the third goal of the game. All of this in the first ten minutes. And there was more to come. Having missed, unmarked, from 5 metres, Pizarro then scored, but was offside. After the break Džeko scored again from the spot to make it 2–2. Seven shots on goal later, the game ended 5–2 in our favour and we'd secured our place in the semi-final.

In the UEFA Cup, which we were in because we'd only come third in the group phase of the Champions League, we knocked out AC Milan, Saint-Étienne and Udinese, and were drawn against Hamburger SV in the semi-final. Exactly the same opponents as in the German Cup semi-final. And because there was another meeting against Hamburg coming up in the Bundesliga, we had four northern derbies awaiting us in 19 days. It promised to be an exciting time. We were on course for a double, which provided us with a distraction from our poor showing in the Bundesliga. For Hamburg, three titles were at stake in our four clashes, for they still had a chance of becoming Bundesliga champions; after 28 games they were only three points behind Wolfsburg and equal third in the table with Bayern. Theoretically everything was possible.

Of course, the slings and arrows were flying around well before the first of our encounters. Nigel de Jong stirred things up by saying that he 'couldn't care less' who played on the day – 'I'll eat the lot of them up.' Rafael van der Vaart described Diego as 'a sissy'.

Tim Wiese's kung fu kick was also pulled from the archives to fire up the contest. He himself chipped into the conversation by saying, 'I think they're afraid in Hamburg. If they get a good battering from us in the German Cup they'll be trembling in the rest of the games too.'

I believe that Wiese is one of those players who needs this sort of friction with the opposition and fans. There are footballers who actually get stronger as the whistling in the stands grows louder. They draw strength from hostility. They have an 'I'll show you' mentality and thrive particularly when they're under serious pressure. This approach doesn't work for me because, as I've said, I barely notice the fans during the game, only my teammates.

In Hamburg Per Mertesacker put us in the lead. Ivica Olić equalised, managing to slot one past Wiese, who otherwise had little to do. In the ninety-second minute David Jarolím hit me with a bad tackle. Referee Knut Kircher immediately pulled out the red card, which meant we were a man up for extra time. But in spite of this advantage we weren't able to score the winner.

So our first duel had to be decided by penalties. Hamburg went first. Joris Mathijsen scored. So did Claudio Pizarro. Then the Wiese show began. Before Jérôme Boateng shot, our goalie advanced towards the HSV defender and looked deep into his eyes. A touch of intimidation. The message: I'm stronger than you. He did the same to Hamburg's remaining penalty-takers, Olić and Marcell Jansen. He also fidgeted wildly on the line, earning Wiese even more whistles than he'd got at the Hamburg end of the ground. But his performance had the desired effect. All three Hamburg players seemed awed. And no matter where they shot, Wiese leapt in the right direction.

He saved all three attempts, while I converted our second penalty and Torsten Frings scored with our third. This meant we hadn't just ruined our Bundesliga arch-rivals' chance of their first title of the season, but we had also given ourselves a chance to win the German Cup.

HSV narrowly won our next clash, beating us 1–0 in our own stadium and thus getting their noses ahead in the UEFA Cup. They'd also be playing in front of their own fans for the return match. The crowd went wild when Olić put them in front in the second game. Everything seemed to point to a Hamburg victory, but we didn't give up and got back in the game through Diego and Claudio Pizarro.

Shortly before the end of the game we were leading 2–1 – and so ahead on away goals – when something happened that I'd never seen before. Under no pressure, the HSV defender Michael Gravgaard went to play the ball with his left foot back to the Hamburg keeper, Frank Rost. A simple pass he must have executed a hundred thousand times before. A pass you'd never talk about because it would normally be too ordinary. But a wad of paper turned this ordinary pass into a remarkable one, and the paper itself into the 'wad of God'.

An HSV fan must have been holding the sheet of paper up before kick-off to encourage his team – it was part of the routine the fans used to spur their side on. And in all likelihood this fan scrunched it up in anger after one of our goals and hurled it randomly towards the pitch, where the wad of paper sat for ages unnoticed in the glare of the floodlights. Until Gravgaard attempted his pass. Suddenly the ball hit the wad of paper and bounced up, hitting Gravgaard's shin and going out rather than back to Frank Rost. This gave us a corner. Diego took it, the ball made its way to Frank Baumann and then into the goal. 3–1 to us – thanks to that wad of paper. It was just as unexpected as my bizarre first goal for Karlsruhe had been.

Although Olić scored again to reduce Hamburg's deficit, in the end we won 3–2. Because of the three away goals we'd scored, they were out of the UEFA Cup. We went on to beat them again in the Bundesliga too.

After the UEFA Cup semi-final a television reporter picked up the paper ball. It became *the* topic of discussion, described and analysed by almost the entire media. It was passed around like a trophy, and even taken to the final in Istanbul. A bidding consortium was set up for the ball of paper, and ultimately purchased the exhibit for 4,150 euros in the auction that ended after the final.

But while the paper ball was able to enjoy its big appearance in Istanbul, I couldn't enjoy mine.

Diego was suspended from the UEFA Cup final against Shakhtar Donetsk in Turkey, and so all eyes were on me. After seven assists in 13 international fixtures so far, great things were expected of me. 'The match will depend on Mesut,' Torsten Frings said before the final. And Thomas Schaaf expressed the hope 'that Mesut can crown his excellent season with this game.'

I'd got half my relatives from Zonguldak to come to Istanbul. They'd made the 330-kilometre journey to the final in camper vans. To this very special (at least for all the Özils) game. But it wasn't just special because I was playing; this was also to be the last ever UEFA Cup final after 38 years.

The competition had been in existence since the 1971–72 season and German teams had won the title six times: Gladbach twice, as well as Frankfurt, Leverkusen, Bayern and Schalke. The last time a German side had been in the final – Borussia Dortmund in 2002 – they had lost 3–2 against Feyenoord of Rotterdam. From 2010 the competition was to be slightly modified and become the Europa League.

I'd slept well the night before the big game. Now I felt good and was ready to fulfil the high expectations of me. But then I didn't play well at all. All the ideas I had in the match somehow went wrong. None of my runs worked. It was as if my antennae, which usually guided me across the pitch with precision, were faulty. I lacked my usual fluency, unpredictability and penetration.

In spite of this we managed as a team to come through the 90 minutes and make it into extra time at 1–1. But we were fully engaged in preventing Donetsk's Brazilian players from building momentum instead of sticking to our own game. And so we were doing exactly what Thomas Schaaf was always trying to avoid: we were being reactive rather than pro-active. In the ninety-seventh minute Jádson, one of the Ukrainian side's five Brazilian players, had a free shot at goal. He took a cross from the right and struck from 11 metres. Standing a metre and a half in front of the goal, Wiese reacted with lightning speed. He thrust out his legs and lunged with both arms down to his right. I watched the ball get closer. Wiese bent his torso as far as he possibly could and stretched out his arms, allowing him to touch the ball with the fingers of his right hand. But all he could do was take some of the pace off the shot. The ball spun into the net. 2–1 to Shakhtar Donetsk. We were beaten.

After Donetsk's victory in the Şükrü-Saracoğlu stadium I just wanted to make myself scarce. I didn't want to watch the cup, which I'd been so set on winning, being raised. But there was no escape. The shower of orange confetti, shot into the air for the victors, pattered down onto us losers. The bits of paper stuck to my sweaty skin. I wiped them away. I hadn't earned them. I didn't want to feel them on my skin. I didn't want to feel anything.

But Thomas Schaaf did something unbelievable. Instead of leaving us alone to brood painfully over the missed chances or criticising us for our performance, he rounded us up on the pitch and immediately started the work of rebuilding the team. 'Listen,' he said, 'I want you to forget this game immediately. Let's put this defeat in Istanbul behind us. Either we can start looking for mistakes, looking for people to blame. Or we can just forget it. And look forward to a great final in Berlin. All of Germany will be watching us. They'll want to see if we can pull ourselves back up. And do you know what? We will pull ourselves back up. Forget Istanbul! Look forward to Berlin. And next week we'll be doing the celebrating! No one else!'

Our fans, too, had an excellent sense of what we needed right then. When we dragged ourselves over to the 5,000 supporters who'd travelled with us, they sang. No whistling. No anger. No reproach. All they did was chant, 'Berlin, Berlin, we're going to Berlin.'

At that moment the Werder fans were simply outstanding. With their singing they helped alleviate at least some of the pain. They made it easier for us to deal with this rotten defeat, and I'll never forget that.

I'm sure a lot of fans don't realise just how important they are. The effect they have on us players. Probably because it often sounds so corny when we call for the support of the 'twelfth man' and urge our fans to cheer us on. But it's really true. Fans can shout the tiredness out of your legs. They can make you keep running despite muscle cramps. Attempt one last sliding tackle. Try to turn around a game that's almost hopelessly lost. Even if, like me, you basically block out the background noise and switch it to mute, nobody can remain unmoved when the level of fans' encouragement rises to extraordinary levels.

I still remember the game when I became aware of how important fans are. It was against Bayern Munich in 2006, when I was still under contract with Schalke. After some poor performances our supporters had announced a fan boycott, in which they remained silent for 19.04 minutes, in reference to the year the club was founded. I was sitting on the bench in the Veltins-Arena, watching the game. It all seemed so wrong. So unreal. You could hear the dull thud of the ball when it was passed, as well, of course, as the Bayern fans cheering their team's skills. It had nothing to do with football and for the first time I sensed how fans can spur you on. Which footballer wants to run up and down the pitch when it's dead quiet? When, on the other hand, your ears hurt because the atmosphere is scintillating, you'll keep running even when your thighs are burning.

When, after 19.04 minutes, the Schalke fans amongst the crowd of 61,482 started chanting again, it was fitting that Levan Kobiashvili scored almost straight away. On the bench I felt stronger, more motivated and more assured than before.

That's how I always want it to be. In every stadium. Loud, passionate, crazy fans who don't only cheer when things go well but are also there for you when things aren't working out.

In 2012 there was a heated debate when I didn't sing along with the German national anthem. I heard critics grumbling, 'The stupid German-Turk doesn't sing.' But do they sing themselves? Are these people there before the game, stoked with passion?

Besides, I think it's a shame that I'm condemned for this, for I'm sure that these people have no idea why I don't sing along. I don't just stand there vacuously, letting the anthem wash over me. While it's being played I pray, reciting the words outlined above. I pray as I always have done. And I'm certain that these moments of contemplation give me – and by extension the team – strength and confidence to bring victory home. And that's what matters.

I'm sometimes disappointed by the atmosphere at international fixtures. When, as reigning World Champions, we played in Berlin in 2016, it was almost as quiet as that time when the Schalke fans had carried out their boycott. Why? What was the cemetery atmosphere all about? Was it fair on the team? Was it perhaps because these days there are too many sponsors in the stadium rather than passionate supporters? The German fans are really so cool.

Luckily the Bremen fans and Thomas Schaaf didn't lack this sensitivity in Istanbul. They knew what we needed. And thus we didn't sink into a deep gloom that could have stymied us.

That evening we had dinner with the team and backroom staff in the exclusive five-star Four Seasons Hotel. I poked at my food unenthusiastically, shovelling carbohydrates into me without any enjoyment. After defeats like that your taste buds are dead. Nothing gives any pleasure. Not even the most well-meaning text message can lift you up. You just want to be alone – you hate yourself because you didn't play to your potential.

To be absolutely honest, after an hour of the Istanbul game I was desperate for the ref to blow the final whistle. I could have begged him to put an end to the misery. Fairly early on in the game I realised that it wasn't going to be our night, especially not mine. I'm able to admit this today, although of course I couldn't have back then. So long as you're on the pitch you consistently want to turn things around. To force a change. Even if you're playing badly. But I can't explain why it doesn't work sometimes.

There are days in the life of a professional footballer when your foot is like a flipper, slapping the ball wildly without any control. No matter what you try, it doesn't work. Even though you've got the determination to play well, you struggle with yourself. You know how everything is supposed to go in theory, and yet it doesn't work in practice. The following day the media write that your attitude wasn't right. That your body language left a lot to be desired. But that's not correct. I don't know a single footballer in the world who would ever say, 'Well, today I'm only going to give fifty per cent. Today it'll be OK if I don't run or pass as much and only take two shots at goal.' You're on a stage with millions of people watching – dozens of cameras are focused on you and studying every move you make. All players want to shine every time. It's certainly never got anything to do with attitude.

The fact is, sometimes it works, and sometimes it doesn't. Sometimes, when you're playing well, it comes as a surprise when the ref blows the final whistle, because you weren't expecting the game to be over so soon. And on other occasions you get the impression that the 90 minutes are never going to come to an end and that you'll have to play for three hours.

After our 120 minutes against Donetsk, the reaction of the press to my performance was predictably critical. According to the *Frankfurter Allgemeiner Zeitung,* I was 'not up to the job of replacing the Brazilian Diego as playmaker'. It wrote, 'The young German international more often avoided the ball than asked for it. He seemed so wrapped up in himself that he was never able to withstand the outside pressure.' And *Kicker* said, 'Without Diego the attack proved to be eyewash. Too fainthearted, too uninspired, too homespun. The man supposed to be his successor failed the acid test.'

I'm not someone who spontaneously reads all these newspaper articles. I don't put my name into Google to find out what the media have been saying about me. But it doesn't completely pass me by either. There are always a number of newspapers

lying around on aeroplanes, which you leaf through out of boredom. Also, all my agents have been avid newspaper readers.
Whenever they come round they bring piles of papers and maga-
zines, which they leave with me. At some point I look through
them and discover what people out there think of me. Of course,
my friends find out what's written too and keep me up to speed.

The slating I got after Istanbul was fair enough. The questions
legitimate. But I agreed with Günter Netzer. The former world-
class footballer was pretty spot-on in his summing-up of my role
in the final. He said, 'Özil mustn't have too much pressure heaped
on his shoulders and fans' expectations shouldn't be set too high.
He still needs time. He can play far better than he showed on the
night.' So I no longer dwelled on the match and the criticism
levelled at my performance, but focused on what Schaaf and the
fans had asked for. I wanted to go to Berlin and show them the
real Mesut.

The final of the German Cup against Bayer Leverkusen was
described as a 'final for two frustrated sides'. This was partly
because we'd limped through the league and abandoned our first
title chance. And partly because Leverkusen, who at one point
had led the table for two rounds of matches, had slipped just as
miserably as we had, finishing up in an equally disappointing
ninth place.

The description was sheer nonsense, of course. Neither we nor
Leverkusen felt frustrated in the run-up to the game. Which
team approaches a final in a bad mood?

I was in the starting line-up, the youngest player on the pitch.
Beside me was Diego, who was playing his last ever game for

Werder. His transfer to Juventus was already a done deal. The grass was wet, the tempo fast. The perfect conditions. Chances at goal on both sides. But both Tim Wiese and Leverkusen's René Adler held firm. It was end-to-end stuff for the entire first half; a game to savour.

Then, in the fifty-ninth minute, a long ball came to Almeida. He just deflected it to Diego, who was surrounded by three Leverkusen players. With his first touch Diego brought the ball under control, with the second and third he sidestepped the men marking him. I'd started just behind the halfway line and now sprinted down the left wing as fast as I could. I took the ball inside the box, shot from 7 metres, and it was in. 10 to Bremen. At the corner flag Diego lifted me into the air. I felt weightless. My most important goal to date, because it remained the only one of the day and it secured us the title.

When referee Helmut Fleischer finally blew his whistle after four minutes of stoppage time, I didn't know what to do at first. On both sides of me I just saw blurs of teammates in green and white shirts, dancing, leaping, throwing themselves into each other's arms. Group hugs everywhere. I was briefly overwhelmed because I didn't know who to embrace first. Should I leap at Tim? Or run over to Thomas Schaaf? Or simply skip down the pitch? As these thoughts spun in my mind, Torsten Frings came racing over and threw himself at me. He put me in a headlock, shouted something and I just shouted something with him. Then I ran to Diego and nudged him ecstatically around the pitch. I was on autopilot. My arms were twirling in the air. My legs were doing as they pleased.

Sometimes they ran, sometimes they jumped. And I just went along with it.

You can't put these feelings of happiness into words. You run to the left, you run to the right. From everywhere, camera flashes flare in the night. You don't know where to look. The spectators in the stands are taking pictures. You fall into each other's arms, but you can't be sure which teammates you've already congratulated and which you haven't.

When the golden confetti from the cannons fell on us that night, I loved feeling it in my hair and sticking to my skin. Today I wanted it, unlike in Istanbul. This time I'd deserved it. I enjoyed the dinner in the Hotel Maritim's banqueting suite too. This time there weren't any problems with my taste buds.

As we ate and celebrated, Diego and I must have discussed the goal at least ten times. 'You saw it so brilliantly,' I told him. And he replied, 'The Leverkusen boys were marking the whole time. But at that moment they gave me a little room for manoeuvre.'

I told Diego that I'd miss him. And I thanked him for everything he'd taught me in the two years we'd been together at Bremen. Then Klaus Allofs gave him a corner flag, which Diego had celebrated and danced around so often in the Weser stadium. 'Best of luck at Juventus. Maybe you'll win a cup there too,' he said, laughing. And Diego replied, 'Thanks for three wonderful years!'

After that evening the media suddenly hailed me as the 'new king', or at least that's what *Bild* wrote. Our manager Klaus Allofs praised me: 'In Istanbul the burden on him was still too great. It was his first major final. This time, beside Diego, it was much better. We know what a talent we have in Mesut.' And Wolfgang Overath, one of the 1974 World Cup-winning squad, said in *Welt am Sonntag* of the situation at Bremen:

In Özil, however, they've found a young player who's quickly managed to make it right to the top. Within a very short time he's become an incredibly important player in this side. He has a huge talent and now has the opportunity to play a similar role to Diego's. Don't forget that when Diego came to Bremen from Porto in 2006, barely anybody knew who he was. It was only with Werder that he developed into an outstanding player. Özil can do the same.

11

MY MOVE TO REAL

KNOWING WHEN TO
THINK OF YOURSELF

After a summer full of discussion about whether I was good enough to be a leading player and ready to fill Diego's boots, the first post-Diego season began with a 3–2 defeat against Eintracht Frankfurt. At home in front of our own fans – hardly the ideal start to a new era. I scored a penalty from a foul, but that didn't alter the result.

In the second game against Bayern Munich I scored again, this time in open play, but after Mario Gómez scored the match ended in a draw. This point against the record-holders did us good. For from then on we had an incredible run, not losing a single game between 15 August and 11 December. We were undefeated fourteen times in the league, as well as notching up four victories and one draw in the Europa League. We were unstoppable in the cup too.

Our goalie, Tim Wiese, even went 619 minutes and 39 seconds without letting in a goal. We had all decided to play a tighter defensive game than in the previous season. Although we'd scored 64 goals, putting us third behind Wolfsburg and Bayern, the inexplicable 50 goals we'd conceded had ruined much of our good play. Which is why we kept telling ourselves, 'We're going to defend our goal with whatever it takes.'

We were better organised and played with more discipline. Taking fewer risks, we were more effective for it. Our focus was on points rather than any prizes for beauty. All the same we did manage the occasional dream game. On 21 November 2009 we thrashed Freiburg 6–0. I set up four of the goals and scored one myself. 'If I weren't the opposition manager,' Robin Dutt admitted afterwards, 'I'd have applauded.'

There was effusive praise from the media. *Tagesspiegel* described me as 'probably the most talented of Schaaf's magical apprentices'. The *Frankfurter Allgemeine Zeitung* insisted that, thanks to me, 'Bremen's former midfield star, Diego, was now forgotten.' And *Sport Bild* ranked me amongst the 18 top players in the league.

In the summer Klaus Allofs had lured Marko Marin to Bremen from Gladbach. He, Aaron Hunt and I worked pretty well together – or at least that's what the press kept saying. With a nod to Krasimir Balakov, Fredi Bobic and Giovane Élber, the 'magic triangle' who'd played breathtaking combination football at VfB Stuttgart in the 1990s, we were hailed as the 'new magic triangle'. *Kicker* even once got us all around a table to do an interview together, in which Marin explained our teamwork: 'All three of us are young, almost the same age. We're all good footballers. This makes teamwork easier. Playing with Mesut and Aaron, it's not hard to shine. It's really difficult for our opponents to adapt to our game. We keep changing position. Sometimes Mesut comes through the middle, sometimes down the left, then I change sides.' Aaron Hunt added that in the end each of us knows 'what the others are planning. Our moves are in harmony. That's all. We have total freedom, we're allowed to change places and we do so.'

Interviews like this are great fun. And of course you feel flattered when someone comes up with a new superlative for you in the paper. It's good for the soul. It gives you confidence. All the same, I care little for all the hype written about me. The real, original magic triangle didn't mean much to me as I was only seven or eight years old when Balakov, Bobic and Élber were at their peak.

Besides, you don't play football just to read inventive descriptions of yourself in the paper the following day. Especially when you're aware just how quickly a magic triangle can lose its magic. Whether I'm called 'The Wizard of Oz' or 'the Diva with the Lumpen Foot', I mustn't let it affect me.

I did, however, take note when Diego sang my praises from Italy: 'Since I left he's had to take on more responsibility. Which he's done impressively. Mesut's now the most important player at Bremen. And he's going to get even better – in my opinion he's going to become a truly great player. Besides his class he's got the intelligence necessary to deal with all the hype too.'

I was also pleased that Klaus Allofs didn't let himself get caught up in the media hysteria either. Whenever journalists intercepted him after victories, asking him to rave about our performance, he said – or at least this is what I once heard in the mixed zone – 'Write what you like. I'm not going to comment.' Thomas Schaaf was equally defensive; the most he would say was, 'Mesut played brilliantly for us last season as well. It's not a surprise for us. Mesut learned a lot in Diego's shadow. And because the master's no longer here, we can see Mesut in a better light.'

Behind the scenes he remained level-headed and quite critical. He didn't like my heading. He also thought that I didn't have the right sense of when I should dribble and when it would be better to play the ball. 'That comes with experience,' he said in training, when he'd keep stopping the play if he thought I'd made another wrong decision. 'You're still lacking the experience.'

After the roll we'd been on in the first half of the season, from the middle of December things came to a halt. Schalke, Hamburg, Frankfurt, Bayern and Gladbach all beat us, sending Bremen to sixth place in the table. At probably any other club in the world, panic would have broken out, with talk of sacking the manager or other such measures. At Bremen things just went on as normal. And because we lost only one of the next 14 games, against Dortmund, we ended up a respectable third in the Bundesliga.

We also reached the German Cup final in Berlin again, where our opponents were Bayern Munich.

Thomas Schaaf had come up with some special tactics for the evening. This was his ninth final in Berlin, four times as a player and five as manager. 'Every approach, every formation has its own risks,' he admitted. But because he'd been right so often we of course trusted his idea.

He left Marko Marin on the bench, opting instead for the more defensive Tim Borowski. I was moved up beside Claudio Pizarro as the second striker.

But I didn't get along at all well up front. I need to be able to work the ball ahead of me, organise the play for the attack. Fathom where there are spaces and play into gaps. Up front I couldn't express myself properly and, more importantly, couldn't set it up for Claudio. In truth, this tactic took both of us completely out of the game. At half-time Schaaf put an end to the experiment.

After eight minutes we had a threefold chance, but neither Pizarro, Torsten Frings nor Aaron Hunt could convert it. After that Bayern was really the only team in the game and they gave us a total lesson in football. Arjen Robben gave them the lead from the penalty spot after a handball by Per Mertesacker. Ivica Olić made it 2–0. Then Franck Ribéry and Bastian Schweinsteiger both scored. In the meantime Torsten Frings had been sent off after a second foul.

In 1972 Kaiserslauten had lost 5–0 in the Cup final against Schalke. Now, almost 40 years later, we were given an equally traumatic thumping. My performance that evening was poor. There's no use trying to whitewash it, even if it was partly down to the unusual position I played in.

Afterwards Thomas Schaaf thought that my weak performance was also down to the fact that since November 2009 my future at Bremen had been the subject of public discussion. 'As a player you've got to come to terms with the fact that you're being confronted with it all the time.'

A transfer had always been a distinct possibility. As 2009 came to a close the British media claimed that Arsène Wenger had earmarked me as a reinforcement if Cesc Fàbregas moved from Arsenal to Barcelona.

I did in fact have my first contact with Wenger at the time. We spoke on the phone. He called me and it was a good conversation. Wenger has a very nice way of talking to people. His voice is calm and he chooses his words carefully. He was also incredibly well informed about how I was doing at Bremen.

'You've developed really well,' he said. 'But now it's time for you to take the next step. In London I can help you reach that stage.'

He asked me if I'd ever been to the city; I told him no. Wenger speaks fluent German, which made our conversation easier. After 20 minutes he said goodbye. 'It was lovely to talk to you. Let's stay in contact and see what the future brings.'

I've no idea how the press got wind of the fact that Arsenal were interested in me. But it really angered me, because after the row over my move from Schalke we'd resolved to be very cautious about future discussions with any clubs that were interested in me.

At the time it wasn't at all certain that I would be leaving Bremen. All my father, my agent and I had agreed was that we wouldn't sign any renewal to my contract with Bremen until we'd seen how the season and perhaps the ensuing World Cup panned out. After all, the contract I had with Werder ran until 2011. Why should we extend this now and rule out other career options for me?

As a footballer your career has a time limit. Your best years constitute a much shorter period than in other careers. Whereas normal workers have 20, 30 or 40 years to develop, we professional footballers have to realise our maximum potential in a time frame of 15 years at most.

We can't have wild stabs at things, experimenting as we please. A wrong change of clubs, an ill-considered signature can break your career. Likewise if you're too hesitant about taking the next step. Real Madrid and Barcelona don't come knocking a hundred times, making you new offers year in, year out. At some point they've got a gap in the squad and they choose you to fill it. If you fail to make use of the opportunity the door can stay closed for the next few years because some other top-flight player will take this free place.

I felt completely happy at Bremen and enjoyed playing there. But I also realised that I was slowly outgrowing the club. That my development might come to an end if I kept playing there for another two, three or four years. That's why we didn't immediately renew the contract in spite of Bremen's offer. It had nothing to do with ingratitude. It was just business.

On the pitch you have to think as a team, but when it comes to sorting out contracts and planning your career, it's just about you. As long as you're helping a team win titles and you're an important piece of the manager's puzzle, the club will do anything for you. But once the club management gets the feeling that there are better players out there, those lovely club bosses become hard-nosed decision-makers. Then the clubs weed you out, despite your contract – and they're no longer interested in what you did in the past.

Bastian Schweinsteiger was forced to learn this lesson last summer. After the 2014 World Cup his ex-manager at Bayern,

Louis van Gaal, really wanted him. But when José Mourinho took over at Manchester United a year later, he had a different view of the game – that didn't include Schweinsteiger.

We just wanted to keep all options open. No more and no less. A perfectly legitimate approach, I think. But I wasn't pleased when, in December, *Sport Bild* printed a story about the threat of players being sold off in the Bundesliga and gave me a 70 per cent chance of 'quitting'. I was particularly annoyed at the choice of words. You quit a club when you're unhappy. When you want to get away. When you have insurmountable differences. As had been the case with me at Schalke. There it would have been justified to talk of quitting. I just wanted to get away from Slomka and Müller. But not at Bremen. Why should anyone quit a club where they are so challenged and supported? Where they've made such great strides in their career? Where they've sensed such great trust from morning till night? There was the likelihood of a move, but in no way was it a done deal. There had been preliminary, non-binding talks. Deliberations that had nothing to do with ideas of fleeing the club. From then on, of course, Klaus Allofs too faced increasing questions about the rumours and my possible move. 'We're convinced that Mesut will continue his career at Werder,' he kept affirming publicly.

In his highly impressive autobiography, *I Am Zlatan Ibrahimović*, the Swedish superstar comments on transfers, 'There's one game on the pitch. And another on the transfer market. I like them both and I've got all manner of tricks up my sleeve. I know when to keep quiet and I know when I have to fight.'

I want to play football and win titles. That's my job. That's what I'm concentrating on. For all the rest I've got an agent I coordinate with.

When I was publicly taken to pieces by Schalke, we tried to counteract the bad publicity. We even invited a journalist, Florian Scholz, the long-time chief reporter of *Sport Bild*, into our home to show him where I came from. And that my family and I were far from living it up. That we weren't money-grabbers, out of touch or swimming in cash. It was a desperate attempt thought up by my agent and my father to combat the image of my being greedy.

Otherwise I want to have as little as possible to do with games on the transfer market. In truth you can do more harm than good. To be honest, what *is* the right way of dealing with transfer rumours? If you walk past reporters without a word and fail to answer their speculative questions, the papers the next day will say that a denial sounds like anything but.

On the other hand you can't always tell the truth because negotiations always take place in strict confidence and under a cloak of secrecy. What would Arsène Wenger have thought, for example, if I had blithely told everyone in Bremen about his phone call? He would probably have regarded it as a breach of confidence and never contacted me again.

Or perhaps I should lie? Would that be better?

It's always easy to sneer when you're an outsider. But not when you're in the thick of things. Every day you have to justify yourself to the countless journalists who stick to you. We professional footballers are expected to give them information. But why should we? Where is it written down that we have to provide answers? When journalists switch from one newspaper to another, I bet they don't tell their colleagues until the negotiations are over. It's probably like that in every business and with every change of job. Just not with footballers.

When Franck Ribéry was courted by Real Madrid the papers said I'd be a logical replacement for FC Bayern if the Frenchman moved to Spain. The transfer rumours continued, and became really heated during and after the 2010 World Cup in South Africa.

We arrived at the competition as the second youngest German squad since 1934, with five players in their first tournament: Manuel Neuer, Holger Badstuber, Sami Khedira, Thomas Müller and me. Michael Ballack, who ought to have been captaining the squad, was ruled out with an injury following a foul by Kevin-Prince Boateng. This was much to my disappointment, because Ballack had always been my great advocate. As I learned, he'd often spoken highly of me to Jogi Löw and his training team. To lose such an experienced player for the World Cup, and one so well disposed towards me, was a real shock. Although in retrospect it might have been a blessing in disguise for both the team and me because it meant we couldn't hide our young players behind anyone or pass the buck. We had to prove our courage. All of a sudden it wasn't just the German media and fans watching us, but the whole world.

In our opening fixture against Australia in Durban Joachim Löw had enough faith to stick me in the starting line-up. He was putting me on the biggest stage I had ever encountered. Although

I'd experienced larger crowds elsewhere – such as in the Olympic stadium in Berlin – I had obviously never had so many people watch me live, because a World Cup game like that is broadcast in over 200 countries. Nor had I ever heard so much background noise in a stadium before. When we came out from the bowels of the Moses Mabhida stadium and stepped onto the pitch we were accompanied by the sound of vuvuzelas. It sounded as if millions of bumblebees were buzzing around.

As I stood there before kick-off, my arms linked with Bastian Schweinsteiger and Per Mertesacker, listening to first the Australian, then the German national anthem, a wave of happiness washed over me. I got goose pimples and shuddered with excitement. My emotions were far more intense than before my first Bundesliga game – more powerful than after my first Bundesliga goal. The wave of happiness just came as a complete surprise and seized hold of me.

I wasn't overwhelmed by the emotion, however; it didn't paralyse me. Quite the opposite. The moment the ref blew his whistle and I first felt the Jabulani, the official World Cup ball, at my feet, I knew that this, today, was going to be my game. I felt as light as a feather and confident. I didn't think, I just played. Which is always the best way to deliver a good performance.

I prefer to play without thinking. I don't want to ponder how I'm going to get past an opponent, but just dribble past him as my instinct tells me. I don't want to wonder where the next pass is going, but kick it into the right space. Mulling it over isn't good. Best of all is when your actions occur automatically and intuitively. Thinking inhibits you on the pitch. And so many of my assists are a combination of prescience and luck – for luck is part of it, as my teammates obviously have to choose the right run to receive my pass.

For this reason I'm not a fan of extremely long and detailed video analyses. Of course, it's professional to consider the opposition's weaknesses. To know how to get past my opponents in the next game. It helps me a little if I know, for example, that an opposition player is less versatile on his left side. But if I focus too much on the other players' weaknesses I'll spend too long thinking and that could cost me a critical second in the actual encounter. Alternatively, I'll pay too little attention to my own strengths and adjust my game too much to that of my opponent. But what happens if the opposition coach tries a trick and lines up another player against me?

My Spanish teacher, who I was to meet a few months later, told me at the start, 'I'm going to teach you the language so you speak it automatically. Because the words and phrases will enter your mind without your having to think about it. I want the language to become part of your daily routine. When you get up in the morning, you don't think how you're going to drive to training, or what gear you should change into when. You just set off, doing everything instinctively, and then you arrive at the training ground. I'm not going to drum grammar or vocabulary into you. I want you to speak Spanish without thinking.' Exactly the same is true of football.

I didn't spend a second thinking in the game against Australia. I made two sidesteps, saw Thomas Müller start running and struck the ball past three Australians to exactly where he was heading. If I'd played the ball a tenth of a second later, i.e. if I'd wasted a single thought on it, it would probably have been intercepted – somehow one of the three opponents would have got a toe to it. But because the pass was instinctive, everything worked perfectly, and Müller was able to play the ball down the centre, where Lukas Podolski came sprinting and put the ball in the back of the net after eight minutes. Miroslav Klose and Thomas Müller both scored to make it 3–0, before I set up the fourth for Cacau.

The game against Australia was the best of my career. It was pure magic. Everything was right. Every pass. Every move. Every tackle. Every double tackle. Every touch of the ball. Simply everything. When I was substituted in the middle of the second half, the German fans got to their feet. A standing ovation. They applauded and called out my name. I could have burst with the pride I felt at that moment.

Obviously I heard what the German manager Joachim Löw said to the TV cameras afterwards. 'Mesut is an extremely important player for us and he embodies the type of football we want to play. His deadly passes are made with such ease, the ball never stops at his feet, but just keeps moving. Mesut Özil was sublime off the ball too. The moves he made were so important.'

I also caught Miroslav Klose's words of praise for me: 'We've been needing a number ten and looking for one. It's great that Mesut decided to play for Germany. The way he kept supplying his teammates with surprising passes is outstanding.'

When we spoke the following day, my brother Mutlu told me that 'Kaiser' Franz Beckenbauer had said, 'What Özil does is extraordinary.'

It was completely crazy, especially because the words came from players, coaches and a legend. But I couldn't let myself get too carried away. One good game on its own wasn't any good either for me or the team. We still had a long way ahead of us.

I felt good in the second match against Serbia too. Within five minutes I'd managed two fantastic passes to Lukas Podolski, though he couldn't convert them. Instead Milan Jovanović scored – and we lost Miro Klose after he collected his second yellow card.

All of a sudden our progress was in danger, despite our excellent performance against Australia. To be sure of making it to the last 16 we had to beat Ghana in our last group game.

Both sides had their chances. In the twenty-fifth minute Cacau crossed to me in plenty of space. An absolute dream pass. I was running alone towards their keeper, Richard Kingson. All Ghana's defenders were 6 or 7 metres behind me. I tapped the ball with my right foot, ran three paces, and then started to think, Dammit! Dammit! Dammit! Should I shoot? Or sidestep the goalie? I knocked the ball forwards again. This time with my left foot. I was already in the box. Kingson was racing towards me, already out of his goal area. We were almost face to face, separated by perhaps 2 or 3 metres. I saw him open his mouth and roar. High or flat? High or flat? What now? High! No, better flat. Bloody head, stop driving me mad. Stop it! Stop!

Kingson flung himself at me, straddling his legs forward. I was still thinking! When I decided to push the ball flat beneath the keeper, he'd long since guessed what I was going to do and his right foot was there. I'd squandered my great chance in a most embarrassing way. And in such an important game too.

'Siktir lan,' I chided myself. How stupid can you get?

I also failed to make my second chance count, even if it wasn't quite as clear-cut as the first. After a free kick by Bastian Schweinsteiger the ball suddenly landed at my feet. Surprisingly, I found myself with a shot at goal from 12 metres. But a Ghanaian got in the way and blocked it.

But then, in the sixtieth minute, I stopped thinking and made it simple. Thomas Müller crossed to me from the right. I stopped the ball, which did a gentle bounce, saw that I had a free shot at goal and struck from 18 metres. The ball rushed past the heads of the Ghanaians and went into the net right beside the left post. The winning goal, which ensured our progress.

The Italian newspaper, *La Gazzetta dello Sport* now called me a 'fixture' in the German team, even though that had only been my thirteenth international cap. In a similar vein, *Tuttosport* considered me 'one of the best players of the World Cup'. In Turkey my goal was celebrated by *Fanatik* as a 'ballistic missile'. And *Bild*'s headline was 'ÖÖÖÖh, what a goal'.

In the last 16 games I provided one assist in our 4–1 victory against England. In the quarter-final against Argentina – a team with such superstars as Javier Mascherano, Ángel di María, Gonzalo Higuaín, Carlos Tévez and Lionel Messi – I crossed to Klose for the final goal in our 4–0 victory. As a team we were doing everything right. And were getting the corresponding recognition from around the world. 'Germany is scary,' *Diario As* wrote, while *Marca* purred, 'The new Germany is awesome. This team is different, it looks to caress the ball.'

Waiting for us in the semi-final were Spain, the reigning European champions. Even they had extraordinary respect for us. 'I've always been a fan of their football. Given the way the tournament's gone so far they may have deserved the title more than us. At this World Cup we haven't yet come across a side that's so strong in attack. We're going to have to be incredibly well prepared,' Fernando Torres said before the game, while David Villa described our performances as 'truly sensational'. Even their manager, Vicente del Bosque, sounded very impressed: 'Against Germany we'll have to play out of our skins. At the moment they're the best team in the world.'

Unfortunately we weren't able to show any of this in the semi-final. As in 2008 – although I wasn't in the team then – we lost against Spain. Back then it had been the European Championship final. Now it was the semi-final. We didn't go in for the tackles. We just ran behind the ball. Their tiki-taka style was unnerving. There's nothing worse for a footballer than to chase after a ball only to be shown that you don't have a chance of winning it. Andrés Iniesta, David Villa, Xabi Alonso and co. wore us down with their play. You try to intervene and win the ball. But it's intensely frustrating after a long sprint down one side to see it disappear at lightning speed to the other.

When, in the seventy-third minute, Puyol headed a corner into our goal, we were finished. I clearly remember Jogi Löw screaming his heart out in the last few minutes. 'Now it's all or nothing,' he shouted from the sideline. When there were only ten minutes left he collared our captain Philipp Lahm, his right-hand man, and gave us the message via him: 'Everyone forward. Even if it means we lose 2–0. It doesn't matter whether it's 1–0 or 2–0. Take every risk!'

We made one last combined effort to avoid defeat. But in vain. We were out. And immediately the nit-picking began, at least for some in Germany. Instead of congratulating the team on its showing up till then. Instead of building it up again, because of course all of us were disappointed.

Out of the blue, Béla Réthy from the television channel ZDF criticised our accommodation during the World Cup. Compared to the Dutch team, whose base had been in a hotel in the centre of Johannesburg, where the players could mingle in the hotel bar with ordinary guests, our team base had been in a no-man's land on the edge of Pretoria, he said. He didn't like the fact that a large area around the hotel had been fenced off. All the footballers saw apart from their teammates were a few journalists and monitor lizards, he claimed. Until our exit in the semi-final our accommodation hadn't been an issue. At times we'd played scintillating football, delighting fans across the world. But now, after one poor game, it was all suddenly our hotel's fault? What utter nonsense!

Most of the Dutch players had an impressive career behind them. Mark van Bommel had won countless medals, in Italy, Germany, Holland and Spain. And he also won the Champions League. But in spite of the fact that, as Béla Réthy wrote, he had sat relaxing at the bar rather than living amongst journalists and monitor lizards, he hadn't won the World Cup or European

Championship. In 2010 in South Africa the Dutch side lost in the final against Spain just as we had.

It was a fantastic World Cup. And we could be immensely proud of how we'd acquitted ourselves with this young, inexperienced team. The fact that we won the last game against Uruguay to secure third place shows how high morale was in the squad.

Shortly after the World Cup, when the national squad came together again, Jogi Löw gave his obligatory speech, in which he said, 'We surprised everyone at the World Cup. We played a good tournament. In South Africa I saw a side that thrilled me. And I'm sure it's going to have success. I know for sure that this side is going to win a major title.' He would prove to be right.

Even after the World Cup, it was still not definite that I would move from Bremen. But the press reports skipped over my successful performances in South Africa to focus on the climax of my transfer saga. I even became a subject for discussion amongst politicians. In a *Stern* interview Jürgen Trittin of the Greens, a well-known Werder fan, said of me, 'Özil is completely overrated. Please tell this to the news agencies, as it'll reduce the likelihood of us selling him.'

Klaus Allofs also weighed in after the World Cup, flattering me with compliments in public, saying, for example, that Mesut was better than Lionel Messi.

Of course, he was required to give his views week in, week out, and make prognoses. In mid-July he told the *Welt am Sonntag*, 'When we spoke personally he told me he's happy at Werder and he hasn't had any concrete offers. I'm not worried about him leaving Bremen.' He said something similar to *Kicker*: 'I don't rule out us being able to renew Mesut's contract.' He also said, 'Losing players on a free transfer is always regarded as terribly bad luck. But if it's not possible financially to extend a contract, though you're determined to hold on to the player from a sporting point of view, then you've got to live with the fact that contracts expire.'

This was the first indirect threat aimed at me, which implied: We don't have to accept any offers. It may well happen that we keep you here and decline all offers.

After the demanding tournament in South Africa I relaxed, as mentioned earlier, in a villa in Port d'Andratx, Mallorca. And it was from there that we conducted negotiations about my future. My agent had even installed a fax machine in the villa. From Mallorca we also flew to Madrid and Barcelona to listen personally to what the bosses at the two clubs could offer me. I also spent hours lying on a sunbed, agonising over whether I should risk switching to Real Madrid and putting myself in competition with Kaká, who at the time filled the role of playmaker with Los Blancos. The answer, though, was pretty clear: Yes, I wanted to take the risk.

The only problem in all this was Klaus Allofs. Behind the scenes he was making every effort to block my move. The nice manager who'd been right behind me for three years, who'd protected me from the rare instances of press hostility and always paid me the kindest compliments, had now become the tough, ruthless boss whose concern was not my welfare but that of the club. And he made no secret of his anger that I was considering a move. 'I don't have to let you go,' he said in one telephone conversation we had. And he also made such comments as, 'We can make you stew on the bench for a whole year.'

My agent called Allofs to appease him. He contacted him again and again. But the Bremen boss wouldn't waver. If he were to let me go, he said, the transfer fee would have to be high enough. We knew that Madrid was ready to pay around 15 million euros for me. Which was three times what Werder had bought me for. An excellent return, especially considering I only had a year of my contract to run. If I remember correctly, however, Allofs wanted 30 million to begin with – a pie-in-the-sky amount.

I was terrified that the deal would collapse. That Klaus Allofs would ruin my opportunity of a lifetime. And so I called him myself. 'It's always been my dream,' I said to him, 'to play under José Mourinho one day'. Then I told him the story about the Milan game, mentioning what I'd said to my agent afterwards. 'There are chances that only come around once in a lifetime,' I continued. I wasn't seeking to threaten him, nor sound angry or aggressive – I just wanted to make him aware of the unbelievable opportunity that was open to me and how important this move was. 'Please don't ruin my future. Please,' I said, almost begging him over the phone. 'The Real Madrid train only passes by once. Let me get on it.'

I completely understand that Allofs couldn't be happy if a player from whom they were still hoping for great things wanted to leave the club after three years. Of course I get his disappointment. And I can even sympathise with his touches of stubbornness. But the threat to leave me on the bench was excessive. Who would benefit by penalising me?

On our last evening at the villa in Mallorca, my friends and I were sitting watching television when some breaking news ran across the bottom of the screen. '+++ Real Madrid signs Khedira +++,' it said. '+++ 14 million for Stuttgart +++. Khedira signs five-year contract +++.'

Images started playing inside my head, in which I kept seeing 'Özil' instead of 'Khedira'. And 'Bremen' instead of 'Stuttgart'. I wanted to be part of the breaking news. I didn't want to wait any longer. And most of all I wanted to finally tell my friends. To get them on board. Break my silence. Put an end to the secrecy. Baris tore me from my thoughts. 'Are you all right?' he asked. 'Yes, fine,' I nodded. I think that now he knew what was up.

At the beginning of August I had to go back to Bremen. Pre-season training had already started; those players who weren't internationals had already been on the island of Norderney and to Donaueschingen, where they undertook their first two phases of training. The third phase was due to take place in the Austrian town of Bad Waltersdorf. Marko Arnautović had just been signed.

When the reporters came racing towards me I uttered some meaningless phrases, which I'd agreed beforehand with my agent and learned by heart, such as, 'As far as I'm concerned only the facts count. The fact is, I'm under contract with Werder Bremen. The situation for the next 12 months is resolved. But right now I can't say what's going to happen after that.'

When, on 5 August, news came through that Kaká had to undergo a knee operation – arthroscopic surgery on the meniscus – in Antwerp it meant I would definitely be going to Madrid.

When we played a practice match a couple of days later against Fulham at Craven Cottage, and Alex Ferguson was spotted amongst the crowd, *The Times* claimed he'd been there to watch me. On 11 August the German news agencies' reports said, 'If we're to believe the sports papers in Spain, it won't be long before we see Mesut Özil there. His move to Barcelona is close to perfect: four-year contract, twelve million fee.' The media were speculating gleefully. And I was sending texts. I'd confided in Sami Khedira early on, because I knew I could totally rely on him. 'Maybe we'll be playing together soon,' I'd written to him at the beginning of August. After the official announcement of his signing, the messages flew back and forth between us. I really pestered him. 'What's the coach like?' I asked. Or: 'What's the team like?' And: 'If you were in my shoes would you move?' Once, something strange happened. My mobile beeped and notified me that Khedira had sent a text. 'Hi Mes,' he wrote, 'I'm forwarding you a text from Mourinho.' Then my smartphone beeped again, and when the promised message came through it read, 'Hi Sami. Have a look, our starting line up for the future.' Eleven names followed. Ronaldo, obviously. And Ramos. And Khedira. And then I saw my name in Madrid's starting formation for the future, even though I wasn't under contract yet. Mourinho must have been very confident to already be telling other players that he was after me.

The exchange of messages with Khedira helped me cope with the interminable waiting. I'm not the most patient of men. Every evening I dreamed of Madrid. Every evening I had this fascination that emanates from Real in my mind. Although I was still training for Werder, my head was full of Madrid. I wanted to be a real part of that team, not just a silent text-message insider.

On 17 August 2010 it was announced that the transfer was complete. In the negotiations over the fee, Real Madrid prevailed over Allofs and paid around 15 million euros for me. 'We were able to get him under contract for a price far below his true value. We couldn't let such a chance slip,' José Mourinho said.

I didn't care one bit about the amount they'd paid for me. The key thing was that I was finally there. My whole life changed overnight.

12

A NEW WORLD

YOUR JOB IS NEVER TO BE SATISFIED

Even before my transfer I knew that Real Madrid was the biggest club in the world. But as an outsider you have no idea of its true dimensions. You have to feel Real to understand it. You need to be part of this crazy entity. Everyone talks about its great history, but these are just words. You only understand the true greatness when you're part of this monstrous club, which swallows you up entirely.

When I put on the white jersey for the first time I felt such a thrill. I was actually shaking and even slightly terrified at how overwhelming it felt. It's not just any old piece of material you're slipping on and taking off again. The moment it touched my skin I realised the responsibility that now lay on my shoulders. The commitment I'd made.

When I first stepped onto the training ground I was in total awe. Put next to the facilities of Bremen and Schalke, there's absolutely no comparison. The gym boasts many more machines than players – you don't have to queue or wait a single second for a teammate to finish. Everything is in abundance, the perfect conditions. A footballer's paradise, if you like.

One of the major advantages at Real is that you can train in total peace and seclusion. There are no distractions. There aren't any journalists who get wind of squabbles during training and then milk them as much as they can. Nor is there any 'spying' during the closed training sessions. At FC Bayern, for example, paparazzi always hang around, taking photographs through holes in the tarpaulin in an attempt to discover training secrets. Reporters permanently stand by the protective screen, listening to the instructions the coach is shouting. None of that is possible at Real Madrid as the ground is too remote. None of the tactical ruses the manager rehearses can slip out. At Real you train as you do at Arsenal: in secret.

Real also owns a hotel inside the training complex itself, so, if a player gets tired between sessions he can retire to a single room to rest. A fingerprint scanner opens the door – you don't even need a keycard.

When I entered Bernabéu stadium, I felt like a dwarf. I looked up at those steep tiers of seats and felt tiny. Really, really small. I don't know why, but I took my first steps on the grass with great care. Complete madness really. But somehow it didn't seem appropriate to stomp all over the sacred turf that had witnessed so many heroic deeds. I imagine there must be hundreds of players all over the world who would pay a fortune for the opportunity to play just once on this pitch, in this stadium. Maybe I'd have been one of those players myself if my chance hadn't come to turn out for Los Blancos.

Everywhere I went I got a sense of Real Madrid's dimensions as a football club. At the World Cup in South Africa there were

20 fans outside our team hotel. When I was away with Real Madrid, thousands of fans would lay siege to our hotel, just to get a few seconds' glimpse of us. I was astonished by the hype surrounding Madrid. It shows the esteem the club is held in throughout the world. No team makes people as crazy as Real. 'Winning on its own is not enough. The victory has to be achieved in a certain way,' Emilio Butragueño, the legendary Real striker, once said. In the days and weeks before I joined Real Madrid I read lots about the club and spent hours Googling everything about it. Which is where I came across that quote. Mad, but true!

The fans and journalists have undue expectations of the club. At Madrid no player is judged by normal yardsticks because the crowds keep getting grandiose performances from Ronaldo and co. They see shooting exhibitions. They're present when Real breaks one record after another. They permanently watch football at the highest level. And they get used to it. At some stage they start to regard the incredible as normal. If Ronaldo doesn't score 40 goals per season they say he's going through a crisis. Real set this standard itself. In Madrid, 'good' isn't enough. Such pressure is really extraordinary. You have to learn how to deal with it.

Right after my first outing I could see which way the wind was blowing. My debut in a Real shirt lasted 58 minutes against Hércules Alicante, who'd been promoted from the first division. 'At particular moments Özil shows the class he has,' *Marca* wrote. 'When the ball is at his feet he's a permanent threat to the opposition goal. In Özil, Cristiano Ronaldo has a high-quality teammate.' The paper's rival, *Diario As*, was more critical: 'We'll see better performances from Özil wearing the Real shirt. On his debut the ex-Bremen player showed both highlights and lowlights.' In spite of his colleague's positive assessment, another *Marca* journalist concluded that I'd moved 'like a priest in a brothel', whatever that's supposed to mean.

To begin with I stayed in a hotel in Madrid. But only briefly, because I was in a hurry to find a home for myself. The first place I found was in Sami Khedira's neighbourhood. In a building that looked like the White House from the outside. I didn't really like it, to be honest, but I didn't think too much about it at first, because I didn't want to spend weeks in a hotel room as I had in Bremen. I didn't feel particularly comfortable there. The house came already furnished. So I sat on a sofa that the owner had chosen. I slept in a bed where others had slept before. I wandered through rooms that looked like a dentist's practice. White, sterile, completely impersonal. The owner's taste certainly wasn't mine. It didn't feel homely at all.

Which is why I moved out again a few months later, and into a house near my friend, Sergio Ramos. It was still being finished, which meant there was no furniture yet. I could – and had to – arrange it all myself. I bought what I liked, without showing much skill as an interior designer; the individual pieces of furniture didn't really match. It was all thrown together higgledy-piggledy. But I thought it was nice and I finally felt at home.

It was the same on the pitch. In the first weeks of training I learned what it means to be obsessed with success. The Madrid squad only has players who never want to lose. They're crazy. They'll do whatever it takes to succeed. No one sits back for even a day. I also trained hard, of course, to get into Schalke's first team or to break through at Werder. But, as I'm sure was the case with all of us, there was the odd day when I wasn't 100 per cent focused on the job in hand. When I didn't push myself to the limit. When I worked to rule, if you like. Such moments were rare, but they did happen. I think everybody is familiar with this. Every normal person, whether they work in an office or on a building site, will have days where they don't try so hard. Until I arrived in Madrid, I thought this was OK, as long as it remained the exception. But throughout my entire time at Madrid I never saw anyone even come close to having days like this. Anybody who watches Sergio Ramos or Cristiano Ronaldo at work soon knows what real effort means.

Normally I don't like talking about teammates. I don't enjoy being asked in interviews about other players, about their performance or potential. But with Ramos and Ronaldo it's different. They're legends. They're unique. And I'm very keen to talk about both of them at any opportunity.

In the Real Madrid dressing room Ramos behaved like the perfect footballer, and served as an inspiration for me. But he's also a wonderful person. From the start he literally took me by the hand. He told me all about Madrid,and explained the rules of the club. Barely had I arrrived than he invited me to his house as if it was perfectly normal. Ramos is a highly gifted musician. Sometimes we'd just sit around at his place, and he'd play guitar and sing.

It was by watching him and Ronaldo in particular that I learned what sheer determination is. How you can really torture yourself. My, oh my, if Ronaldo didn't score in goal-shooting practice it put him in such a bad mood. He'd get annoyed if a single scissors kick went wrong. Even if the 80 he had done before had worked perfectly, the single one he fluffed would drive him into a rage.

I've never seen a footballer as professional as him. Whenever we got back late at night from an away game, he'd always get into the Jacuzzi to give his body a recovery session, whereas most of the other players would drive straight back home and go to bed.

Although Ronaldo is a total superstar, he's remained a perfectly normal bloke. In my early days with the club he'd come up to me when we were warming down and stretching after games and ask how I was. Did I have a girlfriend? What was Germany like? Once we went to watch a basketball match – Real Madrid v Barcelona. We're both great basketball fans. I told him that I love the permanent tension, the continual back and forth. 'Do you like ice hockey or American football?' he asked. 'No,' I said. 'American football rules are far too complicated and I also find it takes too long to get to the real action. I'm not so much of a fan of the NHL either.'

I'm certain that many defenders around the world will breathe a sigh of relief when their opponent Ronaldo takes his football pension and cannot run rings around them any more. It'll feel like redemption when the best of the best retires.

Everyone at Real Madrid wants success. The players are burning to win. The brake is never on during training sessions. The club is home to the most victory-obsessed players in the world, who drive each other on.

During my time with the club there was also a manager who was completely obsessed with winning. When Mourinho started out as Chelsea coach in 2004 he said, full of self-confidence, 'Please don't call me arrogant, because what I'm saying is true. I'm a European champion, and I think I'm a special one.' And it is true. José Mourinho really is special – especially good at what he does.

At the beginning of this book I described the biggest dressing-room bollocking I've ever had from a manager. At half-time against Deportivo La Coruña, when we were 3–1 up, Mourinho criticised me in front of all my teammates with a vehemence I haven't experienced since. He shouted things at me that, given the state of the game and my admittedly lacklustre performance, were perhaps OK in substance. The manner in which he attacked me, however, was not. After I'd enforced the substitution I fled to the shower because it was the only way of calming down. I flung my shampoo bottle at the wall to begin with and slapped my hand against the tiles. Somehow I had to get rid of the aggression that had built up during Mourinho's tirade. I was swearing like a trooper.

But when I gradually ran out of expletives and realised I was starting from the beginning again, I asked myself why Mourinho had attacked me so heatedly. I knew him well enough by then to grasp that he hadn't exploded just for the fun of it. Everything he said and did was very carefully thought through. Which meant that there must also be a message to this bollocking, one he was trying to address to me.

As the hot water slowly brought me back to my senses, I couldn't help thinking of Andreas Müller and the scene he'd made in the Schalke dressing room a few years earlier. Back then Müller had just wanted to lay into me. That was quite clear to me. He wanted to make me look ridiculous and get rid of me in front of my teammates. I soon realised that this wasn't Mourinho's aim at all. His intention was different, but I didn't understand what it was until later.

When I drove home from the Bernabéu stadium through night-time Madrid I tried to recall Mourinho's exact words. Every single one he'd hurled at my face. And the way he'd said it too. I pictured again in my mind how he'd imitated me. But I couldn't find the answer to my question on my drive home. Instead my anger boiled up again when I thought of how he'd made me look like a fool in front of my teammates with his Özil imitation. There was no way I could forget that as quickly as I hoped. But most of all I wondered why the two of us couldn't have had a discussion alone.

As I reached my house and waited for the gate to open I thought of my teammates.

'What a fucking arsehole I am,' I suddenly thought. I was such an idiot! Shaking my head, I slammed my hand against the steering wheel. 'Fuck! Fuck! Fuck!' I'd let my teammates down. It wasn't their fault; they hadn't been part of the argument. And yet I'd refused to help them in the second half. Although I was pissed off with Mourinho, my behaviour had punished them.

That same evening I popped by to see Sergio Ramos, who lived next door. I had a long chat with him and apologised for my desertion. Later, I did the same with the other players. Ramos accepted my apology immediately and just wanted to know how I thought things would go on from here with the manager.

'What do you want from him?' Ramos asked. 'What are you expecting from Mourinho?'

'He owes me an apology,' I replied.

The next day Ramos discussed the incident in the changing room with Mourinho. That's the kind of man he is. He always takes responsibility for others and helps out when things need to be cleared up. Ramos is a genuine guy – a real friend, a player that any team would want to have, both as a footballer and a person.

By now, however, I'd also worked out for myself why Mourinho had reacted so vehemently and bollocked me in front of the others. It was actually quite easy to understand. After all, he had said it quite clearly: I must never relax! He wanted me to leave my comfort zone on the pitch. He refused to accept a 10 or 20 per cent drop in performance just because it was more convenient for me. He wanted to rid me of my nonchalance and toughen me up as a player. He wanted to push me hard so I'd never stop developing. So I'd get better every day. So I'd be in a position to realise when I wasn't pushing myself to the limit. Mourinho also probably felt that trying to drum this lesson into me in one or more face-to-face conversations wouldn't have much of an effect, and that I needed this massive shock in front of all my colleagues and friends to make me grasp the message. He had guessed that I'd be furious and as a result more serious about questioning what might be wrong than if he had just given me a tongue-lashing in private, without any witnesses. Sometimes I do actually need a bit of anger to really perform well or understand things.

No player in the world wants to be insulted by their coach and called a coward or a baby – anybody would dispute an accusation like that on the spot. But, strictly speaking, Mourinho was right. When I came to Madrid part of me believed that playing beautiful football would be enough. After three dream passes and four super solo runs I'd swagger around the pitch, rather than continuing to fight and do my job with the utmost concentration. I was quickly sated, easily satisfied, and then I'd sometimes be happy to go down a gear. But it was exactly this attitude that Mourinho beat out of me.

And I thanked him for it. After a few days I admitted to him that the penny had dropped. And that I was grateful to him for showing me with such clarity what my biggest weakness was. 'I'm not going to leave you in peace until you've exhausted your potential,' he replied with a grin.

He revisited the subject in front of the whole team before the next game. When we were in Barcelona he said, 'Perhaps my little act and choice of words were crass. I'm sorry about that, Mesut. We've talked about the rest of it. I just want the best for all of you. And sometimes you only understand what's best when you have it shoved into your face. But,' he continued, bowing before me, 'don't worry, from now on there will be nothing but cuddles for this fine gentleman.' He laughed and everyone joined in.

I've heard many a dressing-room talk in my life. From a wide variety of speakers. Time and again coaches have tried to stir us players with particular words or give us an extra injection of motivation with short films. Sometimes managers also show a montage of extraordinary goals. I'm not a big fan of this because it often only produces the desired boost for half the players, while falling flat for the others. How is Manuel Neuer going to benefit, for example, from watching Miroslav Klose's great goals? Or if Iker Casillas watches Ronaldo make a successful finish? Or if Petr Čech sees his colleagues celebrating with Olivier Giroud?

The dressing-room talks that have stayed in my memory, which have left a sustained impression, are few and far between. For example, I liked the way Horst Hrubesch prepared us for the U-21 European Championship final against England in 2009. In the dressing room was a screen with a projector. 'Today I'm going to delegate my talk to a man who has come up with the perfect words. You can't put it better than he does. So listen carefully and let yourselves be inspired,' Hrubesch said, pressing the play button.

We'd entered the knockout phase as the runner-up in our group. England, our opponents in the final, had topped it. In the group match we'd drawn our encounter. In the semi-final we'd beaten an Italian side containing Mario Balotelli; now we had our second clash of the tournament with the English, and Hrubesch let Al Pacino do the talking.

He showed the speech that Pacino, the Hollywood star of the cult film *Any Given Sunday*, playing coach Tony d'Amato, gives to his faltering American football team, the Miami Sharks. Most of us knew it, of course, from the cinema in 1999. But we all watched, mesmerised, as Al Pacino knocked it into his players: 'Three minutes till the biggest battle of our professional lives. It all comes down to today. And either we heal, as a team, or we're gonna crumble.' Al Pacino fires up his team with clever, well thought-out words. Every one hits the spot; his message is striking. 'In any fight it's the guy who's willing to die who's gonna win that inch,' he blares out to his players. Then he lowers his voice and says, 'You've got to look at the guy next to you. Look into his eyes . . . You're gonna see a guy who will sacrifice himself for this team, because he knows when it comes down to it you're gonna do the same for him. That's a team, gentlemen, and either we heal, now, as a team, or we will die as individuals . . . Now, what are you gonna do?'

At the end of the clip we all looked at each other. And I saw such determination flash in the eyes of my teammates that it was almost scary. Everybody radiated an unswerving confidence that we could roll over this England team. We shouted at the tops of our voices, slapped hands so hard that it hurt. This video had welded us so firmly together that we beat England 4–0. I set up the first for Gonzalo Castro, scored the second myself, and effected the pass to Sandro Wagner, who made it 3–0. All thanks to Hrubesch's idea of relying on Al Pacino.

In 2010, just prior to the World Cup in South Africa, Joachim Löw hired a very special person to give us a motivational talk during our preparations in Sicily. Jonah Lomu, the New Zealand rugby legend, told us his life story. Normally I'm quite sceptical about this sort of approach, because unfortunately lots of speakers often just talk in platitudes. But what Lomu had achieved in his life was really so impressive that I hung onto his every word and I'll never forget the challenges he defied.

A new world

The son of Tongan immigrants, Lomu grew up in a humble household in a notorious suburb of Auckland. His father drank and sometimes beat him. Lomu went out on the street, joined gangs and was on the verge of slipping into criminality, but when one of his friends was stabbed to death he made the break and decided to direct all his energies into rugby.

Lomu trained as hard as he could until he was chosen for the New Zealand national side, the All Blacks. At the 1995 World Cup in South Africa he took the international stage by storm, although the previous year doctors had identified that he had a rare kidney complaint. Because of his condition Lomu had to take a year out from the game in 1996. But he came back so strongly that he was the outstanding player of the 1999 World Cup too.

His courageous and aggressive playing style brought him worldwide respect. He was described as 'the turbo-charged bull-dozer', 'rhino', 'the unstoppable', 'a force of nature' and 'the black bus'. Weighing 120 kilos, he was able to run 100 metres in 10.8 seconds. 'As soon as I put on the All Blacks shirt I feel like Superman,' said Lomu, who with his stature reminded me some-how of the comic figure Obelix – because he was so strong and yet was such a kind-hearted soul.

He outran his opponents by the dozen. Anybody who got in his way was flattened. But his illness managed to do what no opponent could. It brought him to his knees. He had to undergo dialysis. Then he needed an operation. 'I was this guy who just ran right over opponents, won games and had fun. But all of a sudden I was so ill that I couldn't even run past a baby.'

The power man had to learn everything from scratch again. 'How do I take a step? How do I lift my foot? How do I walk?' He forced himself agonisingly out of his wheelchair, honed his muscles again and lived life with zest once more – until in 2015 he very sadly died at the tender age of 40. Five years earlier, before his visit to our training camp, he was still brimming with energy. 'Nothing can crush you,' he said. 'Just as nothing could crush me. If you fall, stand up again. You can achieve great things.'

I still think about Jonah Lomu today. About his positive attitude to life, even though he had every reason to complain and rail against his fate. Rather than do that he always looked forward in good spirits.

The last dressing-room talks that have lingered in my memory are those from the 2014 World Cup in Brazil. Before each game Jogi Löw got a different player to talk to the team. On one occasion it was Philipp Lahm, on another Roman Weidenfeller. Each one had the chance to express his expectations and view of things, while also opting for his own type of talk. Before the semi-final against the hosts, Brazil, Jogi Löw spoke himself, saying, 'When we go out there now almost everyone will be against us. Which makes it all the more important to stand together on the pitch. To do everything together. All of you on the pitch. All the backroom staff too. We're going to fight together. When someone makes a good play, all of us are going to applaud. If someone makes a mistake, we're going to pick him up. We're going to fight until we're in the final in Rio. We're going to play like champions!'

I don't believe there's a winning formula for dressing-room talks. They just have to suit the situation. And if it's necessary to have a go at somebody in the dressing room, that can help too if – like me – he learns his lesson from it.

To come back to Mourinho again, his big plus was that he was always honest with his players. He always told us what he thought. He never talked about people behind their backs. He was hard, but fair. Mourinho is a thoroughly honest man. That's his strength. He can praise, but he can criticise too. I know managers who have a problem with criticism. Who don't dare criticise their own players. Who pretend to be the strong man to the press, but who are really afraid of challenging great players. Who instead make their assistant manager dish out the criticism. But not Mourinho. And it was precisely that which always went down well. 'I'm never going to tell you you're doing something well if it's untrue,' he emphasised to us. I'm absolutely sure that you'd never hear a bad word about Mourinho from any player during that time in Madrid. I'll even guarantee that not a single player had a problem with him. Because he was always decent. Because he was direct and honest. And because it was this approach that allowed many players to take the decisive step forwards. Like me.

SERGIO RAMOS

'THANKS FOR EVERYTHING, BRO!'

Sergio Ramos is a Real Madrid institution and one of the most successful footballers ever. He's been playing for Los Blancos since 2005. He's won the Champions League with them twice. In the 2014 final he scored the equaliser in injury time against Atlético Madrid, allowing Real to go into extra time, in which they won 4-1. He has won the World Cup with the Spanish national side and the European Championship twice. Ramos looked after Mesut Özil from the day of his arrival at Real and became a very good friend.

When I think about Mesut Özil the footballer I think about magic, talent, quality and the ability to read a game like few others.

When I think about Mesut Özil the person I think about friendship, sensitivity, fondness, respect, joy and warmth.

The truth is that I already knew Mesut the player before he came to Real Madrid. I though he was a different sort of player, with a golden left foot and splendid ball control.

We started to hear his name being talked about and we knew that he could be a great signing for Real Madrid. After so many years at the club, it's my duty to any new teammate that arrives to help them adapt as quickly as possible: help them get to know the city better, the places to live, etc. And I did that with him, but in the case of Mesut it was special. It's really interesting.

Obviously, language could have been a barrier, because he didn't speak Spanish, but we got chatting straight away. His level of English was similar to mine and it was an opportunity for us to practise the language. We became good friends from the start. He happened to move into the house next door to mine and I invited him over to try to help him settle in and spend some time together.

We didn't just share our profession and club, but we also liked the same things. We have similar tastes in fashion and music. It was something that brought us together straight away. He always asked me about where to buy clothes and the type of music I played as we both liked R'n'B and hip hop and that's how we became friends. There was a special understanding right away.

And because of that special friendship we had, in one League game I wore his shirt under mine. It was simply an act of fondness and friendship. Mesut is a very sensitive person with enormous quality and potential and I had the idea of putting on his shirt to remember him if I scored a goal.

Before leaving, he gave me the last shirt he wore for Real Madrid as a gift, with a personal dedication. It is a special souvenir that has a special place in my museum.

In sporting terms we follow each other closely. As it happened, I was lucky enough to win the World Cup with Spain in South Africa in 2010 and he won it in Brazil in 2014 with Germany. I remember congratulating him on becoming world champion, which is one of the most important achievements for any footballer, and I was really pleased with the fact that he could feel the same way I'd felt four years earlier.

We're still in touch today. We talk about our families, our teams, our cities. During his time here in Madrid he was very happy and still has special memories of the club, the city and the fans and that's why he still follows us closely. Mesut, you're unique.

Thanks for everything, bro!

The support of Sami Khedira and Sergio Ramos helped me to feel at home in the Spanish capital.

A total superstar and a perfectly normal bloke – that's my Real team-mate Cristiano Ronaldo.

Barcelona were never 'the enemy' to me, but Real's clashes with them could be fractious and I became obsessed with beating them.

Touchline rivals in Spain – and again in Manchester – but Jose Mourinho and Pep Guardiola could scarcely be more different characters.

I chose Jose Mourinho, the man and the coach, rather than Real Madrid, the iconic club, but he was never afraid to tear a strip off me.

I might have become a team-mate of Lionel Messi at Barca but ended up confronting the great Argentinian in El Clasico.

Beating our great rivals Barcelona to the Spanish championship in 2012 prompted celebrations I will never forget.

After fierce deadline-day haggling between Real Madrid and Arsenal, I was delighted to become a Gunner in 2013.

Arsene Wenger and I pose for the press at the Emirates Stadium after my move to Arsenal – four years after he first made contact.

Sami Khedira and I have a real bond, based on friendship, respect and our shared 'migrant' background.

I like fast cars – and I enjoy the privacy being at the wheel gives me because if I go anywhere on foot I tend to be public property.

The presence of my Germany team-mates Per Mertesacker (left) and Lukas Podolski helped me to feel part of the Arsenal set-up.

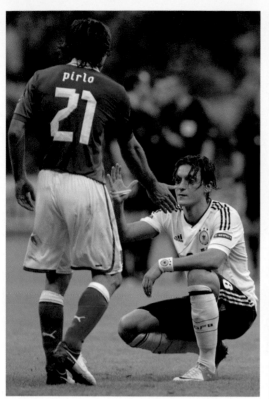

Andrea Pirlo made an amazing gesture after Italy beat Germany in the Euro 2012 semi-finals, coming over to offer me kind, consoling words.

A sweet moment for Lukas Podolski and I as we hold the FA Cup in the 2014 victory parade through the streets of north London.

One of my precious pugs, Balboa, who also loves to play football.

World champions! I lifted the World Cup with the same care as I would if I were holding one of my nieces.

Jogi Low and I have complete trust in each other – for me he's much more than a manager, and winning the World Cup was a fitting reward for his qualities as a coach.

Our base at Campo Bahia on Brazil's Atlantic coast gave the Germany squad the opportunity to sample a life on the ocean waves.

Our 7–1 annihilation of World Cup hosts Brazil in Belo Horizonte was close to perfection.

Bare-chested again! Michel Platini told me it would be an honour to have my shirt from the final – and who am I to deny such a legend.

13

GALACTIC DUELS

FOLLOW YOUR INSTINCT

Mourinho's dressing-room talks are just brilliant. Partly because they're so honest. Mourinho will criticise Cristiano Ronaldo just as readily as he will Sergio Ramos or Iker Casillas. He doesn't have favourites who get special treatment from him. He's not afraid of any player and thus doesn't adopt a softly-softly approach towards anyone. Mourinho always saw us as a team, in which everybody was equally important and treated the same.

After his talks we were prepared to bend over backwards for him and the club. Let's take the example of Barcelona. The entire squad was passionate about beating this superb team. Not just in our head-to-head encounters, but on every other match day as part of the wider duel.

I don't think many people are aware of just how miles ahead Barcelona were of Madrid before Mourinho arrived. Before he was signed to Madrid, Barça was a footballing superpower in both Spain and Europe. It was the best Barcelona side of all time. The Catalans outshone everyone else; they put every other club in the shade. No matter how well a team played, it was never enough against Barcelona. They had an answer to everything. And they drove Real Madrid, in particular, to despair.

In the 2008–09 season Real suffered one of the greatest humiliations of all time at the hands of Barcelona. After the team, led by the then trainer, Juan de Ramos, had been enjoying a strong second half of the season, winning 52 out of a possible 54 points, most football fans were expecting an evenly matched Clásico, the fifth last game of the season. But instead of keeping pace with Barcelona, Madrid were given an object lesson in football and lost 6–2 in the Bernabéu stadium, even though Real had initially taken the lead. 'This is one of the happiest days of my life, and I know that we've made lots of other people happy too,' said Barça coach Pep Guardiola at the press conference following this exhibition of perfect football.

When his team landed at Barcelona airport the following morning they were greeted by throngs of people as if they'd just won the Champions League and had the trophy in their luggage.

All confidence at Madrid was extinguished for the weeks and months that followed. Their arch-rivals Barcelona took the league title and also won the Copa del Rey. The Barça players were the non plus ultra of Spanish football.

And not only in Spain. In the Champions League final they were up against Manchester United, who were full of confidence because the English side had just won the Premier League title for the eleventh time. In spite of this, two days before the final, Pep Guardiola took his leading midfielder, Xavi, aside and told him, 'I know exactly how we're going to win in Rome. I've worked it out. I can see it. We're going to score two or three goals, just wait and see.'

At the press conference, too, Guardiola radiated confidence. 'I know for certain that no team is better than us when it comes to ball possession or courage. We're going to try to instil in them that fear you feel when you're permanently under attack.' To begin with there were no signs of Guardiola's promise. Instead of continually attacking, as vowed, Barça allowed themselves to be pushed back, drastically so, and were lucky to survive the opening minutes without conceding a goal. They won in the end, however – not exactly as Guardiola had predicted, but still 2–0 thanks to goals from Lionel Messi and Samuel Eto'o.

Because the Catalans then went on to win the Spanish Super Cup, and the UEFA Super Cup as well as the FIFA Club World Cup, they bagged an unbelievable six trophies in 2009 – that is to say, the club won every competition it had entered.

To make it perfectly clear, at the time Barcelona and Real Madrid were as far apart from a footballing perspective as the moon and the earth. Or, to use another analogy, Barcelona was like a Mercedes-AMG GT S, with all the cogs working in perfect unison to propel its 510-horsepower engine. With a brilliant driver who could effortlessly manoeuvre the vehicle at high speed down every road. Staying with that image, all that shone at Madrid before Mourinho was the bodywork. At the time Real was like a Ferrari, but with a battered old, maggot-eaten engine under the bonnet rather than a 963cv, and also filled with the wrong petrol.

These were the circumstances in which Madrid found itself when Mourinho, Sami Khedira and I arrived at the club. And it is against this background that our achievements over the next three years must be judged.

We made a strong start to our first season. We won 10 of our opening 12 games, drawing the other two. I managed three goals and six assists. Our performance in the Champions League was excellent too. We won four of the first five games and drew the fifth against AC Milan. My personal record: four assists and one goal.

Then it was time for my first Clásico (a term used exclusively to describe matches between Barcelona and Madrid). I had no idea what was awaiting me. I was prepared for it to be a special game. A derby. A bit like Bremen against Hamburg. Or Schalke against Dortmund. But then the match just steamrollered me, knocked me flat. The Clásico is bigger than anything you can imagine. No other football match in the world has the hype that surrounds this fixture. The Clásico is on its own terms. It is bigger than big. It sets star players on edge. It doesn't just create mayhem in Spain; it has almost the entire world in its thrall. You go by coach to the stadium, at least for home games. Thousands of people accompany you en route, running behind. The coach can only creep along, barely moving forwards due to the masses of people. They let off fireworks. They sing. They jog the coach. And just before it turns into the stadium the people go ballistic. Now they give the coach a thorough shake and hammer their fists on it from the outside. It's louder than a gig. More colourful than Carnival. The hysteria continues into the game. With every skilful play the crowd goes wild. When you step up to take a corner you feel as if 10,000 people are bellowing right into your ear.

This wasn't just my first Clásico; it was also the first duel between Pep Guardiola and José Mourinho as managers of Barça and Real respectively. When Mourinho moved from Italy to Spain, Guardiola said, in one of his first press conferences after the summer break, 'Mourinho is going to make me a better coach. It's important to have him working in Spain because he's one of the best managers in the world. He'll make all of us better.' In the end Mourinho drained him of energy and was perhaps part of the reason why Guardiola left Barça.

I can still see the game being played out before my eyes. We travel to the Camp Nou as league leaders, with 32 points, one more than Barcelona. The media are expecting the closest Clásico of all time, because only a few months previously Mourinho managed to defeat Barcelona with Inter Milan.

The game is being played on a Monday, which is unusual. Elections had been taking place in Catalonia, which was why the match had to be rescheduled.

I'm in the starting line-up, between Cristiano Ronaldo, Ángel di María and Karim Benzema. Xavi scores for the hosts in the ninth minute. Soon afterwards Pedro makes it 2–0. Then David Villa scores twice in two minutes. 4–0 to Barcelona. Jeffrén slots in the final one shortly before the end. In the meantime, Ronaldo gets into an altercation with Pep Guardiola. The Barça coach prevents Ronaldo from taking a quick throw-in, dropping the ball at his feet rather than handing it to him. The Portuguese player shoves Guardiola and there's a brief scuffle, which Andrés Iniesta and Víctor Valdés get involved in too. In stoppage time Sergio Ramos is also sent off after fouling Messi. On the way back to the dressing room he starts an argument with Carles Puyol and Xavi.

For me the drama is over after 45 minutes when we're 2–0 down. Never before has a side coached by Mourinho suffered such a heavy loss. 'This is a defeat that's difficult to swallow. It's not the kind of defeat where you actually deserved to win or kept hitting the woodwork,' Mourinho says afterwards. 'One team played to the limits of its potential, the other one played really poorly. We have to look at it positively. If, as a team, you win major titles, you've got every right to cry for joy. If you lose as we did today, you've got no right to cry; you have to get back to work. If I had the choice I'd like to play again straight away.'

I recall Xavi saying, 'They never got to the ball. We put them to sleep.' Barcelona's goalie, Víctor Valdés, was almost bursting with pride: 'I got dizzy following the ball. In the end I decided not to watch too closely. In any case our boys had the ball.' Guardiola was convinced afterwards that this game would 'stay in the memory and take its place in football history, not just because of the scoreline, but because of the manner in which we won. It's not easy to play that well against such a strong team – against a team that dispatches its opponents both in Spain and abroad. We must be proud of our performance. It's a victory with worldwide significance, because we've done it in our own particular way. No other club in the world trusts its players as much as we do.'

These were sentences that burned into me. That pained me. That I'll never forget. This 5–0 was the worst defeat I'd ever been involved in. I felt terrible and humiliated as I crawled back into the dressing room, plagued by self-doubt.

Our performance had been a disgrace. This defeat was unforgivable. Words like 'disappointment' are inadequate to describe it. The whole world was watching. We let down every single employee in the club. The doctors and physiotherapists who did their best to prepare us physically for the game. We even felt thoroughly ashamed in front of the coach drivers and kit managers. And, of course, in front of all the fans, who'd spent money on the trip and the tickets.

My aspiration, and that of everyone who plays for Real Madrid, is that we should be the best footballers in the world. Real Madrid is a collection of superstars, an assembly of the best of the best. But that night these best players neither gave their best nor played well, not even averagely. Quite simply, we failed. After a humiliation like that you feel self-doubt. Apparently – or so it occurred to me – I wasn't as good as I'd always thought. Perhaps I'd just wildly overestimated my ability.

Our profession is wonderful because it proceeds at such a fast pace. For the most part we can rise again as heroes in no time at all, make amends for our mistakes or failures. But even after the next victory over Valencia and the one after that against Real Zaragoza, the hammering we'd taken still hurt. The embarrassment remained. It stayed in our heads. Even though Mourinho did his best to relieve the ignominy. Right after the game he gave us a brief talk. 'Forget the game,' he said. 'It was a bad defeat. Nothing more and nothing less. One game over the course of a long championship. Don't think about it any more. I'm sure we're going to break Barcelona's dominance in this country. I'm sure we're going to be champions. But we won't do it if we allow this defeat to get on top of us.'

I was impressed by the way Mourinho reacted. He could have just as easily punished us with extra training. But he knew exactly how every player felt at that moment. He realised that we were down on the ground. And that we didn't need another kicking.

Mourinho showed his phenomenal understanding of how his players felt on several occasions. Once he gave me some time off in the middle of the season when he noticed that I was utterly exhausted and needed a break. He came over to me and said, 'Mesut, have some rest. Have some fun. Enjoy a few days without thinking about football and do exactly what you feel like.'

I've never seen that from any other manager. He took me out of operations so I could recover my strength. Normally the opposite happens – the manager refuses to dispense with his best players for a second. Even if they're slightly under the weather, the coach would rather his top footballers play at 80 per cent than not at all. But seeing that I wasn't completely right mentally, and that I had some intensive weeks behind me, Mourinho's reaction was superb. After five days he rang me and asked how I was. 'Are you any better? How are you feeling?' he asked. You can't take enquiries like this for granted in our professional world. Most coaches expect you to be in good working order. And if you're not, they ditch you.

On that Monday in November, the Barça Mercedes with its perfectly meshed cogs hadn't just outpaced Real, it had lapped us.

Guardiola had won the first round. But luckily we had four further chances that season to pit ourselves against the high-fliers and close the gap.

We stayed on Barcelona's heels in the league, second place behind them in the table. In the Copa del Rey we made it to the final. And in the Champions League José Mourinho let us know that after 2,562 days, 74 matches and 9 coaches we were in a quarter-final again. For seven years Madrid hadn't got past the last 16. In the quarters we knocked out Tottenham and then had Barcelona in the semis, giving us the opportunity for the perfect showdown.

In other words, there would be four Clásicos in 18 days. Four Guardiola–Mourinho duels. Four unequal showdowns – unequal because although Mourinho's work was immaculate, he was still at the start of his Ferrari inspection and repair. He was still in the process of taking it all apart and putting it back together again. He was still looking for the perfect tuning. And, of course, he was also looking for the weak spot in Barcelona's champion team.

And indeed he did find a way in. Viewed from a distance Guardiola appeared to be a master of focusing on his team, concentrating on the work with his squad and preparing them for the next opponents with the highest possible degree of passion. He was totally focused, never wasting a drop of energy on other things.

But that's exactly what Mourinho made him do. He succeeded in breaking Guardiola's strict focus on the next game by continually unsettling him. He created distractions that robbed the Catalan of strength. Mourinho actually managed to strip energy from Guardiola and Barcelona, disrupt them and lure them to another battleground. At the same time he injected us with the unswerving determination to beat Barcelona.

'You don't have to be enemies to be able to give your best, but it's better if you are,' he said on several occasions during my time at Madrid. 'Especially if you're very successful and tend to have a relaxed attitude.' I took this completely to heart. Although I never regarded Barcelona as an enemy, never saw the club as bad, I was obsessed by the idea of having to beat them. In every league game, no matter who our opponents were, it was in my mind that we mustn't lose or Barcelona would pull away in the title race. I imagined them delighting at us losing points and this thought made me even crazier about winning.

At Schalke I saw the onus that's on the players to beat Dortmund, for the sake of the fans and everyone in the club. At Bremen I realised how sharp the divide is between Werder and Hamburger SV. I saw how the German press went berserk in the run-up to these duels, trying to inject even more spice into the encounter. I experienced the verbal sparring that went back and forth between Dortmund and Gelsenkirchen. The attacks from the River Weser to the Elbe and back again. But none of this was anything like the Clásico.

This was already the biggest duel between football teams in the world, but it was made even bigger and more interesting by the two managers standing on the touchline.

Under no circumstances did Mourinho want to lose the first of the four Clásicos that were coming up. He instructed Pepe to stick right beside Lionel Messi at all times. 'He's got to feel your breath,' he told him in the team meeting, when he put us in a more defensive formation than I'd ever encountered while playing for Real Madrid. For this reason I stayed on the outside to begin with.

When you come out of the dressing room in Madrid and you're waiting in the players' tunnel to go out on to the pitch, it's the most intense feeling you can imagine. In most stadiums around the world the teams are just lined up alongside each other. First the captain, then the goalie, then the rest of the team. On one side the home team, on the other the visitors. Usually you shake a few hands and engage in some small talk with players you know or who are friends, before it's time to file out onto the pitch. The atmosphere is fairly relaxed and harmonious. Not in Madrid, where the two teams are separated by bars. You can't really say hello. The atmosphere is different from the start. Less friendly. You feel like a gladiator about to engage in the fight of his life.

Here in the tunnel your senses are sharpened, and the minutes you wait there seem more intense and to pass more slowly. It's one of the many moments you experience as a footballer where things feel distorted. The voices of your teammates, who are generally mumbling a few motivational phrases to themselves, sound more muffled. The clacking of boots sounds more menacing than usual. Looking though the bars into the faces of Iniesta, Messi and Villa, you don't see anything nice there, no smile – nothing that could be construed as a weakness. All that's lacking to make this the perfect re-enactment is the war paint.

My second Clásico, the first of this block of four, takes place on 16 April 2011. We stay deep and, to begin with, stick well to our task of disrupting Barcelona's game. Pepe carries out Mourinho's order to mark Messi closely to perfection. He goes in hard at him five times, spoiling his enjoyment of the game. He demoralises Messi to such an extent that towards the end of the game he furiously wallops a ball into the crowd, striking a spectator.

There are goals too. Both from the penalty spot. Messi scores after a foul on David Villa. Ronaldo after a foul on Marcelo. 1–1. Our first point against our arch-rivals after five defeats on the trot. Our first success since May 2008.

In spite of this, Real Madrid legend Alfredo Di Stéfano criticises Mourinho's defensive tactics, which reveals what really counts in Madrid. Sometimes even a confidence-inspiring point isn't enough if the team hasn't played beautifully enough to win it.

Four days later we meet Barcelona again in the cup final in Valencia. This is Pep Guardiola's tenth final as manager of the Catalan team. And he's won nine of them. Madrid hasn't won the Spanish Cup since 1992–93, almost two decades.

Once again Mourinho has me in the starting line-up. This time I'm to play as a deep centre forward and disturb their defensive lines, which works pretty well. We also manage to contain Barça; they virtually have no shots at our goal.

There's no score for 101 minutes. It's a very intense period of extra time. The referee has given six yellow cards for harsh challenges. Messi has also been warned for unfair play because he tried to take a free kick from too close.

In the 102nd minute Di María crosses from the left. Ronaldo spirals into the air and heads the ball in. 1–0 to us – the winning goal. A title for us. Admittedly a minor title, because the Spanish Cup isn't regarded as highly as the championship. But the fact that we've won it against the *über* team – against the perennial victors, against an almost perfect side – enhances the value of our win.

After the final whistle Messi flees to the dressing room in tears. He's devastated to have lost a final. He's forgotten what it's like not to be the shining hero after a final. His tears are a very important signal to us. For now Barcelona finally have to take us seriously. After a tough, intense struggle, we've regained their respect, which has been lacking in recent years.

While Mourinho prepares us for the remaining two clashes with the Catalans he also launches a few verbal missiles in the direction of Barcelona. He wants to drain Guardiola of more strength. And he succeeds in drawing the Catalan into a slanging match in the media, which is completely unlike him. In the first press conference before the Champions League semi-final Guardiola says, 'Off the field Mourinho has won all year, all season, and will continue to do so in the future. He can have his own Champions League off the pitch. Let him have his fun; I'm perfectly happy with that. He can take it home with him and enjoy it there. In this room [i.e. where the press conference is taking place] he is the bloody boss. He knows the workings of this world better than anyone else. I don't want to have to compete with him for a moment longer in this field.'

The match itself is another heated affair. Álvaro Arbeola and Dani Alves are both shown yellow cards in the first half. On our way back to the dressing rooms emotions are running high. Arbeola shoves Keita. In response Barça's substitute keeper, José Manuel Pinto, goes at him and gets the red card. Soon after the resumption Pepe crashes a little over-keenly into Dani Alves with his outstretched leg and also gets the red card. This is a serious handicap, because now we have to play a man down for half an hour in such an important game.

Mourinho doesn't agree with the card and applauds the referee ironically. Afterwards he complains to Thorsten Kinhöfer, the fourth official, after which he's banned from the touchline. Mourinho defended Pepe and put himself behind the team, an important signal for us.

Unfortunately Barcelona exploits its numerical advantage and Messi scores two goals in our stadium, which are painful in the extreme.

In the official press conference Mourinho again attacks the referee for sending Pepe off. It turned the game on its head, he claims. 'Why did the referee do something like that in an evenly balanced game which was still undecided?' he asks. And then says provocatively, 'I'd be ashamed to win the Champions League in that way, like Guardiola. If I were to tell the referee and UEFA what I really think about what happened this evening my career would be over in a flash. Madrid has been denied a place in the Champions League final. We'll leave with pride, with respect for our world, the world of football, which sometimes disgusts me. It disgusts me to live in this world, but it is our world.'

Because of his severe criticism of the European Football Association, Mourinho is given a five-match ban from games.

This is reduced to three on appeal. Which means he can't be there for our return match and coach us. We finish 1–1 – impressive for a game in the Camp Nou, but we're knocked out all the same.

In spite of this there are clear signs that there's more parity in the Clásicos. Gone are the days when Real had no chance against Barça. Gone are the days of the shameful 6–2 or 5–0 thrashings. Twice we drew with Barcelona, once we won – and that in a final too – and once the Catalans won, putting them into the Champions League final.

In those four clashes an unbelievable 25 yellow cards were handed out, in addition to which there were four sendings off and Mourinho's ban.

The battles lasted for the best part of three weeks. They were energy-sapping, especially for Guardiola, who admitted afterwards that it was a 'very tough time, with lots of stress: highly intense and absolutely exhausting'.

Once we'd been knocked out of the Champions League Mourinho was even more determined to destroy Guardiola's supremacy in Spain. 'When I was the manager of Inter Milan, it took me three games to work out how to beat Barcelona and adapt to Guardiola's side,' he told us. And, full of confidence, he assured us, 'We'll be at that point soon.'

We get our next opportunity right at the start of the following season, my second year at Real. As cup winners, we meet league title-holders Barcelona in the Spanish Super Cup, which they've won for the past two seasons.

I put us in the lead in the thirteenth minute, having been set up by Karim Benzema. David Villa equalises, then Messi and finally Xabi Alonso score to make it 2–2. We've got every chance in the return game three days later at the Camp Nou, which will prove to be one of the most intense matches I've ever played.

We scent the opportunity to snatch another title from the Barcelona side who are spoiled by success. They're going to do everything they can to preserve their dominance, and so this game is being played for high stakes.

Iniesta puts the Catalans in the lead, Ronaldo equalises. Messi scores, Benzema makes it 2–2. Then Messi gets another goal. 3–2 to Barcelona. Anything but deserved. Particularly as Barça put on an unparalleled diving display. No sooner do we move to make a tackle than they're already airborne. At the slightest body contact they contort as if they've been seriously injured. The moment one of their players is lying on the ground, no matter how harmless the incident, the rest of the team surrounds the alleged offender. I've rarely played a game with so much mass confrontation.

They provoke us in turn with their non-stop comments. A little provocation here, a little provocation there. That evening Barça is anything but a team of goodie two shoes. But of course we get the majority of yellow cards. A total of five until five minutes before the end of the game. Barça are given two.

In the ninety-third minute the Catalans are in possession of the ball on the halfway line, and still leading by a goal. I can predict that the result's not going to change from here. Xavi eases the ball over Alonso, Fàbregas takes it elegantly in the air with his right instep, knocking it to his feet. All of a sudden Marcelo comes flying towards him. His left leg outstretched, he slices with his right like a pair of scissors. He brings Fàbregas down with full force, right between Barcelona's and Madrid's substitute benches. A completely unnecessary challenge that cannot go unpunished.

Within a few seconds, the place is in total chaos. From the outside the whole thing looks like a bundle of white, red and blue jerseys, shoving, threatening, insulting and cursing each other. Within the action it's a scrum, with even the physios and men in suits getting involved. A large number of Barça players are gunning for Marcelo. They rush up and hassle and insult him in a really uncalled-for way. His red card is appropriate. The fierceness with which he's attacked after the foul isn't.

I stand in front of Marcelo in an attempt to protect him. I pull him back so he doesn't do anything else stupid. In moments like that you're no longer in control of your senses. Marco has given everything for Real Madrid. He's thrown himself into every tackle. He's fought for every ball. He's fought splendidly and defended the honour of Los Blancos with all he's got. When, in a situation like that, you commit a bad foul and the opposition gangs up on you, with all the emotions flying around and the adrenalin levels it's easy to do something stupid. No player in the world consciously head-butts or slaps others. Nobody punches an opposition player deliberately or with a clear head. These sorts of things occur in exceptional circumstances. And that's precisely what I was trying to protect Marcelo from. But while I'm trying to be sensible, all of a sudden David Villa comes up from behind like a cowardly dog and gives me a smack on the head. That really takes the biscuit!

There's no place for such cowardly behaviour. Not in the Camp Nou, nor in the Estadio Santiago Bernabéu. Nor in any other stadium around the world. Not even on the recreation ground. Hitting someone from behind, even if it's just a gentle slap, is sneaky and mean. You can't get out of the way or defend yourself. Quite apart from the fact that hitting another player is wrong anyway.

As soon as I realised that David Villa was the offender I blew a fuse. I was trying to protect Marcelo and calm the situation down, and then I was attacked myself. Instead of standing by my teammates I became a raging bull. The smack in itself hadn't been a bad one, neither brutal nor especially painful. But the sneaky nature of it made me livid. I wanted to get Villa back for it. At that moment I lost all sense of reason. I just wanted to pay him back. Lacking all self-control I ran across the pitch with the intention of socking him one. I felt that my pride had been dented and I wanted revenge. I swore that he'd regret what he'd done.

Pepe and Ricardo Carvalho held me back. I screamed at them to let me go. I tried to wrest myself free. I really was out of my mind. Barcelona's Adriano also came over in an attempt to calm me down, which now I give him – as an opponent – huge credit for. At the time, of course, I had little appreciation for it.

After I'd been shown the red card, as had Villa, I wanted to collar him up in the tunnel to give him the thrashing due to him. This time it was Marcelo and Mourinho who thankfully stopped me.

At the time I was mad at everyone who was holding on to me. I was convinced I had to give David Villa a lesson. Today I'm very pleased that the episode turned out as it did. Perhaps I'd have felt better for a few seconds if I'd given Villa the punishment I believed he deserved. But what would have happened then? I'd have probably entered the Real Madrid history books as a thug! As a bully! As a crazy idiot! All my assists would have been forgotten. It's possible that people wouldn't have talked about my footballing abilities any more, only my fit of rage. My reputation would have been in tatters. Just because of a single moment of madness.

While Villa and I were having our altercation on the pitch, Mourinho had already had his own lapse of sanity. During the tumult he'd crept up to Barcelona's assistant manager, Tito Vilanova, and poked him in the right eye with the index finger of his right hand. I've no idea what had got into him. Even today I bet he can't explain to anyone why he did it. But I'm sure, at any rate, that his behaviour wasn't premeditated. With all his deliberate provocation and games with the media, Mourinho remains a real gentleman.

Later on, he apologised for the eye poking. 'I shouldn't have done it. I'm not an idiot. I work hard with my players to get them to control their emotions. I made a mistake and I'm not going to try to look for excuses.'

The criticism heaped on us by the media after the Super Cup only welded us together even more strongly as a team. We swore that, no matter what was written and said about us, we wouldn't let it knock us off course. We wouldn't allow ourselves to be driven apart. We'd be there for each other, protecting and driving each other on.

In the games that followed we scored six goals against Zaragoza, Vallecano and Sevilla, five against Granada, Espanyol Barcelona, Real Sociedad, and even seven against Osasuna. After 33 matches we topped the table, with only two defeats against our 27 victories. And till that point we'd scored a whopping 107 goals. In second place was Barcelona, with four points fewer. A victory against us and the championship would be open again with four games to go.

But by now Mourinho had worked Barcelona out. For which he'd needed one more lesson in the Spanish Cup. After having won the first leg 2–1, Barça were soon 2-0 in the lead in the return leg too. But somehow we weren't at all affected by the scoreline and we decided to make the play ourselves rather than stay on the defensive against them. In the Camp Nou I set the ball up for Ronaldo, who made it 2–1, then Benzema made it 2–2. It was a demonstration away from home that intimidated the Catalans. And gave us the last shot of confidence we needed to maintain our position in the championship.

Mourinho reminded us of all the trophies that Barcelona had collected over the last few years. 'They're not going to win a fourth championship in succession. Together we're going to stop them,' he said, making us hungrier than ever for the title.

And we actually won our thirty-fourth game of the season in the Camp Nou. Sami Khedira put us in the lead and Alexis Sánchez equalised. Then I got the ball. I'd already provided 18 assists in the league. Now I set up a nineteenth goal, this time for Cristiano Ronaldo.

In my first year with Real Madrid I'd scored ten goals and set up a further 28 in all competitions. In the second year I managed seven goals and 29 assists, the highest number by any player in the Spanish league. And – jumping forward – there were 24 assists and ten goals in my third season. Three years of sensational figures in a row, although it must be said that it's easier to shine personally at a club with such world-class credentials, where every position in the team is filled by a player of the highest quality.

If I make a decent cross, there's a high probability that one of these attackers will get the ball in the back of the net. With our victory against the Catalans we took the decisive step towards the championship, which we indeed won after three years of complete dominance by Barcelona. Mourinho had knocked our Ferrari engine back into shape, repaired all the broken parts and driven the sporty number down the road with great passion and total control. By the end of the season we'd scored 121 goals and only conceded two defeats to our 32 victories.

Thanks to Mourinho we'd managed to crack Barcelona. In only two years we'd caught them. It was an incredible achievement. We were a formidably strong team. Mourinho had turned us into an impressive unit. He was the manager who put an end to Barcelona's superiority. That was his biggest achievement.

The title was a similarly weighty achievement. It's easy to jump into a reliably performing, perfectly tuned racing car and bag title after title. But getting into a car that's not running smoothly and tinkering with it until you start winning races with it, that makes you proud.

In my career up till then I'd been runner-up in the Bundesliga twice, once third and once only tenth. In my first year in Spain I was runner-up again. And now, at the sixth attempt in my career, I had my first championship title.

It's very gratifying to have achieved this success at Real. I can't imagine there's a footballer in the world who hasn't dreamed of putting on the Los Blancos shirt at some point in their career. Only a few footballers are granted the opportunity to score for Real. And even fewer can savour the moment of celebrating winning a title with the club. I was fortunate enough to be one of these. In addition, after this sensational season the readers of *Marca* chose me in their Spanish XI of the year.

When Guardiola announced in 2012 that he was leaving Barcelona he said, 'I've given everything and there's nothing left. That's the long and the short of it. And I've got to recharge the batteries.' Together with Mourinho we taught the '*über* manager' how to lose again. We drained him of energy. Mourinho did everything right. The fact that away from the pitch he engaged in conflict to unsettle a team that had written football history was worth its weight in gold.

Real Madrid is the most intense club I've ever played at. It sucks you dry. One season at Madrid is like three or four at any other club. I changed immeasurably as a footballer over this period. Although I learned a lot tactically, especially as far as defence was concerned, there was one other important insight I gained: on the pitch you have to listen to your feelings. If a coach gives me guidelines for play that are too strict, I feel cramped. If my body tells me I have to push left, that's what I do. I can't just stay firmly in one position. As a player you have to take decisions. As a player you have to have freedoms. If you're a creative player your coach mustn't shackle you. You mustn't be a puppet. But it also stands to reason to say that you mustn't abandon the team's tactical plan altogether.

I had already suspected at the 2010 World Cup in South Africa that thinking disrupts the magic of the game. But I didn't realise it fully until I was at Madrid.

The third year was OK, by normal standards. But not by the club's ones. We came second in the league, behind Barcelona. In the Champions League we reached the semi-finals for the third year in a row, but were knocked out by Borussia Dortmund after Robert Lewandowski scored four goals in one game against us. In the Spanish Cup we made it to the final, even knocking out Barcelona en route, in the semi-final. But because we succumbed to Atlético Madrid in the final, we failed to win a single title for the first time since I'd been signed by Real. Not acceptable in the club's galaxy.

14

LONDON CALLING

WHEN ONE DOOR CLOSES
ANOTHER ONE OPENS

José Mourinho left Madrid in 2013. The Italian Carlo Ancelotti took over as manager, and my time at Real ended too. In surprising fashion.

There are plenty of different stories about my departure. Countless rumours. Endless speculation. Many claims. And even more interpretations and explanations. A great deal of nonsense was written. I was particularly irritated by the allegation that I'd told shameless lies during this period.

The only truth, which is not without self-criticism, is as follows. At the time my father, Mustafa, was acting as my agent. He was convinced that by now he understood enough of the business and didn't need the help of other agents. He thought he was sufficiently strong and worldly-wise to go face-to-face in discussions with a man like Real's president, Florentino Pérez, and able to negotiate with him as an equal.

I don't want to blame my father for this. He learnt a lot from watching Roger Wittmann, Michael Becker and Reza Fazeli. Until then he'd been my closest confidant and had always acted in my interest. As my biggest critic he'd pushed me for years and spurred me on to ever better performances. He had a great deal of confidence in his ability because he'd helped his little Mesut become the player who'd ended up at Real Madrid via Schalke and Werder.

Up till then my talent and success had always meant that several clubs, all a rung up from the one I was currently playing for, embarked on an auction for me, which meant it was easy to switch instead of having to make an early renewal of my contract with my existing club.

On several occasions up till then my father had watched how my agents were able to make demands that were generally met, because they were acting from a position of great strength. But now the situation was slightly different. Naturally, after three good years at Real Madrid, our negotiating position once more wasn't bad. No player apart from me and Lionel Messi had managed more assists in the Primera División since 2010 – we were equal with 47.

But there was no auction for me. In summer 2013 no other clubs were making enquiries to buy me out of my contract, which still had two years to run. And why should they? I had no intention of leaving Real Madrid. Nobody imagined that a transfer was in the offing. My father and I were both aiming to get an early renewal of my contract for a few more years. I would continue my successful career at Real and finally win a Champions League medal. That was our only goal.

Then my father took over the negotiations. He contacted Florentino Pérez and arranged a meeting with the construction giant, where the sole topic of discussion was to be securing another long-term contract with Madrid, admittedly with better terms.

When I arrived from Bremen I was a nobody, with little international experience – I had only six Champions League matches under my young belt. I was also a newbie in the German national side. After three years in Madrid I'd played another 31 games in Europe's premier competition. Under Jogi Löw I'd become a regular in the German team, with 29 further appearances wearing the eagle on my chest. And so I was due a higher salary at Real Madrid.

During his time as a professional at Manchester United, Juan Mata said something that was very true: 'Taking the world of professional football as a yardstick I earn a normal salary. But compared to 99.9 per cent of the Spanish population and the rest of the world it's an indecent sum. Out of respect for the rest of society we have to admit that we earn a ridiculously high amount of money. It's incalculable.'

My mother worked like crazy in a job that gave her little pleasure – cleaning up other people's filth isn't any fun. And she earned a pittance. My salary, by contrast, is enormous. Do I work harder than her? I'd never say that. Do I have more fun than her? Of course I do! Is it right that I earn so much, while she got so little? Absolutely not!

For that matter, my earnings are all above board. I pay my taxes regularly and honestly. I don't hide money from the taxman with 'dirty dealings', as *Der Spiegel* claimed at the end of 2016. I featured on the cover of the December issue of the magazine – a terrible black-and-white photo of me looking very serious. The creative publishers had replaced my pupils with lurid yellow euro signs. The headline was 'The Money Experts', leading to an article detailing supposed tax dodges by Cristiano Ronaldo, José Mourinho and myself. In the introduction it said, 'For eighteen months the Spanish tax authorities were after the German international Mesut Özil. Then they slapped him with a demand for several million.'

The edition containing these allegations appeared on 3 December. The evening before, my agent Erkut had called to warn me about the story in advance. I was already in the team hotel with Arsenal, because we had a game against West Ham the following day.

'You're on the cover tomorrow,' Erkut began. 'The *Spiegel*'s running the story.'

We weren't surprised that the story was being published. The editor of the article had emailed us a few days earlier with a whole host of questions, none of which we'd answered. All we did was state that we'd be defending ourselves against the false claims. I sat on my bed, listening to Erkut. 'We're going to stay cool. They can't touch us,' he said.

'Erkut, we haven't done anything illegal, have we?' I asked him, as I had done so often since we'd received the magazine's questions. Just to be sure. Of course, I don't do my own tax declaration; I let experts who I trust sort it out. I don't have the time and, to be honest, I don't have the know-how either. That's exactly why, after the Spanish authorities asked me to pay extra tax, we sought the advice of Spanish, German and British tax experts who explained the situation to me and shed light on all the details. 'No, Mesut, everything's above board. They can't pin anything on us,' Erkut said calmly, before going through the situation with me again point by point.

'As far as your image and personality rights are concerned we've been totally straight. You assigned them to a company based in Germany, Özil Marketing GmbH, a perfectly legal and normal procedure. So you haven't only been paying tax, you've also created jobs for eight people who are also paying tax in Germany.'

The Spanish authorities had investigated the set-up, Erkut summed up, and very quickly approved it. 'We didn't hide anything. We made it clear that everything is taxed correctly in Germany. The question of image rights has absolutely nothing to do with this extra tax payment.'

At the start of 2016 I did actually – and this is factually correct – pay 2,017,152.18 euros in supplementary income tax. We immediately appealed to the Spanish tax authorities against this demand. The reason being that, up till then, clubs always paid the commission due to agents. It's the same everywhere, be it Bayern Munich, Paris St Germain or Arsenal. The agent commission is paid by the club.

That's how it has operated for years and been accepted by the authorities. Real Madrid, for example – and this was reported correctly by the *Spiegel* – paid 1.2 million euros to my then agent, Reza Fazeli, and Arsenal 1.47 million euros to my current agent, Dr Erkut Sögut. These payments were declared by both the clubs and the agents and appropriately taxed. But now, Erkut explained to me, the cash-strapped Spanish authorities were suddenly putting a different interpretation on the law. Without, it must be said, any change in the legal basis.

They were arguing that the commission paid by the club was a financial benefit to me and therefore must be included in my tax declaration.

As I've already said, the authorities had never asked for this before. And that's why we weren't withholding anything or defrauding anyone when we didn't register this information in my tax declaration. The Spanish authorities were just trying to fill their empty coffers by every means possible.

To avoid difficulties we began by acquiescing to the – from our perspective, unreasonable – demand for two million euros, but lodged an appeal in the belief that the additional tax would be deemed unlawful by a higher-level authority and we'd get the money back. From the outset we refused to pay a fine of 789,963.36 euros imposed by the authorities and appealed against this too.

I listened to Erkut explain all this again. I was reassured by his clear and forthright assertions: 'You haven't got any offshore companies. You haven't evaded any taxes. You've always submitted your tax return on time. Since the beginning of your professional career in Germany, your home country, you've paid millions of euros in tax in accordance with the regulations. You've put millions into the German coffers. You could have set up your marketing company abroad. But you left it in Germany, thereby providing more tax for your home country. And this is the thanks you get. This is pure sensationalism from *Spiegel*. It's just about shifting copies. At your expense. You're the scapegoat of this *Spiegel* campaign. It's a smear campaign, a really dirty one, but you're going to get through this, no doubt about it.'

I just kept listening. Very calmly.

'It's just going to make us stronger. You've already got through plenty of other things. We'll hit back with facts. We've even got a tax clearance certificate from the Spanish authorities. Real Madrid confirmed in writing that they were liable for tax on Reza Fazeli's commission. He provided us with the same written confirmation. Everything's fine. And your best response is to score goals, OK? Goals and assists. Show everybody that none of this nonsense is getting to you.'

'I trust you. I'm relaxed. Everything's all right, Erkut. It's good that I'm prepared.'

That night I slept normally because I was convinced my team were doing the right thing. And because I had nothing to reproach myself for.

When I played the following day against West Ham United in London's Olympic Stadium I wasn't thinking about the matter any more. I put us 1–0 up and assisted a goal for Alex Oxlade-Chamberlain – so much for that.

But I don't know that I'd have been so relaxed had I known what was going on at the same time in my agency in Düsseldorf. The telephones would not stop ringing. After the claims in *Der Spiegel* my employees were getting threatening calls, being insulted and sworn at. I should piss off out of the German team, some callers demanded. I was a disgrace, a lousy crook sullying the German shirt. Unbelievable claims, based on an inaccurate

Spiegel investigation, which was also broadcast on 'SpiegelTV' on the RTL channel. To stop this character assassination going any further we filed for an injunction against the magazine on the day of publication.

One thing is certainly true. The transfer fees that are now paid in football are crazy too! We footballers are commodities whose value to a club varies, depending on the differences in our performances. And also on our individual market value. I realise that football is growing and growing, becoming ever more global, causing prices to continue spiralling upwards.

But we have reached a level that is unhealthy and difficult to explain to the fans. As far as I'm concerned, no single sportsperson in the world, no matter how good or popular, is worth 50, 60, 80 or even 100 million euros. Those are astronomical sums. Especially as I can't see any correlation whatsoever. It's no longer just about a player's class. Sometimes – at least this is the impression I get – it's all about club directors being able to bask in the knowledge that they've achieved a new record transfer. Increasingly they just want to show off.

Of course, Paul Pogba is a good player, but neither he nor any other footballer is worth 100 million euros or more. What on earth would you have to pay these days for someone with the unique abilities of Zinédine Zidane? These are just unreal sums.

I've never forgotten where I came from. My best friends who, when I was a child, helped me get my bike from the rat-infested cellar, are still by my side today. They assist me in my company – Mesut Özil Marketing GmbH – and I pay them for their work.

I've bought my mother a wonderful little house and I support her financially so she doesn't have to work any more.

Having said all this, there's a simple reason why my father demanded a higher salary for an early extension of my Real Madrid contract. It was to do with how the club valued me. As in any other job. Besides, it's usual practice with contract renewals that salaries are adjusted accordingly.

If someone produces good results, they should be paid accordingly. If an apprentice, through hard work, ambition and overtime, has evolved into a skilled professional who takes a business forward, they deserve a pay rise. If a footballer matures, improves tactically and helps break Barcelona's dominance, and if he also permanently plays at the highest level, he cannot continue to be paid the same as a newcomer.

A contract renewal must benefit both sides – this was the message my father was supposed to bring to Florentino Pérez. This was our starting point for negotiations and nothing else.It had nothing to do with greed. Nothing to do with not being able to get enough. It was about being paid fairly. Unfortunately, this was not reflected by the first offer that Real made us.

I'm not going to criticise Madrid for this. In the early stage of negotiations the two sides have differing views that converge as talks progress. One side gives way on a certain point, the other offers something else, and it goes on like this till both parties are happy. It must be very rare that both sides immediately reach agreement in initial talks.

But it was a new situation for my father. He was not used to being put under this sort of negotiating pressure. He suddenly found himself operating in an arena where he was not, as he'd hoped, an expert with a solution for all eventualities at his fingertips. In retrospect I have to admit that because he hadn't conducted dozens of negotiations with top club directors, he lacked the detachment to deal appropriately with such a challenging offer. Which is why he unfortunately didn't have the cool head that was probably needed.

My father can be terribly stubborn. Sometimes that's a good thing. And I've certainly benefited from this occasionally, as was evident in the episode in the Turkish Consulate General in Münster, when he managed to get my passport revoked. But stubbornness was not appropriate when dealing with a man such as Florentino Pérez, who expects people to dance to his tune. And it definitely wasn't right to storm angrily out of Pérez's office, slamming the door noisily behind him.

Rather than intimidating the Real boss, this behaviour merely provoked him, which meant there were now two stubborn-headed men firing on all cylinders. Both of them were determined to show the other who was the stronger, or at least that's how I saw it.

At first I was convinced that this pig-headed duel wouldn't last long. That the two of them would make up as quickly as they had fallen out. After all, both sides wanted the same thing: an extension to my contract. It was with this expectation in mind that I went to a press conference on 28 August 2013 with my new sponsor, Adidas.

Journalists were there from all over Europe. Television cameras were filming and photographers snapping away. I was ready to answer their questions honestly and put an end to the speculation flying around about me in the media again. In front of everyone present – and you can still see this on YouTube – I said, 'I've got a contract with Real Madrid and I'm staying with Real Madrid.' In the individual interviews I gave to *Marca* and *Bild* afterwards, I then reiterated this in similar words, outlining in more detail what my actual intentions were: 'I'm proud to be playing for this club. I feel very happy here. Why should I leave? I haven't given a transfer a moment's thought. As far as I'm concerned there's no other club worth considering. I can promise now that I'm going to fulfil my contract with Real until 2016.'

If I had had the slightest inkling that I would break this promise less than 120 hours later, I'd never have made such a clear commitment. I'd never have chosen words that could blow up in my face and be held against me for all time as lies. I don't sit in press conferences talking tosh without weighing up the effect my words could have. I wanted the speculation about me to stop. And I also wanted Florentino Pérez to realise what Real meant to me.

I couldn't know that the duel of stubbornness was no longer just a silly showdown, just banter between men, but had gone so far that it had consequences for me. I'd fallen out of favour with my club's big boss, even though I'd done nothing myself. I was at risk of being dropped. I had to do something, quickly. For the sake of my career. Not playing any more was out of the question, especially if the decision had nothing to do with my performances.

And so, although I found this hard to do, I called a number that I'd saved in my phone back in 2010.

'Mr Wenger,' I said, 'I promised that you'd be the first person I'd contact if I were ever looking for another club. Now I am.'

Arsène Wenger told me that he had been keeping an eye on me the whole time and that he liked how I'd developed. And all of a sudden I had that positive feeling again, the one I'd had during our telephone conversation back in 2010. I sensed that this man, who I'd never met personally, had a very high opinion of me and trusted me. Exactly what I needed at this difficult time.

Of course, I'd hoped that Pérez would back down and not punish me for the argument between him and my father. That he'd approach me again. But he didn't. The relationship had cooled.

Two days after committing to Real Madrid I contacted another club because it seemed to be the only possible way out. Time was flying. There were thousands of things to sort out if I were to actually move to London. Was I sure that's what I wanted? That this was what would make me happy?

I took Luka Modrić – my teammate who'd played for Tottenham between 2008 and 2012 – aside. 'What's London like?' I asked him, and talked honestly about what I was considering. 'It's the coolest city in the world,' he said. I believed him. There wasn't time for more questions.

On the evening before our fixture in the Santiago Bernabéu stadium against Athletic Bilbao, our third league game of the 2013–14 season, my friend Baris asked whether we could have a chat. He sensed that there was something weighing on my mind.

That I wasn't totally at peace with myself. 'Are you really sure?' he asked, when the two of us were sitting together. 'Do you really want to move?'

It's true to say that my transfer from Real Madrid to London was the most difficult decision of my life. When I left Bremen I was 100 per cent certain that it was the right move. I knew that I owed a lot to Werder and that I was giving up something great. But the future was so attractive that I didn't have to think for a second whether my decision was right or wrong. My heart and my head spoke in unison: my mission at Werder was over.

But now I was on the verge of leaving a city where I felt really happy. I loved running onto the pitch in the Bernabéu. I loved being able to put on my Real shirt, first number 23, then number 10, which Ferenc Puskás, Günter Netzer, Robinho and Wesley Sneijder had worn before me. I felt such strong support from the fans. And most of all I felt my mission here was far from over. I still harboured the desire to win the Champions League with Real. And with the help of my teammates at Madrid I wanted to become the top footballer in the world. My journey with Real was not yet at its end. But the last thing I wanted was to stray through the Spanish football universe like a rocket in a tailspin and maybe come crashing down to earth.

And then there was this man with the calm telephone voice, engaging personality and clever words that convinced me that he really wanted me in his team. Wenger had been watching me intensively for three years and he gave me a much better feeling than Carlo Ancelotti at Real was doing at the time.

So there was that cool city with that attractive football league. There was that club where Per Mertesacker and Lukas Podolski played. A club with a melodious name, but which hadn't won a title since its FA Cup victory in 2005. And there was that manager.

'Yes, Baris. I think it's the right move,' I replied after I'd told him everything that was on my mind.

When I drove to the Bernabéu for the last time on 1 September 2013, I found it a real struggle. When I took my place on the bench beside Álvaro Morata, Casemiro and Iker Casillas I had a lump in my throat. For the last time I was part of this team in this magnificent stadium. For the last time I heard the Spanish songs of our fan choir. For the last time our club anthem, 'Hala Madrid y nada más'.

After we'd won 3–1, thanks to two goals from Isco and one from Ronaldo, I told my closest friends – Álvaro Arbeloa, Sergio Ramos, Karim Benzema and, of course, Sami Khedira – that I would in all probability be leaving.

Afterwards I made my way to the airport. The next day the German national squad was assembling in Munich to get ready for the forthcoming World Cup qualifying matches against Austria and the Faroe Islands.

When the plane took off I peered out of the window. For the first time ever I watched the runway beneath me get smaller and smaller. The terminals at Madrid's Barajas airport became tiny dots until they, like the rest of the city that had received me so wonderfully for the past three years, vanished once we broke through the clouds.

I'd taken off and landed at this airport hundreds of times. But till then I had never really looked at it. As soon as I'm on board the plane I usually get into my seat, put on my chunky head-phones that block out any external noise, plug them into my tablet and watch films. I don't take any notice of the safety announcement or the take-off. I'm not someone who looks out of the window. Apart from this one time, on my last flight from Madrid for the time being. I even noticed tears welling in my eyes. 'Hala Madrid.'

All the German players were supposed to be at the hotel in Munich at 1 p.m. Including me, but I had another important meeting and so had to let Jogi Löw in on my transfer plans too, and ask him if I could join the squad later. Although I was going to Munich, my first stop was to undergo the routine medical check. I ought to have done this in London, but as the transfer window was about to close and time was running out, Arsenal's director of football, Richard Law, and the team doctor came to Hans-Wilhelm Müller-Wohlfahrt's medical practice and carried out the necessary tests.

At the same time my father was sorting out the final contrac-tual details with London. While Arsenal and Real were haggling fiercely. At the end of the day, less than an hour before the trans-fer window closed, I signed my new contract at 11.16 p.m. and was now an Arsenal player.

Ex-Bayern keeper Oliver Kahn said of my move, 'In the choice of whether to sacrifice Özil or the Argentinian Di María for Bale, Real's coach Ancelotti has plumped for the German.' He also said that I hadn't managed to make myself 'indispensable' in Madrid. The *Frankfurter Allgemeine* wrote, 'The competition in Madrid became too intense for the artist with the ball who lacks the necessary bite.' Elsewhere it said that I was 'escaping'. Then quotes suddenly appeared in the Spanish press, purportedly from Pérez, which claimed that I was 'obsessed by women' and 'not a good professional'. When it later emerged that these quotes had been made up, they'd already been reprinted in half the papers of Europe. Worked up by Pérez's supposed accusations, my father had also gone on the counter-attack and replied in their duel, 'Just because someone earns a lot of money, it doesn't automatically make him a man of honour. And Pérez isn't a man of honour. Mesut is now meant to be the scapegoat. And me the greedy father who's just been waiting for the big money. A stitch-up, a rotten business.'

All I can say and want to say about these claims is that I don't know Gareth Bale personally. I'm not jealous or upset that Real bought him for something around 100 million euros. After all, it's not his fault that Madrid wanted him and laid this money on the table. He's never played a part in my life and it would be utter nonsense to claim that I feel hatred for the man.

Nor did I ever have a problem with Carlo Ancelotti personally. We only had dealings together in a phase when it was difficult for me at the club. We never really got to know each other. We weren't able to build up any mutual trust.

Likewise I didn't have a problem with Florentino Pérez – that was my father: a small, but important difference.

When I looked at my phone on the evening of the signing there was a variety of messages. Including one from my brother Mutlu, who was on holiday in Turkey with his wife. He'd left a message on my voicemail. He'd been asked at the hotel reception if it was true that I was moving to Arsenal. The papers were full of rumours to this effect. Until then I hadn't had the time to let the people closest to me know personally. Everything had gone so quickly. My mind just had to keep working. There hadn't been time for breaks. No opportunity to catch my breath. No lengthy pondering.

When I called Mutlu and told him that I had actually transferred to Arsenal, he was gobsmacked. 'I hadn't been expecting that,' he replied. José Mourinho, too, was astonished. 'You didn't say anything to me. I thought you wanted to finish your career at Real Madrid,' he texted me.

On the day that Gareth Bale was unveiled at Los Blancos, thousands of fans bellowed at full volume, 'Özil no se vende!' – 'Özil's not for sale!' Sergio Ramos also complained when my transfer was settled: 'If I had any say in the matter, Özil would be one of the last players I'd let go.' Even Cristiano Ronaldo sounded critical: 'Özil's departure is very bad news for me. I'm furious about his move.'

The Spanish press featured polls in which up to 80 per cent of Real fans said it was wrong to sell me. All of these showed me that I hadn't done much wrong in my three years there.

Once I'd arrived and settled in London, I thought long and hard about the circumstances surrounding my move. I wondered whether everything had been done in my interests. Whether the hassle with Pérez and the headlines in the press had been necessary. Couldn't things have been done differently?

Of course, it would have been easy to make my father the scapegoat. He had been obstinate with Pérez. He hadn't made up with him. And so he was to blame. No, no, it's not that simple. Year in, year out my father was there for me and always supported me. He helped me in difficult times. He took many right decisions, thanks to which I was able to begin my stellar career in the first place.

Just like anybody else, my father isn't perfect. And ultimately the negotiations with Pérez and Real Madrid were out of his league.

When the German squad met again in October 2013 in Düsseldorf, I asked my father to come to the team hotel. It was just before my twenty-fifth birthday when I told him that he was no longer going to be my agent. A really difficult conversation. I think it's always difficult for parents when their children cut the umbilical cord. When they announce they're moving out of home. Or even to another city to study. It breaks the heart of most parents, because many of them refuse to believe that their children will now be able to cope on their own.

Breaking with my father wasn't just moving out; it was the end of a business relationship. A notch up. He took it very emotionally at any rate. I didn't want to hurt him. I didn't want him to think he'd done something bad or wrong. I just wanted him to understand that I needed a change in my life, the last step in the process of growing up.

Obviously I had no intention of banishing him altogether. From now on I just wanted to stand on my own two feet and thus be completely responsible for my decisions. I resolved that from now on only I would stipulate the when, where, how and why when it came to key decisions.

Unfortunately, however, my father did not congratulate me for having taken this, as I thought, mature decision. He was angry. And hurt. So hurt that, as the administrator for my Twitter account, he deleted it in a fit of obstinacy, which meant that the several millions of fans following me disappeared.

This happened on 23 November 2013, a Friday evening. I wanted to go to bed earlier than usual, as the following day we had a home fixture against Southampton. About 10 p.m. my phone rang several times – friends telling me that my Twitter account no longer existed. Quite apart from the fact that it's stupid if your fan forum simply vanishes like that, it also does huge financial damage. Hubert Raschka, who in the meantime had been helping me with my media and PR work, told me that from a commercial perspective each social media contact is worth several euros. So with his action my father didn't just extinguish me from the internet, but also almost destroyed a million euros' worth of advertising. Luckily, with Twitter's help Hubert Raschka was able to completely recover my account that night and block my father's access to it.

Raschka remained on my team. Besides my brother Mutlu, who I trust blindly, I also hired Dr Erkut Sögüt, a trained lawyer, to help represent me. We consult closely on decisions relating to my career.

In the end the separation from my father didn't go as calmly and smoothly as I'd hoped. He felt as if he'd been booted out, and even went to court to claim his commission, as he had secured the sponsor contract with Adidas. There's conflict in every family – times when you don't want to be with each other. For the most part these arguments take place within your own four walls, without much involvement from your neighbours. Unfortunately our dispute was made public, owing to a mistake made by the judge at the court in Düsseldorf. In actual fact we'd already come to an agreement in private, well away from the public gaze. In spite of this the court announced in a press release the date originally scheduled for the hearing, which had been cancelled because of our settlement. They apologised for this afterwards and the spokeswoman told us that it had occurred due to an 'internal misunderstanding'. If it hadn't been for this blunder nobody would have found out about our dispute.

I very much regret the quarrel. It's a sad chapter in a very long, very sound and harmonious father–son relationship, which is the reason why I've come as far as I have as a footballer. I'll never forget that.

15

SAMI KHEDIRA

'HE FOUGHT LIKE A LION'

Sami Khedira arrived at Real Madrid the same year as Mesut Özil. Long before Özil's transfer was made official, the two of them exchanged text messages about Los Blancos. Together with Real they went on to win the Spanish championship. Later the two became World Champions with the German national side. Khedira played 102 games for Real, and won the Champions League with them in 2013-14.

Although I'd already played with Mesut – we were U-21 European champions together in Sweden in 2009 – I only got to know him properly in Madrid. It's funny when you look back on it. Two German internationals, with Turkish and Tunisian roots, get to know each other well in Spain. And all because of a Portuguese man: José Mourinho. He brought me to Real Madrid after the World Cup in South Africa. On a trip to Los Angeles just a few weeks after I'd joined Los Blancos, he told me in the dugout that he was looking to sign Mesut too. Cool, I thought, because at 23 and without any Spanish at the time, Real was full on. With Özil there I'd have someone I could relate to and my life would probably be easier.

Mesut then got in contact himself, pestering me with text messages about what Madrid was like. He confided in me that Barcelona were trying to sign him too and he had to decide between the two. To be honest I was still busy digesting the size of this club, this crazy attraction for fans and the media. 'The club is absolutely huge,' I wrote. 'An enormous step.' But I also explained to him that if José Mourinho really wanted you, this would give you 'absolute certainty'. 'If Mourinho wants you, he'll nurture you. Every day he makes me feel I'm important.'

Then, a few weeks later, Mesut was there. We got together in our new home and chatted about how the two of us had got here. Going into all the details. From the first contact to the final signature. At some point Mesut said with a smile, 'Because of Mourinho I'd had my sights set on Madrid for ages. But I also chose Real because of you. When I heard that you were going to Madrid I was finally convinced. It made me feel more assured.'

Since then Mesut's had to listen to me go on about how it's only because of me that he's had such a great career. For the first league game we sat side by side on the subs' bench. Mourinho left us out for the match against Mallorca. We hadn't been expecting that! We were convinced that we'd be part of this landmark fixture.

As the game in the Iberostar stadium plodded along we huddled together in disbelief. 'What have we done wrong? We've moved to Real Madrid and we're not playing.' Luckily our frustration didn't last long. In the second league game against Osasuna, Mourinho had both of us in the starting line-up. From that day on we were part of the regular 11. In the dressing room everyone talks to everyone else. Small talk, the odd joke, music and some chat about the game, of course. But it's not where you get to know people well. Mesut and I also spent a lot of time together in private. Anybody who knows Mesut just from the football pitch or interviews knows the player, but not the man. Mesut is deeper and more complex than many would expect. He's incredibly caring and helpful. Characteristics that aren't common in the football industry. In private he's often putting others first out of concern for their well-being.

There are critics who accuse him of not being a leader. It's true to say he doesn't go shouting his head off on the pitch or in the dressing room. But he looks after teammates and young talents who are new to the squad. That's a crucial quality in a leader.

There are people who accuse him of hiding in big matches. Besides the fact that no footballer can be at his best in every single match, his body language is often misunderstood. Some things appear casual because with his great talent he finds them easy. I've rarely seen him look fiercely determined, even though I know he's busting a gut for the team. There's no doubt that in his early days, when things really weren't going his way, his shoulders would sink and he might not exude the perfect attitude, but I think this has totally changed now.

At the European Championship in France he had a brilliant game against Italy in the quarter-final. Not just because he scored a goal, but because he fought like a lion. In the semi-final against France, too, he led from the front. I was able to watch him closely because I was on the bench injured. His body language reflected his determination.

Which sort of brings us back to Mourinho. I was there when Mesut got the biggest bollocking of his life. When an argument such as you rarely see broke out between him and the manager at half-time in our game against Deportivo La Coruña, which we were winning 3–1.

The fierceness of Mourinho's attack was incredible. In the rough world of professional football his choice of words was OK, perhaps, but took some getting used to, shall we say. A good performance by Mesut wasn't good enough for Mourinho. He wanted to see him play outstandingly every time. And Mourinho has a very provocative way of trying to get to you. He managed to find Mesut's sore spot. I was sitting next to Mesut and saw how he rolled his eyes and turned red. All of a sudden he took out his shin pads, kicked off his boots and pulled down his socks. Even though Mourinho hadn't said a word about substituting him.

Now Mesut began mouthing off himself, virtually substituting himself in the game. All I thought was, 'Oh no, that's it. They'll never talk to each other again.'

But things turned out differently. Mesut began to think about the bollocking and question himself. And what I find admirable is that Mourinho didn't hold Mesut's reaction against him. A few days later everything was good again.

Then, in our first Clásico, Mesut and I were on the receiving end of a terrible 5–1 hammering. Afterwards we spoke a lot about what had gone wrong, and knew that we must never allow another humiliation like that to happen. 'We'll have them,' we swore. 'We'll thrash Barcelona. They'll get a taste of their own medicine.'

In the following season we did exactly that. After 34 games we were leading the table, four points ahead of Barcelona. Now we were due to play them in the Camp Nou. A Barcelona victory would leave the championship race wide open again. But we didn't let that happen. In the seventeenth minute I put us in the lead, then an hour later Barça's Alexis Sanchez equalised. A few minutes later Mesut got the ball. He was a few metres behind the half-way line and quite far out on the right. Di María passed to him, then he sprinted away from his three opponents in the expectation that Mesut would pass back to him as he ran. Ninety-eight per cent of all footballers would have done precisely that. But not Mesut! As quick as lightning he'd seen that Cristiano Ronaldo was starting to run from behind Javier Mascherano. Not many would spot that. But after that, to play the ball 60 metres past Mascherano into Cristiano's stride – that is great artistry!

We won 2–1, thereby taking the decisive step towards the championship, now seven points in the lead after 35 games. 'We've arrived in the footballing elite,' we told ourselves at the celebrations to mark winning the title, and we planned the next step. 'Now we're going to win the Champions League with Real too.' Unfortunately, after three unsuccessful semi-finals, we were unable to achieve this accolade together.

I'm eternally grateful to Mesut for our three years together at Real. I made a great friend who really has so many talents. But is Mesut talented in the kitchen too? That's debatable! He once invited me over to dinner. 'Let's cook together this evening and watch a film,' he suggested. I like trying out dishes from all around the world. I don't get to eat much Turkish food, so I was looking forward to this occasion. Half an hour before I was going to set off for Mesut's house he called and asked what I'd like to eat. Then he read me out a menu from a delivery service. This wasn't exactly my idea of cooking. In his defence, however, let me say that his 'sucuk', a Turkish garlic salami, is in a class of its own.

When Mesut left Real in 2013 it hit me hard. I'd heard about the negotiations with Arsenal and knew that there were a few problems with Real, but I'd never imagined these were insurmountable. In negotiations it's only normal that each side starts by stating its own aims.

On 1 September we were in the team bus on the way to the Bernabéu. Mesut was sitting next to me, dead still. He hardly said a word, nor was he bothered that our new coach, Carlo Ancelotti, hadn't picked him in the starting line-up for the game. When I asked him what was wrong he said, 'I think I'm moving to Arsenal.'

That was really a shock for me. In spite of everything I hadn't thought he'd actually leave Real. In the dressing room after the game he told me, 'I'm going. Both clubs came to an agreement during the match.'

Boy, that came as a blow! Not just because we'd lost an excellent player, not just because a great role model was leaving, but because Mesut is my friend.

Together Mesut and I have achieved almost everything, including the World Cup in 2014, but to be in the same team that wins the Champions League is still on our wish list. Who knows . . .?

16

OUT OF THE GOLDEN CAGE

OR, BE THE MAN YOU ARE

I spent my first few weeks in England in a top luxury hotel. It looked like a palace – like something straight out of a film adaptation of a Rosamunde Pilcher novel.* It was a grandiose country house hotel called The Grove in southern England.

I looked out of my window onto a golf course, with a lawn like I'd never seen in my life before. Mown with such precision. No yellow patches. No bumps. No gouges like the ones on our football pitches when a defender slides along the turf with his boots. As I stood at the window, lost in my thoughts, I sometimes wondered what it must feel like to have a kick around on that lawn.

My friend Baris accompanied me to London to help me get set in my new life. In Madrid my cousin Serdar was busy packing

* Rosamunde Pilcher is a British writer whose works are especially popular in Germany, where more than 100 of her stories have been adapted for television.

my old life into crates and sorting out things such as giving notice on my rental contract.

I had come to London with practically nothing. When I'd booked my flight to join the national squad I'd assumed that I'd be going back to Madrid afterwards. I'd even booked a return flight back to Spain. But now my life had completely changed in less than five days. A new language. A new city. More rain. Less sun. Driving on the left. A new colour shirt. New fans whose hearts I had to win over. New media. A new journey to the training ground. A new boss. A new way of playing. Everything, really everything was new.

Imagine you're getting up one morning and nothing is as it was before. Normally you prepare yourself for such a big change. You look for somewhere to live beforehand. You take a language course. You read up on the customs of the country, or at least I think most people would. You spend weeks packing up your things and gradually prepare yourself mentally for the move. I did none of this. I knew nothing about London, except for what Luka Modrić had said in his brief assessment. It was almost as if someone had clicked their fingers and I had been suddenly transported from Madrid to London.

Several times I wondered how my neighbour Sergio Ramos was. What Ronaldo was doing. How my dogs were in Serdar's care.

I'm not a sentimental person by nature. But I missed Madrid even though I felt excited about my new adventure. After all, the decision had been mine. I'd been the one to tell Wenger that now there was the chance we might work together. The impulse for all this had come from me.

And yet I couldn't just forget Real Madrid from one day to the next. I couldn't easily wipe this beautiful capital city from my heart. I'd loved Madrid. And I still did. It's only when you leave Real that you realise what makes this club so special. You quickly get used to certain things. If you spend a while there, at some point the huge circus around the club starts to feel almost normal. But when you leave Real, you first have to absorb the fact that everything's different.

From the hotel Baris and I embarked again on the search for somewhere to live. For my fourth apartment or house in six years. And I came across one between the parks of Hampstead Heath and Highgate Wood. We found a house that the former supermodel, Claudia Schiffer, was also keen on. Why did the owner rent it to me rather than her? No idea. Certainly not because he was after a pretty face. Perhaps he's an Arsenal fan.

When I arrived at the Arsenal complex for the first time barely anyone was around. It was a yawning void as the club had given the players a day off from training. Only Alex Oxlade-Chamberlain was there, doing a special session. As I was inspecting my new dressing room he came up to me with a big smile, took me by the arm and said, 'It's great you're here. We could do with a player like you. I'm pleased.'

I'm normally reserved to begin with when I go somewhere new. I sit in the dressing room and watch what's going on. Each changing room is governed by its own rules. It has its own hierarchy. There are loud and quiet players. Those who talk the whole time and call the shots. And the more introverted ones who you barely notice in the dressing room. Some have lockers in total chaos, others are obsessed with tidiness.

In truth, a dressing room is not much different from a classroom at school. Where you'll find the class representative, the swots, the clowns, as well as nice and nasty pupils. There are those who get on well and others less well. Those who listen dutifully and studiously write down what the teacher says, and those who aren't interested and are easily distracted.

As a newcomer you have to work out what makes each individual player tick. You have to learn which players are most like you. To give me an idea I always spent a few days at the beginning observing the squad. That's what I'd done at Schalke, Bremen and Madrid at any rate.

But at Arsenal I didn't have the chance to start by sitting quietly in the corner and studying my new team. That's because one of my teammates was Lukas Podolski. Poldi never gives you a moment's peace. He and Per Mertesacker collared me straight-away and did everything to ensure that I was given a wonderful welcome into the Arsenal family.

I went to watch boxing with Poldi in London. The frequent team evenings also helped me to integrate. They were held roughly every couple of months, and organised by the team committee, of which Per is a member. Once, for example, we had a fancy-dress party. Everyone had to pick a piece of paper at random and then appear in the corresponding outfit that evening. I was lucky; I picked out Superman. Poldi was the Hulk. But there was also someone – I really can't remember who it was – who had to go as a short, fat, Italian plumber. With overalls, cap and big moustache. Of course there wasn't just a Super Mario at our party; we had a Luigi too. But neither is my idea of a hero. There were hardly any team evenings like this at Real Madrid. If we did get together it was at lunchtime. In Bremen they were held every month,

Arsène Wenger, too, helped me acclimatise to London. He and his entire family made every effort to ensure that my friends and I felt comfortable in London from day one.

When I left for my first game with my new team – an away match against Sunderland – Wenger asked his ex-wife Annie to look after my friends and family so they weren't hanging around on their own in London. She invited them all to her house. Mrs Wenger cooked for them and her daughter Lea was there too. Our game was going on at the same time. During the match Mrs Wenger was highly emotional. She sat on the floor, watching her husband's team play. When, in the eleventh minute, I set up Olivier Giroud's goal that put us in the lead, she leapt up with a homemade cheesecake in her hand and danced around the room. Or at least that's how it was described to me . . .

Before the game, which we won 2–1, I had to undergo the Arsenal initiation ritual. Fortunately Per Mertesacker had warned me about this in advance, which meant I was partially prepared for it.

Every newbie at Arsenal has to stand on a chair and sing, surrounded by the rest of the team. Now, I don't have the most beautiful voice in the world, unfortunately. Even with all the technological wizardry at his fingertips in the recording studio, Jan Delay wasn't able to disguise this. In 2010 the German hip-hop artist, a former member of Absolute Beginner, came up with the idea of recording a song with me. Jan Delay, who's a big Werder fan, wrote the rap 'Large' for us, in which I sing – if it can be described as that – the following: 'My captain says, Hey, you chicken, compared to you I'm a European champion. What's up?' In one verse we took the mickey out of Bremen by singing, 'We stink of fish 'cause we're from Werder.' And I rapped about my ambition, which unfortunately I didn't quite manage to fulfil: 'I'm young, born in the 80s and I'm gonna win the cup in South Africa.'

It was a real hoot and I'd do it again any time. I can't sing for toffee. I can't hit a single note and have no sense of rhythm. As a child I never learnt to read music or play an instrument. I'm totally unmusical. But because I thought Jan Delay was cool and his idea was amusing, I didn't have a problem joining in with a large serving of self-deprecation.

Shortly before the game in Sunderland I wondered whether I should sing this song to mark my debut. But because of my hopeless voice I decided on a song that everyone knew and everyone could join in with. Ideally my voice would be lost amongst the general caterwauling. Climbing onto the chair, I launched into 'Kiss Kiss' by Tarkan. I began really quietly, my teammates started booing, so then I got louder until, with no inhibitions and enjoying every second, I was squeaking at the top of my voice, 'Kaderim puskullu belam. Yakalarsam.' And all the rest joined in, 'Kiss. Kiss.'

With my singing I'd endeared myself to my teammates. Even if my performance didn't come close to Petr Čech's following his move from Chelsea to Arsenal in 2015. When we stopped in Singapore before the start of the season it was his turn. He came up with a brilliant rap in which he talked about certain players, dedicating individual verses to them. He didn't say anything about the manager, except for, 'I'd rather keep quiet about you, or I'll find myself on the bench.'

When I sang I took care that none of my teammates filmed it on their phones. Čech also rapped without any incriminating 'proof'. Only one song has been captured on video. The one that the Arsenal fans sang for me some time later. They created a special song for me, which they sang in the stadium and also in the London Underground. It goes, 'We've got Özil. Mesut Özil. I just don't think you understand. He's Arsène Wenger's man. He's better than Zidane. We have got Mesut Özil.'

The first time I heard this I couldn't believe my ears. When thousands of people are singing for you, you get overcome with happiness. I loved the Schalke fans. I was crazy for the Bremen supporters. The Madrilenians regularly made my hair stand on end. But I'd never had my own personal mini-anthem before.

Whenever I hear the song I feel as if I've grown. As if I'm not just 1.80m, but am towering above people who are 1.90. My shoulders grow broader. My head becomes clearer. And the desire to be part of Arsenal's next victory becomes greater. Just once I'd love to go on a tube train where thousands of fans are singing my song, without anyone knowing who I am.

But I'm afraid that's never going to happen. I lead a far too secluded life in London for that. I can scarcely leave my house. Why? Because it's no fun to wander around in public when your face is familiar. Besides, never underestimate the paparazzi in London. When I was still quite new in the British capital and had just moved into my house, they laid siege to me in an extraordinarily intrusive way. Photographers stood outside my front door day and night with their cameras and high-zoom lenses. Not only that – there were incidents that shocked me to the core.

Lukas Podolski had recommended a Turkish restaurant called Likya near Golders Green, where I was planning to go one evening with a few friends and my agent. I just had to get out, empty my head a bit, because in the Champions League I'd just missed a stupid penalty against Bayern and we were behind for the return leg of our last-16 match.

I got into the car, the wrought-iron gates to my drive opened and we carefully drove out. At once photographers were on us. They followed us through London, virtually sticking to my bumper. Completely irresponsible.

After a few kilometres I pulled over, got out of the car and spoke to our pursuers. 'Look, guys, I'm out for a private evening. We just want to go for something to eat. Please respect my privacy.' I was perfectly friendly towards them. But it didn't help one bit. No sooner had I set off again than the pursuit continued. So we decided that rather than go for dinner we'd return home. When I arrived I saw that even more photographers had gathered outside my property.

'Mesut,' my agent Erkut said, 'please drive really carefully. You mustn't even brush one of those photographers.' I rolled onto the drive at a snail's pace while the paparazzi snapped away though the windows. A dreadful explosion of flashes you'd just want to run or drive away from. All of a sudden there was a crunch. A photographer's elbow slammed against my wing mirror, which clanked to the ground. I thought my eyes were playing tricks on me. Then the photographer gave a loud scream and his face contorted with pain. He was holding his elbow and rolling his eyes as if on the verge of collapse. A moment later he cried out, 'He drove into me. The guy wanted to run me over.'

I sat in the car as if paralysed. I hadn't done anything. My car had been entering the drive at less than 5 kilometres per hour. Nobody had been that close that I could have touched them. 'Did you see that?' I asked Erkut, who was looking as shocked as me. 'Yes,' was all he said. And then, a few seconds later, 'Keep calm. Let's not react.' This was the lousiest attempt anyone had ever made to provoke me. Even worse than the coward David Villa in that Barça–Real game.

The nasty paparazzo act continued. He called an ambulance that arrived a few minutes later and attended to him. The police came too and rang at my door. They breathalysed me – of course the result was negative – and allowed us to describe the incident from our point of view.

The officers remained totally calm and were suspicious of the story that the paparazzi, who were all saying the same crap, had dished up. 'If you like,' Erkut suggested, 'you can check the footage from the CCTV cameras that are all over the place here, in the street and on the houses. You'll see that Mesut did nothing of what those men are claiming.' The officers believed our story anyway. But it was a good feeling that, had there been any doubt, we could have got hold of clear evidence that the paparazzi were lying.

The journalists wanted to see me lose it. They were craving pictures showing me leaping out of the car and going for their colleagues, which they could then sell on to the newspapers for a tidy sum. When that didn't work they tried to present me as a reckless driver. I know that being photographed is part of my life. I know that being in the public eye means you have less privacy. But this attempt to manipulate me and make me look bad went way too far.

A similar thing happened a few years before, after my grandmother died. She passed away during the 2010 World Cup. On that occasion too I was hassled by a disrespectful pursuit.

A few days before the last-16 game against England my dear grandmother Münevver died at the age of 73. My father had originally decided not to tell me until after the World Cup so that I wouldn't lose concentration during the tournament. But my brother felt that I ought to be told the sad family news straightaway. Because the funeral was due to take place within a short time, he was worried that a journalist might get wind of the news and publish it. 'Just imagine if Mesut found out about it from a paper rather than us,' Mutlu said. My father agreed with him.

My grandmother always spent several months in Germany each year. She'd stay with us in the flat. A wonderful time for us children, full of love and warmth. She always called me after my games and congratulated me if I'd scored a goal or assisted.

Now she was dead. It was bad enough that I couldn't say goodbye to her personally. It was bad enough that I couldn't be with the family at her funeral in the Uzunalioğlu Mahallesi mosque near Hışıroğlu. But to be pursued after the World Cup by photographers who took photos of me standing by her grave, that overstepped the mark.

It was the moment when I wanted to say goodbye to her. When I wanted to be alone in my grief and sadness. When I wanted to be just the private Mesut Özil rather than the footballer, the celebrity. I was someone who'd lost a person I loved. Who just wanted to reminisce, which is very hard to do when your peace is disturbed by cameras clicking away behind you.

I don't think many people can imagine what it means to be permanently in the limelight. It's often nice, and of course I enjoy it too. But when the focus is on you round the clock it can be a real burden too. I have a great life, a very exclusive life that many people couldn't afford. But my fame also has its price. Because the truth is that I live life in a golden cage.

José Mourinho once said, 'Football has given me everything. But football's taken everything from me too.' A very accurate comment. Thanks to football I've been able to make a good life for myself, and also for my parents and family, free of all financial worries. Football has opened up a world to us we would never have been able to enter in normal circumstances.

Football has made me rich. But I'm also mighty poor at the same time. Poor in life experience. I can only lead a private life within my own four walls. I can't wander down an arcade from shop to shop, or go for a stroll with my friends. I can't go out climbing on the high ropes or to the cinema. At best I have to go in disguise and even then my cover's usually blown. People will immediately stare at me to see how much popcorn I'm eating and whether I'm drinking Coke or water. Every movement will be captured by some mobile and then broadcast around the world. And I have to endure hundreds of selfies.

That isn't a problem in theory. It's also part of the job I enjoy doing. But not in those rare moments when I'd like to be completely private. Sometimes people can't understand the rare occasions when I refuse a selfie. They think, 'Why should he react like that just because of a photo?' But they don't realise that I've already had 40 or 50 selfies taken that day. It doesn't occur to them that I might want to move on, have an appointment, or just don't happen to feel great.

I would have loved to get to know London better. I'd love to go on the London Eye, that big wheel by the Thames. Discover the city on the top of a double-decker bus. I'd love to be a tourist, an unknown person, to be able to do all these normal things that everyone does from day to day.

For me every day is the same. I train or I play. Then I drive home and hang around with my mates. In truth I hardly know London at all. It must be a fantastic city with so many sights. But because it's so stressful I rarely leave my golden cage, but instead play a permanent game of hide-and-seek.

This is why I'm already looking forward to my retirement from football. When I'm less popular, when the media and fans pounce on other players and I'm able to catch up on many of the things I've missed. I learn about the world mainly from the television. I watch documentaries for hours – BBC History programmes as well as ones about the world's tallest skyscrapers. And most of all I like watching animal documentaries – I'm especially keen on lions.

After the 2012 European Championship I vanished into thin air. I was really annoyed by our elimination at the hands of Italy. By this stupid 2–1 defeat in the semi-final.

When we were knocked out two years earlier in South Africa, I could cope with that. Although it was disappointing, the team was still so young and inexperienced that we had to admit that even reaching the semi-final was a huge success. The defeat there was acceptable. I could be pleased with many positive things even though we'd fallen just short of our goal.

It wasn't so simple after our defeat against Italy. I couldn't stand seeing blue football jerseys. It made me furious when I heard the name Mario Balotelli. After the semi-final I couldn't stand that man, even though he'd never done anything to me personally. But for me his name was associated with that bitter failure that was somehow unacceptable.

I was livid with myself. And at my performance. I was hurt by the discussions in Germany where overnight the papers were full of criticism again. There was a 'loser gene' in the German team, they said. And it was claimed that Joachim Löw had lost 'some of his magic'. In the press conference following the defeat he was asked by journalists whether he was going to chuck in his job as German manager.

Once more: our performance in the semi-final must be viewed critically. There's no getting away from it. We weren't good. But we were the youngest team in the tournament, so it's hardly surprising that our performances fluctuated, even if none of this was on purpose. And we did reach the semi-final, where we had our opportunities. Mats Hummels had a big chance early on, which wasn't a goal only because Andrea Pirlo cleared the ball from the line. A little later Gianluigi Buffon foiled a long-range shot from Toni Kroos with a good save.

It was perfectly legitimate after this to say it was 'unlikely' we would win the World Cup in 2014. But to claim that the semi-final had been contested between 'wimps and men', as the tabloids did, was insulting and bore no relation to the game. 'Even when the anthem was being played, many of the 27.98 million Germans watching on TV had the feeling: we're going to lose tonight,' *Bild* wrote. It went on, 'The Italians belted out their anthem with fervour and power. Even Mario Balotelli, the son of Ghanaian immigrants. The goalie Buffon with his eyes closed. It was with this passion that the Italians strode onto the pitch.' At the end *Bild* concluded, 'Show me how you sing, and I'll tell you how you'll play . . .'

If there was truth to this logic we would have succumbed to the defeat of our lives in the semi-final on 8 July 2014 in Belo Horizonte.

I'll never forget the expression on the face of David Luiz, Brazil's captain, in the tunnel shortly before kick-off. On his right shoulder was the hand of Júlio César, the Brazilian keeper. Each player had his right hand on the shoulder of the player in front. And that's how the Brazilians marched into the Estádio Governador Magalhães Pinto. Eleven players, lined up like pearls on a string. Very closely linked. As they entered the Brazilians had to scuttle a bit with short strides, so as not to step on the heel of the man in front.

We go into the stadium as we always do. Each for himself. First Philipp Lahm, then Manuel Neuer, behind him Mats Hummels, Thomas Müller, Toni Kroos, Benedikt Höwedes, Miroslav Klose,

Sami Khedira, Jérôme Boateng and then me before Bastien Schweinsteiger.

We don't grip onto each other. We don't form a chain. I wonder what the assessment would have been had we lost. Would the media have claimed that the Germans weren't as closely bonded as the Brazilians? Would it have been said that the Brazilians were a team of 11 friends in which everyone fought for each other, whereas the Germans only thought of themselves, as was clearly evident when they filed onto the pitch?

When our national anthem is being played I go through my usual procedure prior to kick-off. I pray. And don't join in the singing. Jérôme Boateng doesn't sing either. Nor does Sami Khedira.

All of the Brazilians are singing. Without exception. Although the term 'singing' is a pure understatement. If you watch Luiz Gustavo, see the ardour with which he bawls the Hino Nacional Brasiliero, it can be terrifying. It seems as if his singing could be heard in the whole of Brazil without amplification. David Luiz and Júlio César are shouting the house down. With such power! With such determination! With such might! With such passion! Every single Brazilian sings louder, more passionately and enthusiastically than our players.

If this rule of football really did exist – 'Show me how you sing, and I'll tell you how you'll play . . .' – then Brazil would have devoured us. They would have beaten us 7–1. Not the other way round.

After our defeat to Italy, Pirlo, who'd set up the first goal with a dream pass to Balotelli, came up to me and took my arm. 'You're

My first Arsenal goal – a first-time finish from Aaron Ramsey's cross against Napoli in 2013.

My new team-mates certainly seemed to appreciate the goal against the Italians!

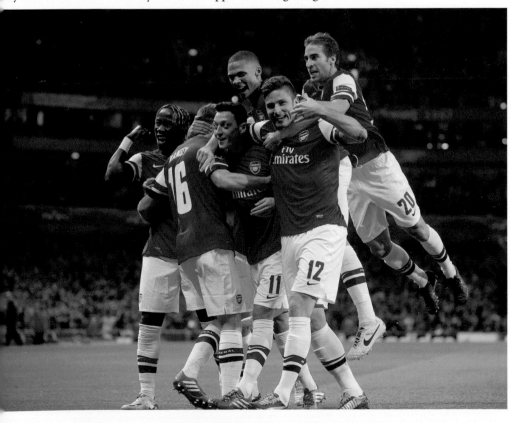

Per Mertesacker vents his fury after I didn't applaud our fans following a 6–3 loss at Manchester City, leading me to apologise on Facebook.

A better day for my relationship with the wonderful Arsenal supporters as we enjoy our FA Cup final victory over Hull with them in 2014.

Silverware in my first season with Arsenal! Prince William looks on as I lift the FA Cup following our fightback against Hull at Wembley.

After three months out with an injury in 2014–15 I was delighted with this goal at Brighton in the FA Cup on returning to the starting 11.

Making up for lost time again, my shot beats Brad Guzan in our 5–0 Premier League victory over Aston Villa soon after the Brighton tie.

Arsene Wenger sets great store by set-pieces. This free-kick brings us the second goal in a superb 4–1 win against Liverpool.

Retaining the FA Cup in 2015 was very satisfying, particularly after we turned on the style to blow away Aston Villa 4–0.

Mastery of the ball is the key at any level of football. Alexis Sanchez has it, and I believe we have a special understanding.

My shot flashes through Chris Smalling's legs, nutmeg-style, for our second goal in a 3–0 defeat of Manchester United in 2015.

Warm congratulations from Nacho Monreal and Arsene Wenger after my goal against an old Bundesliga foe, Bayern Munich.

At last! I volley past the Bournemouth keeper for Arsenal's first goal in four games before celebrating in what's become my trademark fashion.

The guys join me to mark my first hat-trick in professional football, in Arsenal's 6–0 win over Bulgaria's Ludogorets in 2016.

A slice of history as I become the first Arsenal man to score at West Ham's new London Stadium, launching a 5–1 win in 2016–17.

a class player,' he whispered to me. 'Your team has played a great European Championship. You'll win a cup some time.' It was almost like a father taking his son by the arm and psyching him up after a failure. So intimate. So close. So respectful. But most of all so honest. It wasn't just superficial jabber, a gesture for the cameras. Not a brief pat on the shoulder before switching to celebratory mode. Pirlo was really very sorry to see me looking so worn out and sad. He knew exactly what it felt like for a competitive sportsman to be knocked out like that. It was an unbelievable gesture that I made a mental note of – and recalled two years later when I copied it myself.

When we thrashed Brazil 7–1 in the World Cup on their home turf I caught sight of David Luiz standing on the pitch. He didn't know what to do with himself and was just drifting aimlessly across the Belo Horizonte stadium. And so I grabbed him, pressed him close to me, his head on my chest, to whisper a few words of comfort in his ear. I even apologised for the scale of our victory.

Even though Pirlo's words helped me at that difficult time in 2012, it still took a while to get over that defeat. So I booked a holiday, almost away from civilisation. Away from the mobile network, from being permanently contactable. Away from my normal life. Away from football. Out of the golden cage. And into deepest Africa. Into a world where goals and passes aren't crucial. Where I'm not centre stage, but animals and nature capture the imagination.

In the wilderness of Africa I managed to forget these blue jerseys. I learned to laugh again. And most of all I had the freedom to move around without anyone being interested in who I was. I didn't have to answer to anyone about why I hadn't kept chasing Pirlo before he passed to Giorgio Chiellini. The Australian mother who'd given her daughter this trip as a reward for having finished school was as uninterested in a photo or autograph as the couple that had been coming on safari every summer for the past ten years.

They had no idea that only a few days earlier I'd been playing football in front of an audience of millions. As far as they were concerned I was just the bloke who was too stupid to stick to the simplest of the safari rules we were given at the start. Our guide had expressly forbidden us to pack any food in our rucksacks or go for a wander. For some reason I didn't take the warning so seriously when on the first day I took a look around the area surrounding our lodge. I thought a few bananas would be fine in case I got peckish – a typical sports snack to keep you going in-between meals. But I'd barely left the building when I was targeted by a troop of baboons. At least 20 animals, some of them 80 centimetres tall, followed me with the intention of snatching my rucksack. One even leapt onto it and tried to wrench it open. I was just about able to shake him off and escape back to my room. Because the monkeys were waiting on the roof of the lodge for me to come back out I had to call a ranger and confess my mistake to him.

Soon afterwards I had my second encounter with a wild animal. Suddenly there was this impala standing right in front of me, staring at me with its deep black eyes. A beautiful beast. So graceful and finely sculpted. With fur that looked so soft I wanted to touch and stroke it. But it also had these corkscrew-like horns, which must have been around 90 centimetres long and looked rather menacing. One strike and I would have been badly injured. So I stood still and didn't move. Because the antelope didn't make any move to leave either, the two of us stood face to face for what seemed like an eternity. Then the animal got bored, vanishing into the bush with a huge leap.

On the third day I saw lions, from just 2 metres away. They were lying around on the savanna. Under a tree. Completely peaceful. No fences or ditches. Two-hundred-kilo colossuses. It's awful to think that these majestic animals, whose hunting grounds in the wild extend to several hundred kilometres, are crammed into tiny enclosures in zoos.

Although the lions were doing little more than occasionally moving their heads from one side to another, closing and opening their eyes or sometimes giving a hearty yawn, I couldn't stop staring at them. I could have stayed for days watching these beasts.

I love lions because I think they're very like me. We're proud, afraid of nothing and would defend our families against any danger. Because of these similarities I got myself a lion tattoo – although it took a number of attempts before I actually dared do it. I went to the parlour several times with my cousin, who I'd also persuaded to get a tattoo. We even enquired about designs, but for a long time I lacked the courage. It wasn't until I was badly injured in October 2014, and out for three months with a torn ligament, that I finally had the tattoo inked.

I was in Donaustauf in Bavaria, undergoing rehab with Klaus Eder. When I wasn't having treatment I went stir-crazy. So I found another a tattoo parlour. On 1 April Serdar sat in the chair first and had a tattoo. When I saw his face contorted with pain I got scared. 'I think I'd better leave it,' I said to him when he'd finished. And called out, 'April fool!'

A joke. This time I didn't back out again; I had a large tattoo inked in one sitting. The torture lasted eight hours. Tears were in my eyes at the first jab. When the fine needle made its way along the open wound, prick by prick, it was so painful that I just wanted to run away from the tattooist. After four hours my skin was numb and I no longer felt anything.

I'm proud of the lion and my motto, 'Only God can judge me', inspired by an idea that came to me on the African steppe. My journey to the African continent was one of the few occasions when I've broken out from the golden cage. One I've lived off for a long time and which opened my eyes to this world.

In 2012 in Africa I discovered a new world. In 2013 in London I also got to know a new world, at least from a footballing perspective. Arsène Wenger manages Arsenal differently from the way Mourinho ran Madrid. His rules are stricter. For example, he always insists that we take off our boots before entering the dressing room. Wenger brought this ritual back from Japan after having coached Nagoya Grampus over there. That Arsenal dressing-room floor is so clean you could eat your dinner off it.

Being at Arsenal is a bit like being at school. Wenger doesn't allow mobile phones in the massage room, for instance. They're strictly banned. He also likes us to appear in similar dress, as if we were wearing a school uniform. Before the game he decides whether we're going to play in short- or long-sleeved jerseys. He won't have one player wearing short sleeves and another long. Sometimes, when it's cold, I'd like to wear a long-sleeved T-shirt under the jersey. But it's not allowed. And absolutely no long-johns of the sort that Arjen Robben in Munich often wears in winter.

For all his positive personal attributes, Wenger is a strict man in other ways too. Once my two pugs, Balboa and Capon, ran away. Somehow they managed to squeeze through a weak point in the fence and escape. Obviously I was very worried about them. But my search was fruitless – they'd gone. And in a huge metropolis like London, in an area with busy streets. My friends ran around the entire neighbourhood, calling out the dogs' names. They even asked whether they could go into the gardens of the next-door houses. But my pugs were nowhere to be seen. Wenger had scheduled training for that morning. I couldn't just ring him and ask whether I might on this occasion stay at home to look for the dogs. It would have sounded like a poor excuse. As if I were still woozy after having been up drinking all night and couldn't play. So despite my concern for the dogs I hurried to training.

We have to be there half an hour before the session starts. Luckily my teammates covered for me and didn't tell him that I'd only got to the ground five minutes before. 'Coach, my pugs have disappeared. Can I go and look for them?' I asked nervously, after he'd seen with his own eyes that I wasn't offering some poor excuse but was actually fit and alert. But Wenger didn't under-stand the fuss. 'Your pugs will come back,' he said coolly and calmly, sending me out onto the pitch. I couldn't comprehend how he could be so hard. We were, after all, talking about dogs – practically family members – who'd disappeared. I couldn't bear the thought that they might be lying in a ditch somewhere, having been run over, and suffering internal injuries that would lead to a horrible death.

But it was hopeless. Wenger wouldn't budge. I couldn't resume my search till after training. In the meantime my friends had plastered the whole neighbourhood with posters. And that evening a call came from a pet shop where the two runaways had luckily been handed in.

*

From a sporting point of view the first few months were great. In the first Premier League match Arsenal had lost against Aston Villa. The team then won the next two games against Fulham and Spurs. And after that, starting with the aforementioned game against Sunderland, I was part of the squad. After 614 seconds in an Arsenal shirt – I was given number 11 – I assisted Olivier Giroud's goal. Ninety per cent of my passes were successful. Wenger was happy, publicly praising my debut as 'outstanding'. After our victory against Stoke City we climbed to the top of the table and didn't lose this position until a 1–1 draw against Everton and a 6–3 defeat to Manchester City in our 17th game. But we soon reclaimed the top spot and remained there for the following four games.

So far things had gone pretty well. I'd assisted nine goals in the league and scored four myself. But I gradually felt that my body was starting to flag. That ought not to have come as much of a surprise, as I'd missed pre-season training with Arsenal due to my last-minute transfer. What's more, this was the first time that I hadn't had a winter break. Up till then there'd always been a little time around the end of the calendar year to give my body a rest. But in England I had to play on 23 and 26 December too.

At the beginning of February we went to Liverpool. We were leading the table again with 55 points, followed closely by Manchester City and Chelsea. After that came the Reds with 47 points. After 53 seconds the Liverpool player Martin Škrtel scored. In the tenth minute he made it 2–0. And after 20 minutes we were already trailing 4–0. We were in total confusion with no idea how this was happening. Liverpool were doing what they liked with us. We couldn't find anything to stop them. And I'll admit that I looked terrible too.

After the game, which ended 5–1, the media lashed into me. Especially because of the huge transfer fee that Arsenal had paid, they evidently found it unacceptable for me to have the occasional off day. They expected me to shine each time, and when I didn't, the *Independent*, for example, wrote that my performance was 'loose and lazy in possession'. It also said, 'He's one of the best in the world when the score is 2–0. But you wouldn't want him in the team when it's the other way around.' In his response to the criticism Wenger backed me up: 'Mesut's been a professional footballer long enough to know that he'll be questioned if his performance isn't good enough.' I shouldn't put myself under pressure because of the transfer fee, he advised me. 'I just want him to enjoy the game and play well. He's happy on the ball, which is the most important thing – because he's got quality.' He also insisted that I was 'an exceptional player'.

Per Mertesacker also tried to nip the criticism in the bud. Defending me, he said, 'Here the ball goes up and down at light-ning speed. Everyone here wants to hurt Mesut and show him that it's a different league to Spain, where you can play beautiful football. That's why I knew in advance that he'd flatline at some point.'

I really value such support. But it didn't help much. For I was still being hit by a torrent of criticism. Once one person had taken a pop at me, others decided to have a go. Like a chain reaction.

Under the heading 'Özil's not going to win us the World Cup', an article by Jochen Coenen in *Sport Bild* said:

Can you recall a really big game that Mesut Özil has transformed? That he's put his stamp on? No? That's hardly a surprise because there hasn't been one yet. He's messed up the last two important games with Arsenal [. . .] In the European Championship semi-final against Italy in 2012 he scored the goal in stoppage time to make it 2–1. And that's it. In the 1–0 World Cup semi-final defeat against Spain two years earlier he was a total failure. When he was playing for Real Madrid he was regularly substituted in the Clásicos against Barcelona. The list could go on and on. Of course he has lots of ball contact. But that's all airy-fairy stuff if, at the end of the day, nothing concrete comes from it. The bitter truth is that Özil's not going to win us the 2014 World Cup either. Because when push comes to shove he hides away.

Naturally there was more talk about my body language too. According to the *Süddeutsche Zeitung* it was a 'welcome object of study for all sorts of observers. When the ball isn't actually glowing at his feet Özil can sometimes look like a little boy standing around looking lost because the big boys aren't letting him play.'

Our 5–1 defeat was followed by a 0–0 draw in the league against Manchester United. In the FA Cup we took revenge on Liverpool and progressed to the quarter-finals. But then I missed a penalty following a foul in the eighth minute of our Champions League last-16 game, at home against Bayern Munich, which they won thanks to goals from Toni Kroos and Thomas Müller. After a 1–1 draw in the return leg, they progressed to the next round. As far as the *Daily Mail* was concerned, I was now the German who'd cost 42.5 million pounds but couldn't take a penalty.

Kicker, too, started a great 'Özil debate' at the beginning of March. Ignoring the fact that I'd scored eight goals in our qualifying matches for the World Cup in Brazil, they raised the question of whether I could hack it in big matches. The answers were given by experts who, fortunately, were for the most part united. Andreas Möller, for example, couldn't understand the criticism I was facing. He was convinced that as a squad we were capable of playing an outstanding World Cup and that I had definitely earned my place as the number 10 in that squad. Günter Netzer and Wolfgang Overath also made positive comments. Netzer praised my skills and said that I'd also help the team, even if I wasn't one of its leaders. Wolfgang Overath clearly recognised what my problem had been during this slump in form: 'Mesut Özil can shape the game and determine the tempo, he plays the concealed and final pass, he looks left and plays the ball right, and he's a threat to the goal. A young man like that is ever reliant on his self-confidence. But there are always phases when you lack this self-confidence. Highly skilled technicians are very sensitive towards this.' Only Uwe Bein gave a critical answer, which he has every right to do. On the basis of my performances he said that I wasn't 'a player for big matches'.

I followed these debates from a distance and held back from commenting publicly myself. I knew that the time would come when I'd give the right answer on the pitch.

But in the middle of March I had a thigh problem that put me out for four weeks, preventing me from helping my team turn their fortunes around in the Premier League.

During that period Arsenal lost 6–0 against Chelsea, in Arsène Wenger's thousandth game as Arsenal. And against José Mourinho of all people. 'I feel embarrassed for him,' he'd once told the press. Mourinho had called him 'a specialist in failure'. After the match Mourinho said, 'We came to kill and in ten minutes we destroy. After that, easy.'

We plummeted to fourth place, where we managed to stay for the rest of the season. In the end we'd only lost one more game than the champions Manchester City as well as Liverpool and Chelsea. We were seven points off the lead. Really annoying. For a long time I'd believed we'd be champions in my first year with Arsenal. Of course, I'd dreamed that anyone winning the title would want to win it again.

But we still had a chance to bring the season, which had begun so promisingly, to a successful conclusion.

In the FA Cup quarter-final I had a perfect game against Everton. One of those days full of 'altered perception' as I call it. Where you play and know that the ball belongs to you. Where you're faster and more assured than your opponent. Where your ego is large and everything you do works. Where time doesn't play tricks on you.

For time is a funny old thing. Sometimes it flies by, as the saying goes. And sometimes – at least this is what people claim – it seems to stand still. All nonsense, of course. Time always passes at the same speed. Everywhere in the world. Always in the same 24-hour rhythm. Just not on the football field! At least the way I perceive time is subject to big fluctuations.

Sometimes time stretches, then it compresses again. Sometimes I'm astonished that the 90 minutes are over. Then there are games where I'm longing for the final whistle to be blown, but the minutes just refuse to tick by. But this is just one of many instances of altered perception you encounter as a footballer.

Proportions change too. On good days, when I step up for a free kick, for example, the goalkeeper behind the wall of opposition players seems tiny, far too small to ever get to my ball. Because my self-confidence is high, it really feels as if it's someone the size of a Lego figure who is between the posts of the 7.32-metre-wide and 2.44-metre-high goal. Sometimes, however – though luckily this is rarer – things are the other way around. Then it's the goal that seems tiny and I can barely see a free space to slot the ball into. Now the goalie's a monster who'll fish my shot out of the air with his Kraken-like arms no matter where I put it. And without even having to dive.

Sometimes I'm facing four opponents who are rushing wildly towards me. But because I know how they'll move to win the ball off me I can easily dodge them. It's as if they're running at me in slow motion and I'm able to react to their movements in real time – a little bit like Keanu Reeves in *The Matrix*, when he dodges bullets that are fired at him.

Or, to put it more simply: when you're sure of yourself you believe you can still do a lot with the ball when the opponent is only a metre away. Then you trust yourself to dribble. You are going to determine the next move. If you're unsure, you feel hard-pressed in the same situation.

I know it might sound funny but I'm convinced that many sportspeople have experienced this altered perception. I seem to recall that the tennis legend Roger Federer, who I'm a great admirer of, once described something similar. That the tennis ball looks bigger and bounces more slowly when he's feeling really good. And that in these situations he hits the ball even more accurately, sending it right to the edge of the line and out of reach of his opponent.

The quarter-final against Everton was one such magical day. I felt as if I were holding a magic wand that I could use to direct the game as I pleased. I felt fantastic, I was totally sure of my game. After seven minutes I scored to put us in the lead. Later I assisted Giroud, who made it 4–1. I was declared 'man of the match', and with our entry into the semi-finals the media's attitude changed slightly. All of a sudden our world wasn't dismal and bad any more; the *Daily Telegraph* commented, 'Arsenal revived their season with this FA cup performance. This was more than a win. This was the return of hope.'

We'd beaten Tottenham, Coventry City, Liverpool and Everton. In the semi-final we defeated Wigan Athletic, setting up a final against Hull.

After a few minutes we were already trailing 2–0 in this crucial game. Once again we'd completely gone to sleep in the opening stages. But this time we fought back and after normal time we had recovered to 2–2. In the 109th minute Aaron Ramsey then made it 3–2 to us, which was the final score.

In the nine years before they had signed me Arsenal had gone without a trophy. Now they won the oldest football competition in the world, first held in 1871–72.

After the final whistle I raced over to a television camera and screamed, 'Ja, Gunners, ja!' It was just the emotion of the moment; I was expressing my joy at the victory. A few fans no doubt found it amusing to see me bellow into the camera with such passion. And in German, too. But that didn't bother me. Instead I continued to use this exclamation whenever I had success, even using it as my personal hashtag on Facebook and Twitter. #YaGunnersYa has since achieved cult status. It's been known to be used more than 50,000 times a month when fans discuss me and Arsenal.

I like this exchange with my fans. Every message is a piece of me that I consciously give away and share with my followers. I particularly like the efficiency required by Twitter. Only 140 characters. No stylish flourishes or embellishment. Just boiled down to the message. Twitter is my favourite social network.

I consult Hubert Raschka, my PR man, before sending every message. We have a WhatsApp group in which we discuss each tweet. Sometimes Hubert makes a suggestion, sometimes I do. We're like two directors with equal say.

Thanks to social media platforms I have very different opportunities to engage with my fans. For example, Hubert once found a video of a wedding speech on YouTube, in which the groom says, 'I think everybody in this room knows that this person has made me the happiest guy on the planet [. . .] All that I hope is that this special someone knows from the bottom of my heart how much they truly mean to me. I know that it's difficult to find someone who makes you feel this way. I'm never ever going to take it for granted. So can we please raise a toast to . . .' Then, to the amazement of everyone there, he says my name.

I thought the video was so sweet, funny and warm that Hubert and I decided to show my thanks for his admiration. So we tweeted, 'Well said. I'll congratulate you both personally after your honeymoon and I'll also invite you to an #AFC game.' Of course they took up the invitation.

So Arsenal finally won another trophy in 2014. Somehow this seemed to be my competition. I'd won it with Bremen, Real Madrid and now Arsenal. And then we won it again the following year. After we beat Aston Villa 4–0, a journalist in the *Sun* wrote, 'I have to take my hat off to Mesut Özil. I have criticised him for much of the last two seasons. But the artistic German reserved one of his best displays for yesterday.'

Contrary to what some people claimed, I had won big games too. Proper finals. All-or-nothing matches. Being actively involved. And with real passes.

Because of the size of my transfer fee, the expectations of me in London were higher than ever before. I was even more sharply in the focus of the media, being scrutinised more carefully than normal. And I received more frequent and harsher criticism than I'd ever had at Schalke, Bremen or Madrid. But I didn't take it all to heart. For I know that the most important thing is not to lose faith in myself and my ability. Despite the criticism coming from all quarters, I trusted the fact that my way of playing could be successful. And so I didn't just manage to win titles, I also developed as a person and left the golden cage, at least inwardly.

17

WORLD CHAMPIONS IN BRAZIL

A SUCCESSFUL CONCLUSION NEEDS PASSION AND DISCIPLINE

All of a sudden the other people around me are unimportant. I'm even ignoring the beeping on my mobile that that's telling me I've got a text. I don't want to look at the screen and get distracted right now. I want to hold on to this moment. Capture the impressions and simply enjoy this unbelievable beauty.

I'm standing on a rusty ferry, sailing over the João de Tiba, a river in Brazil, on the way to our World Cup base in Campo Bahia.

When we boarded LH 2014, the 'Fanhansa', in Frankfurt just before 10 p.m., to head to Brazil after our pre-tournament training, I knew that the World Cup was beginning. But I, at least, didn't feel immediately overwhelmed by emotion. We knew that the next few weeks would be a special time. We knew that soon the whole world would be watching us. But in the end this was just one of many, many, many flights we took each year. You take off, you eat, watch films, turn from left to right, from right to left, sleep and then land somewhere. This time in Salvador de Bahia, around 3.40 a.m. local time. A stopover. An airport like any other. Sometimes the plastic seats at the gate are green, sometimes grey, sometimes yellow, sometimes white. Sometimes comfortable, sometimes uncomfortable. I think that airports look the same all over the world. Not a surprise really, given the 600, 700 or 800 flights I've taken over my career so far.

Out of the plane, loiter around, back in the plane. Onward flight. Next stop: Porto Seguro. Another step closer to the World Cup. But still no knockout blow of emotion. The routine is far too mechanical for that. Gather your things, get up, out of the plane, into a bus. Onwards to the team base. After the long journey, even though it was very comfortable, you just long to finally get there, get into your room and collapse onto your bed.

But now we're suddenly on this ferry that's bringing us to our base. None of the players has stayed on the bus. We're all outside enjoying the air that somehow smells different than in Germany. The engine of the ancient ferry is rattling loudly, startling a few birds in the mangrove forest. A few crabs have smuggled themselves onto the boat as stowaways, and are hiding beneath rusty iron girders. The sun is shining golden on the river.

We pass colourfully painted fishing boats with blue, green and yellow stripes. Trees with gigantic roots hang in the water.

I've rarely been so overcome by my feelings. This glimpse of the Brazilian jungle reminds me of my African safari and the sense of freedom I experienced there. 'It's the World Cup. Now it's the World Cup. We're here,' I think.

Our set-up is perfect. Not just in the camp. There are technical innovations too. For example the German Football Association provides us with software that we all have installed on our mobiles. This allows the players to do some homework on our forthcoming opponents from the comfort of our rooms. Just a few clicks and I know the strengths and weaknesses of my counterpart. I can get as much information on him as I need. I can look at him as often as I think is right.

Our World Cup motto, which the coaching team is fostering by example, goes, 'A good start requires enthusiasm. A good finish discipline.' And so we, too, start the tournament brimming with enthusiasm. Against a Portugal team containing Pepe, Coentrão, Nani and of course Ronaldo.

Cristiano has the first chance early on in the match, but Manuel Neuer saves the shot. Then Mario Götze is brought down in the penalty area. Pereira could only stop him by grabbing and pulling him. Thomas Müller scores the ensuing penalty as cool as a cucumber.

I feel good. Toni Kroos plays me a dream pass that I take in the Portuguese box. Götze comes running from behind; he's in a better position than me so I give him the ball. But his shot is just deflected, otherwise it would certainly have gone in.

Soon after, however, a header from Mats Hummels makes it 2–0. And then the great Thomas Müller Show continues. First he powers through the Portuguese defence and scores our third, then he steals another goal to make it 4–0. A hat-trick in our opening game.

A match like that can inspire you. A successful first game gives you self-confidence and a sense of ease. It means that our plan has worked and we don't have to ask too many questions of our performance.

We have a tougher time of it in our second game against Ghana, however, even trailing 2–1 for a while, before we eke out a 2–2 draw. In the final group fixture we beat the USA 1–0 and claim a place in the last 16.

There Algeria put up an inexplicable fight. We really have our work cut out and don't manage to win the game in normal time. If we hadn't had Manuel Neuer on our team, who, as so often in this tournament, puts in another sterling performance, there could have been a debacle.

But we don't give up. Two minutes after the start of extra time André Schürrle scores with his left heel. In the 119th minute I make it 2–0. From 5 metres I slam the ball so hard at the goal that keeper Raïs M'Bolhi can't get his hands up quickly enough and it fizzes in between the heads of Madjid Bougherra and Essaïd Belkalem. A case of millimetres. Thank goodness, for in the last minute of extra time Algeria's Abdelmoumene Djabou actually scores to make it 2–1.

The international press crucifies us. 'In 120 minutes Germany forfeited any status it might have as a favourite for the World Cup,' the Brazilian paper *O Globo* writes. The *Neue Zürcher Zeitung* says, 'The favourite teeters, but doesn't fall.' And the Swiss *Tages-Anzeiger* comes to the conclusion, 'With hair-raising mistakes in defence Germany almost skittled out of the World Cup. For now the good morale has gone.'

Right after the match Per Mertesacker has to do an interview with ZDF reporter Boris Büchler. His opening question is

'Congratulations on getting into the next round, the quarter-finals. Why was the German game so plodding, so vulnerable?' Per's reply and the interview as a whole have since attained cult status. 'I couldn't care less,' he answers back stroppily. 'We're now in the last eight and that's all that counts.'

An argument develops between a critical Büchler who keeps probing, and a Mertesacker who stands up to him. At some point Per asks, irritated, 'Do you think being in the last sixteen is like a carnival parade?' then finally finishes the interview with the words: 'What do you want? Do you want us to be successful in the World Cup or play beautifully and be knocked out again? I ... I just don't understand all these questions. We've got through, we're really happy, we've given our all and we're now going to get ready for France.'

I thought Per's reaction was truly remarkable. I could never have been so quick-witted. Essentially these weren't bad questions and comments about the game. At another time, perhaps the following morning, Per would have probably answered them in a more relaxed way – I expect he would even have agreed with Büchler that we had to raise our game. But the timing of the question was clumsy. Just imagine that boxer Wladimir Klitschko is in a bout against David Haye. Each man is taking some heavy blows. Both are staggering. Either could find himself on the canvas with the next punch. The fight is wide open, nobody can pick the winner. At the last moment Klitschko manages a final upwards hook and sends Haye to the floor. Shouldn't the first question to him be how he managed to land that last fantastic punch? Instead of talking about his weak defence?

For 120 minutes against Algeria we were on the verge of being knocked out. The opposition players demanded everything of us. And made it far more difficult than we'd expected. Of course it came as a surprise. Of course the game wasn't pretty to watch throughout. But when you've spent 120 minutes running, sliding, throwing yourself into tackles, even though your muscles are burning and already full of lactic acid, you don't want to have to talk first about the bad aspects of the game. Because however tense or close it was, we were in the quarter-finals. And in the end that's the only thing that counted.

In the next round, too, we have to dig incredibly deep against a French team featuring my friend Karim Benzema. We take an early lead with a header from Mats Hummels, but miss the chance to make it 2–0. Jogi Löw substitutes me in the 83rd minute to waste a bit of time.

From the coach's perspective this substitution is perfectly understandable. I'd never be so arrogant as to hold it against him. Especially as Jogi Löw and I have great trust in each other. For me he's more than a manager. He always has a sympathetic ear; even off the pitch he's an excellent listener. There are some people you only have professional contact with and nothing else. But with Jogi Löw it's different. Such as the time he paid me a visit in London. As I knew that he'd been a coach in Turkey, including with Fenerbahçe of Istanbul, I invited him out to my favourite Turkish restaurant, Likya. Löw was in his element, even ordering in Turkish. He still speaks the language remarkably well, albeit with a funny accent. That evening he downed Turkish tea by the litre.

Although I'm not his captain, I sense that Löw values my opinion. At this dinner he spoke to me about a number of young players, and wanted to know whether they might be of use to Germany. Whether I saw them as up-and-coming internationals. It's hard for me to evaluate the younger guys in the Bundesliga, however, because I don't see them play much and very rarely play against them.

When Jogi Löw takes me out of the France game there are still seven minutes to go. Seven minutes that which are pure agony for me although – or perhaps because – I spend lots of time on the pitch during this World Cup. In all seven matches I'm in the starting line-up, and in four of these I'm on the pitch for the entire game. But it drives me crazy that I can't make an active contribution any more. There's nothing worse for a footballer than to have to watch, unable to help your teammates. This sitting on the bench is almost torture. Especially during such a tense conclusion. Especially when the game's on a knife-edge. Of course, I've got 100 per cent faith in my teammates. Of course, I know the quality that each of them has. But you still want to get involved. You want to launch into tackles and stop attacks. Or put the result beyond doubt with another goal.

I love sitting in front of the telly. Or the games console. But I hate sitting on the bench in a situation like that. For from that vantage point I have to watch France make one last assault on our goal in the fourth minute of stoppage time. Laurent Koscielny, my Arsenal teammate, makes another pass towards our goal. It lands at the feet of Benzema, who, after a double pass with Olivier Giroud, suddenly appears unmarked in front of

Manuel Neuer. He gives the ball a crack with his left foot from 6 metres.

I hold my breath. Please, no extra time. I watched Benzema score 81 goals during our time together at Real Madrid. Thirteen of these were from his left foot. And these were only the ones in proper matches. He scored hundreds more in training. But at this instant it's not Germany against France; it's Benzema against Neuer. The ball flies towards Manuel as fast as an arrow, fired as hard as a cannonball. If I were him I'd probably try to duck for fear that the ball might knock me unconscious. But Manuel doesn't budge one millimetre. He stands there like a colossus. Legs splayed. Body fully tensed. Not a trace of fear or doubt. His eyes somehow locked onto the ball. And then he throws his right hand up. He manages to parry the ball and preserve our lead. The match is over and we're in the semi-final.

Where Brazil are waiting for us. The hosts. My friends have told me about the hype that's taken over the whole of Germany. They say that some companies, such as Volkswagen in Wolfsburg, have given their employees time off, for the duration of the game at least.

All the Brazilians are completely delirious too, of course. The drive in our coach to the stadium for the semi-final against the host nation is accompanied by nine police motorbikes and two police cars. A helicopter is flying above us. Our bus wiggles its way through a sea of green and yellow. Practically no one in the mass of people we pass is dressed normally. I see painted bodies, wigs, flags.

Our coach is easily recognisable as the German team bus. It's different from in London, where the Arsenal buses are indistinguishable from any other. Every English team travels to the stadium in an identical model, with no markings. From the outside it's impossible to tell which team is in which bus.

I always sit at the back. It's what I did at Real Madrid. It's what I do at Arsenal. And it's what I used to do in the school bus too. I'd always sit on the back seats.

I don't take much in on most journeys. I sit in my seat and listen to music. Or watch series. Some players are already in their own bubble on the bus, focusing on the match. Whereas I can still laugh at the jokes in the programmes I'm watching. I can still have fun. But I respect it if teammates are already going through their personal, individual routines of preparation. I leave them to do their thing in peace.

On the way to the semi-final I look out of the window more than usual. Because I'm fascinated by this play of green and yellow outside. In a similar situation at Real Madrid I would probably have thought of the Barcelona fans: 'You won't be celebrating tonight!' But the people here are just brilliant – what confidence and joy they're walking to the stadium with! It's amazing how every person bar none is completely behind their team. And the way they belt out the national anthem with their team before the game too. United like the biggest choir in the world. Even *I* get goose pimples.

It seems an eternity that I stand there, taking in this remarkable backdrop to the stadium. It's almost two minutes before the ref blows his whistle and Miroslav Klose, who's at the centre spot, can play the ball. In FIFA's strict schedule there's no provision for starting earlier, even if everyone's ready. In a tournament like this everything is timed to the second. Everything to ensure the perfect entertainment. The game kicks off at 5 p.m. precisely.

The Brazilians want to strike at us in the opening minutes of the game. They immediately drive into our half and win a corner after only 42 seconds. We're forewarned because our coaching staff have prepared for this. Brazil scored from a corner against both Chile and Colombia. One goal was by David Luiz, the other Thiago Silva, but he's missing from this evening's game, having collected two yellow cards. So is Neymar, the corner dangerman, who fractured a lumbar vertebra when he collided with the knee of Colombian Juan Zúñiga.

In the third minute Marcelo has a shot at our goal from 18 metres, but misses by a good metre. Then Müller gets the ball and crosses it to me from the right. Maicon hasn't noticed that I've slipped away from him and he can't get to the cross. From the corner of my eye I see Khedira racing forward and chip the ball to him. He whacks a drop kick, making perfect contact. It's only Toni Kroos's backside that prevents us from going into the lead.

The ball goes back and forth in the first few minutes. We sound things out. Check out what the opposition will allow us to do. Then something happens that no one can have expected. Brazil loses control of the game. Of their home fixture. Despite the support of the entire country. After 9 minutes and 40 seconds Hulk prances around a bit on the left, but shies away from a tackle by Philipp Lahm. He shifts responsibility, in the form of the ball, onto Marcelo, who passes it into no man's land, where

Sami Khedira snaps it up. From that moment the game is ours. And we don't give it back again.

In the eleventh minute we have a corner. Toni Kroos will take it, as he has in so many practice sessions over the past few weeks. Including the goalkeeper, there are nine Brazilians in the box. Only four of us are there. But the advantage we have is that we know exactly where each of us is about to move. We've got insider knowledge; the Brazilians can only react. We're now determining the rhythm of the game. Dominating the situation. If Toni's corner lands where it's supposed to, Thomas Müller will be there.

Miroslav Klose, Mats Hummels and Benedikt Höwedes come towards the ball. Not Müller. He takes a few steps in the opposite direction, but he's not followed by David Luiz who's marking him. I'm right on the edge of the area in case the ball is knocked out or Thomas doesn't get to it.

Corners are a bit like chess, only with lots of pieces being moved at the same time. If all the moves work perfectly, it's checkmate, i.e. a goal. As happens at that moment in Belo Horizonte.

No German has ever scored a goal against Brazil at a World Cup before. The only meeting between the two sides came at the 2002 final, which Germany lost 2–0.

Now Müller scores. Then, between the twenty-third and twenty-sixth minute – or within the space of 178 seconds, to be precise – Miroslav Klose gets a goal and Toni Kroos scores twice.

It's the most unbelievable period of play I've experienced on a football field. Every one of our passes works. Every run is perfect. Every idea is a stroke of genius. We surpass ourselves with every successful play we make. At the same time we rob the Brazilians of every last speck of self-confidence. Each one of us wants the ball because he has a plan. None of the Brazilians want the ball because they're too afraid of making a mistake.

You might expect such dominance if a full-strength Real Madrid side were playing against a ninth-division XI. But not here. I still can't explain why this semi-final should go the way it does. I don't know what it was that intimidated and unsettled the Brazilians so much. These great footballers with their individual class. Was Neymar's absence so decisive? Or was he playing around in their minds too much? At any rate, before the anthems Luiz and César lifted his shirt up into the air. One online journalist from the *Daily Telegraph* commented during the game, 'It's like Brazil have been shot with tranquiliser darts.'

I find the whole thing unreal. Surely it can't be true. After Toni's second goal I look up at the scoreboard and really do see four goals for us and none for the Brazilians. After less than half an hour's play. That's never happened before in World Cup history. In none of the – as I read later – 832 encounters since 1930.

Later David Luiz said he thought he was stuck in a nightmare from which he was desperate to wake up.

When I look around I see the first Brazilians leaving the stadium in despair. At a throw-in I'm standing right on the touchline looking at a man with tear-stained eyes. The make-up he'd painted flags on his cheeks with has smeared. I feel sorry for him. As I do for the country as a whole, this united sea of tears that in the end has to digest a 7–1 defeat. We destroyed their dream of a title. Every goal was a stab in the heart of this proud nation with their great reputation and their samba football that had inspired all visiting nations. A German 'machine' had steam-rolled the helpless Brazilian national side in four minutes.

Of course, I was proud and delighted that we'd made it to the final. But the dominance with which we humiliated the Brazilians was a historic annihilation. An annihilation this country hadn't deserved. I felt I had to compensate somehow for the fact that we'd destroyed their World Cup dream in such a way. I wanted to express the true feeling that many of us had. In a short message, 140 characters long, which would be irrevocable; nobody would be able to change it. And so I tweeted, 'You have a beautiful country, wonderful people and amazing footballers – this match may not destroy your pride! #Brasil'.

It was a message from the heart that I really wanted to get out. It was a collective feeling, a truth with which I spoke to many people from the soul. More than 92,000 people liked my tweet and more than 124,000 retweeted it, which meant that my message, which I'd written in English, became the most viewed tweet of the year.

The most remarkable thing was the reaction of the Brazilians we met on our way back to Campo Bahia. No trace of hatred. No outrage that we'd thrashed their team. In spite of their sadness at having been knocked out, they were good losers and showed us respect. From time to time, but rarely, you're confronted by contempt from fans of teams you've beaten. But we felt none of this in Brazil.

On the flight back Wolfgang Niersbach, president of the German Football Association, grabbed the microphone and spoke to us: 'It's no exaggeration to say this is a historic result. In the years and decades to come you can say to your children, when you have them, and your grandchildren, that on 8 July 2014, in Belo Horizonte: I was there. In ten, twenty, thirty years' time people will still be asking: How was that possible?'

It's lovely to be admired from all sides. And, of course, I felt flattered to hear such words. But at that moment, deep down, I couldn't really care less about them. For amongst all the euphoria there was one thing we mustn't forget. We'd only won a semi-final. We may well have done it in unforgettable fashion, but I didn't want to tell my children about a 7–1 victory in a semi-final. At some point I wanted to tell my children about winning the World Cup. What it feels like to have that golden trophy in your hands.

What use would it have been to enjoy this moment and feel like king of the hill if five days later there was a renewed discussion about the German loser's gene? About us sissies? About the generation that can't win a title? Up until the semi-final against Spain in 2010 we'd also earned lots of respect for our performances. But Spain won then.

That's why I blocked out Niersbach's words – for the time being, at least. Jogi Löw and his team also impressed on us that we hadn't achieved anything yet. And that's exactly how we continued to work until the final. No training session was casual. Nobody was arrogant or thought of settling back for even a second.

Although the 7–1 victory helped us go into the training sessions with great confidence, it didn't take away our sense of reality.

When we leave the team base at 1.50 p.m. on 13 July 2014 to go to the Maracanã stadium for the final against Argentina, the feeling is somehow different from usual. Nervousness would be the wrong word. I think that the people in the stands, the players on the bench, the presenters and journalists are more nervous than we are for a final like that. I really believe that none of us players was properly nervous. Because nervousness is not a good companion. You can't go into a final feeling nervous.

You have to go into a final in the knowledge that no millimetre is too far. That no tackle is unimportant. That no slide is unnecessary. That it's important to remain positive and be there for your teammates. And of course you must be absolutely convinced that you can win the game.

Nonetheless more thoughts than usual flashed in my mind that day. Things like, 'Today you could become a legend.' You want to banish these thoughts and keep them out of your head. You want to stay cool, but you can't. The coach journey seems longer than normal. You're brimming with vitality, you can barely control your energy, so great is the desire to start running around, passing and shooting. On the bus you feel locked in. Cooped up between seats.

Because Jogi Löw doesn't let us use mobiles in the dressing room I write my mum a text from the coach. 'Pray for me to stay fit and for us to win.' Seconds later, as if she'd had her phone in her hand, just waiting to hear from me, she writes back, 'Mesut, I always pray for you. Before each game. We love you. You'll do it.' And then she sent a smiley.

When we're sitting in the dressing room it's louder than any other I've been in throughout my career. The 74,738 spectators are making a noise that penetrates underground. Even with the door closed we can hear the singing and chanting. It's faint, but it still finds its way into our changing room.

You feel so hot because of the atmosphere in the Maracanã that it's barely necessary to warm up. In an adjacent room I play keepy uppy with Per Mertesacker and Julian Draxler. In bare feet. Just a bit of fun before the big showdown.

There are people who denied we had the necessary will for success as a national side. They thought we weren't mature enough to win the biggest title of them all.

Anybody who looked into the eyes of the German players that day would know that such claims are utter rubbish.

When I'm on the pitch, a few seconds before kick-off in the most important game of my life, I feel like the little Mesut. Like the boy who was once addicted to playing football every day in the Monkey Cage, as our pitch in Gelsenkirchen was called. Who in the mornings at school would look forward to playing with his mates in the afternoon. Who would forget the time and the fact that he was hungry. Who didn't care what the weather was like and if the pitch was the right length. Who just wanted to play and win. Without any pressure or obligations, simply for the fun of it.

I love this feeling of being carefree. Because it makes every game so simple. So relaxed. Luckily it stayed with me the entire match. I felt free the whole time. Never under pressure for a second. I wasn't thinking that I had to prove something to the world. I wasn't thinking about having players like Lionel Messi opposite me. I didn't worry about the skills of this exceptional footballer.

Manuel Neuer is in the form of his life. Benedikt Höwedes defends brilliantly. Jérôme Boateng is always in the right position. Mats Hummels gives us security. Philipp Lahm exudes calmness and confidence. Bastian Schweinsteiger fights like a lion who's been wounded but refuses to die. Toni Kroos always knows what to do with the ball. Although Christoph Kramer doesn't realise it, he plays a really important role until he's substituted. Thomas Müller makes Argentina tremble. Miroslav Klose gets completely stuck in.

Everyone on the pitch is playing the game of his life. When André Schürrle crosses to Mario Götze in the 113th minute I immediately get the feeling that something magical is about to happen. Mario chests the ball down, strikes with his left foot and scores the all-deciding goal. 1–0 to us.

I still can't really explain what happens then. At the moment when the whistle blows I'm completely overwhelmed. Players in blue jerseys collapse onto the ground, burying their faces in the grass. Men in white shirts fall to the ground too, but these do it for joy. Because the fact that they've won has bowled them over emotionally.

I can't remember what I did. Who I hugged when. What I said to whom. All I know is that everything is spinning. I want to shout and cry. I never want this moment to end. Pelé, the Brazilian legend, once said, 'Without the Maracanã I would not be the person I am.' Without the Maracanã none of us would be what we are today – the first European team to win the World Cup in South America.

I'd really like to find the right words to describe what it feels like to lift the golden trophy in the air. But I can't. Because this feeling is so strong that you can't describe it in words, or at least I can't.

That night chaos reigns inside my head, albeit a nice chaos. One moment you're still standing on the pitch, the next you have a medal put around your neck, and the next moment Philipp Lahm is lifting the cup into the night and a firework display erupts into life above us.

So much happens that my head can't process all these moments all at once.

Suddenly Michel Platini is standing in front of me. I don't have a clue where he's come from. Three years in a row, from 1983 to 1985, Platini was European Footballer of the Year. With Juventus he won virtually every title going. 'I don't take the shirt from every player,' Platini says that evening to me. 'But I'd love to have yours. It would be an honour.'

When such a great footballer asks for your jersey, you give it to him. Platini's words were probably the biggest compliment I've been paid in my career. It was an expression of respect, just between the two of us. A really intimate moment.

For this I was happy to risk more criticism from some quarters in the media. Because I'm the only German player in the World Champions team photo standing there bare-chested, some people thought I was trying to show off my muscles. Total nonsense. When I get my first feel of the cup, strange thoughts enter my head. Why is it smaller than the cup given to the Champions League winners? At 73.5 centimetres, the silver

Champions League trophy is almost twice as tall and considerably heavier. But I don't actually care about the answer, and the question vanishes as quickly as it arrived.

I don't yet know what it feels like for parents when they hold their baby in their arms for the first time, unfortunately. Up till now my only experience has been the emotional feeling of holding my nieces Mira and Lina for the first time. I think that I handled the World Cup trophy with the same care as I had my two nieces. All I thought was, 'It's beautiful.'

The coach ride back to the hotel, the party and the flight back to Germany pass by in a flash. We keep bawling the same songs. Do high fives. Take souvenir photos of the cup. But I don't grasp what it really means to be World Champions until we drive through the streets of Berlin and celebrate by the Brandenburg Gate. I'd never imagined that we could delight so many people with our play. That we could have put so many people in a good mood, having given them such euphoria, satisfaction and happiness. On that day we get smiles from many, many people.

Once I was at a Michael Jackson concert. I admired the perfection with which he staged his show and choreography. The audience went crazy and cheered him with a passion that was infectious. After the concert I wondered what it must feel like to stand up there on the stage and experience this adulation.

Well, I did experience it in Berlin. This moment was worth everything. Every tough training session. Every severe dressing-room bollocking. Every harsh criticism. The hassle with the Turkish authorities over a document. Every whistle. Every critical comment.

For all those things had meant that today I was able to stand on this stage with these wonderful people. It was a feeling I wanted to savour again in the summer of 2016. To soak up this football euphoria once more, and experience again the feeling of belonging to a tight-knit group. The admiration.

We could have become European champions. We were the best team in France. We managed to knock out our nemesis, Italy. And in the semi-final we played really great football.

After half an hour the French were spiritless, on the verge of collapse. It didn't matter whether it was Griezmann, Giroud or Pogba – all of them were panting like horses that have had to draw a plough across a field without water. When I ran past them I heard them breathing loudly like I'd virtually never heard before in a footballer. They were gasping for air, as if their heads had been held under water for a minute. We were doing lots and lots of things right. We were on the way to creating a bit of history.

But sometimes even doing lots and lots of things right isn't enough. The penalty scored by Griezmann seconds before the half-time whistle breathed life back into the tottering French team. They recovered themselves in the dressing room and gathered new energy. So much so that in the end they beat us 2–0. After the match Giroud, himself in disbelief, asked me what we were doing to them in the first half. After we were knocked out I howled like a little child, because this defeat hurt unbearably. We had to be European champions in 2016. We'd had such a big chance.

On the flight back I barely said a word. From Frankfurt I immediately jumped on the next plane to Los Angeles. Once again an escape. Once again I put my mobile well away. I didn't want to read any reassuring texts, or hear any sympathy. Nobody would have been able to find the right words.

I didn't watch the final. I didn't want to watch two teams – both of which I'm sure we could have beaten – play each other. In 2016 we squandered a great opportunity. But it wasn't a one-off. This German team still has sufficient quality to take the European title. It'll come in 2020, I'm convinced of it. Just as I'm sure that my personal collection of trophies at club level is not yet finished.

I've won titles in three countries. Won the Spanish league with the greatest club in the world. And I've won the biggest trophy you can possibly win as a footballer. Does that mean I'm content with my tally of trophies so far? No! Because it could have been more. I absolutely want to win the Premier League title. I absolutely want to hold the Champions League trophy in my hands.

But most of all I want to feel the magic of this wonderful game of football as often as I can.

18

ARSENAL

THE TOUGHEST CHALLENGE

I'm 28 years old now. I've played in Germany, Spain and England. I've taken something from each of these countries and soaked up experiences from each club. I've learned to cope with setbacks. I've learned by watching how the biggest stars in the world prepare for games. Germany has given me a lot. Spain has enriched me in an incredible way. But it's been during my time in London that I've learned one of the most important lessons of all: how to be a real man.

The Premier League is the toughest challenge I've experienced in football so far. If you can't take it here – and without whining – then you're history. It's something I had to get to grips with in the first few weeks and months after my switch from Real Madrid.

Whereas in Spain the entire game is based on elegant ball play – even in the teams from lower leagues – in England you have scratching, biting and fighting to contend with. In England, football is one tackle after another. There's barely any respite. The next opponent is already at your feet.

Generally, this doesn't happen in Spain because the ball is

constantly on the move. Pass – pass – pass – pass – pass. The opponent rarely has the opportunity to intervene because the ball is already on the other side of the pitch. Sometimes in England you fail to notice how hard it is during the game itself and how many attacks the body sustains. You're so full of adrenalin that you don't feel the pain. But then, under the shower, you discover the 'misery'. After some matches my shins have looked as if someone has gone at them with a hammer – covered in blue marks.

I've had scratches on the neck and bruises on my back, shoulders and chest – from opponents' elbows welcoming me into the Premier League when the referee wasn't watching. Some opponents also gave me a right earful on the pitch soon after my move from Spain. I'd never heard anything like it before. Nowhere is there as much chit-chat as in England. There are some players who are permanently rabbiting on. And of course it's not exactly friendly stuff. For example, after I'd been brutally brought to the ground in one of my first encounters, the opponent hissed, 'It's not Real Madrid. We're not in La Liga.' And as my new best friend turned away he muttered a clearly audible, 'Come on, get up boy,' with a malicious grin.

In an attempt to fight back I'd go running to the ref to begin with and try to 'work' him. Every player does it. We all try to influence the referee verbally, to raise his awareness if we're worried about getting hurt. We complain so that the next time he'll watch more carefully and spot if we're kicked or elbowed. I do this just like Franck Ribéry, Arjen Robben or Lionel Messi – all players who get kicked a lot because opponents are trying to disrupt their rhythm. And because sometimes it's the only way to stop them.

But, to my great surprise, I was forced to realise that even the English referees have their very own form of communication. In my early days at Arsenal they dismissed my appeals in a way that made me think I'd misheard them. They'd say things such as 'Don't whinge. You've got to deal with it. Welcome to the Premier League.'

Sledging from the opposition. Cutting comments from refs. And football that's harder than anywhere else – that's the Premier League. That's English football. And that's the football I've got used to and love today.

At Arsenal I've grown tougher. I've learned to take so much more. I've toned a few more muscles than during my time at Real Madrid so I'm in a better position to meet the physical challenges. But it's a very fine line. I wouldn't gain anything from spending hours on the bench, wildly pumping iron. If I were too muscular I'd be less nimble and sprightly. I reckon I've put on about a kilo and a half of muscle mass. Enough to survive the physical batterings, but not so much that I'm too brawny to run.

Otherwise I haven't changed that much as a player – partly on the advice of Robert Pirès, the Arsenal legend, who has become a close friend. Between 2000 and 2006 he won the Premiership title twice with the Gunners. In 2002 he was chosen as the best player in England. After his career he often looked in on Arsenal, even training with the injured players sometimes, so I got the chance to get to know him better. Over the years he has become more than a friend. He's an advisor, a confidant – someone I can discuss problems with and whose opinion is incredibly important to me.

When the media started having a go at me again, demanding that I become more selfish and score more goals myself, I asked him what he thought. I wanted to know if he judged these criticisms to be correct. He encouraged me to stick to my way of playing. 'Let them say what they like,' he said. 'You've got a unique style. You're not like Ronaldo. You're different. You see spaces that barely any other player does. You can read a game. Trust in your extraordinary ability and don't adjust your game merely because this is what outsiders are telling you to do.'

It did me the world of good to hear this assessment from him. Pirès has been a European and World Champion, as well as contesting a Champions League final. He knows what he's talking about. And he's honest. He's not someone who tells me what I want to hear and doesn't dare criticise me. Quite the opposite. After poor performances I had to listen to him say quite a lot, which I value enormously, and which is why he'll always be an important person in the background for me.

When I got an offer from China in the summer of 2016, however, I didn't need his advice. Because the offer was too absurd. The Chinese were prepared to pay me 100 million euros net over a period of five years. A fairy-tale amount of money that went beyond the limits of my imagination.

In spite of this it took me less than three minutes to decline the offer. My agent, Erkut, called me to let me know about the bid. He told me the name of the club and the amount. 'I think we're agreed what we're going to do, aren't we?,' he said over the phone,

'I just wanted to inform you that the offer's been made. It's my job. You won't consider it, will you?' Of course he was spot on with his supposition. 'I'm nowhere near the end of my career,' I replied. 'I still want to win titles with Arsenal. The Premiership – at least. I don't want to play in China no matter how much they're willing to pay. No way.'

And so the matter was settled. In the knowledge, by the way, that Chinese President Xi Jinping is a fan of mine. On one occasion Arsenal's managing director came to tell us that the president had contacted the club asking for my jersey with a dedication. In fact he wanted a Germany shirt, which of course Arsenal couldn't help out with. We promised to sort it out and that same day a courier picked up the shirt from my house.

Recently I was also asked for one of my jerseys by the daughter of Dennis Bergkamp, a legend who left his stamp on London over a period of 11 years. She said she's a big fan of mine – and of course I granted her wish. It is also these little things – the support both loud and quiet – that make me feel very happy at Arsenal. The two club photographers, David and Stuart, are part of my circle of friends, which is highly unusual. I've never allowed photographers at any other club to get so close to me or trusted them as much.

At the start of the year I went with Josh Kroenke, the son of our owner Stanley Kroenke, to watch an NBA game between the Denver Nuggets and Indiana Pacers that was taking place in London. We sat next to each other and were completely on the same wavelength. And I find the same is true with my team-mates, which is the most important thing of all. At the beginning of every training session we play rondo, an exercise where five players on the outside pass the ball to each other while two in the middle try to win it – the whole thing is played in as small an area as possible and the aim is to pass as rapidly as you can. At Arsenal it's generally the same seven of us who play it. In my group, if everyone's fit, are Alexis Sánchez, Theo Walcott, Gabriel Paulista, Per Mertesacker, Alex Oxlade-Chamberlain and Aaron Ramsey.

They are a great bunch of guys and we have huge amount of fun with this exercise. I take particular pleasure in annoying Aaron Ramsey. When I play the ball to him for the first time I pass it so it bobbles and is difficult for him to pass on. Or I make an especially weak pass so that our opponents in the middle have a better chance to intercept the ball when Ramsey tries to pass it. And he tries to do the same with me. Sometimes you need a bit of amusement like this. It makes training more fun and of course players should be able to have a laugh during the hard and highly focused work.

At the end of every session I usually stay out with Shkodran Mustafi for a little shooting competition. We take turns to stand at the edge of the box and get one of our goalies to throw us the ball. We then have a maximum of two contacts to take the ball and shoot it back at the goal. I usually win this shooting duel, and so I'll shout across the pitch, 'What? We paid Valencia 41 million for him? Why?' Mind you, if he wins he doesn't hold back with his comments about me.

As far as preparation for matches or announcing the line-up are concerned, Arsène Wenger doesn't particularly differ from my previous coaches. He won't tell us the formation until the day of the game. But there are two things that mark him out.

First, I've never practised set pieces so frequently and intensively with any other manager before. It's one of Wenger's passions. He places great importance on trying out free kicks and corners. Again and again and again he gets us to practise all manner of variations.

Second, he's the most gentlemanly coach I've ever played under. When he comes into the dressing room in the morning he shakes everybody's hand. A firm handshake and he'll look you in the eye. If he happens to miss a player and see him for the first time on the ground, the personal greeting will take place there. In winter he even takes off his gloves before shaking hands.

I actually think that every club should have a morning routine like this. I like it when people show their respect for each other. But the manager's handshake is not usual; Wenger's the odd one out here. It was not for nothing that at the beginning of the year in an interview for the German football magazine, *Kicker*, I emphasised what an important figure Wenger has been in my life. He watched me for years, followed my progress, then hired and nurtured me. He is entitled to criticise me in any way he likes. He can throw anything at me if I've played poorly. Because what he says is important. Because he's good at getting things into perspective.

Even the devastating loss against FC Bayern in February 2017 – obviously a very painful chapter in my time at Arsenal. This dreadful 5–1 defeat is undoubtedly one of the darkest hours of my footballing career. It's in the top five of the most humiliating defeats I've suffered. Our failure in the Munich Allianz Arena is almost as difficult to bear as the semi-final loss in the 2016 European Championship. As unacceptable as the Clásico calamity against Barcelona in my first year at Real Madrid. It hurts as much as losing with Germany in the 2010 semi-final against Spain in South Africa, or two years later in the European Championship against Italy, also in the semi-final.

In truth, we were positively prepared for the game. On the Monday before the match Arsène Wenger had revealed to us in London his game plan against the German record-holders. His talk lasted ten minutes. It was short and sweet, but he was very clear about his ideas – and they were good ones. Our intention was to go all out for Bayern's central defender Mats Hummels, to prevent him from opening up the game, which he does so brilliantly. We wanted to force him to play the ball to Javi Martínez, who's also a fine central defender, but whose greatest strength isn't opening up the game. In this way we hoped we'd be able to stop Bayern from building up the play at an early stage and disrupt their rhythm.

Wenger also warned us about Douglas Costa and his speed over the first 5 to 10 metres, as well as Arjen Robben. Of course, I could go on and on writing why our game plan didn't work. I could look for excuses. But I'm not going to. What went on between us in the dressing room after the match is nobody's business. Nor is what Arsène Wenger considered our failures to be in his post-match analysis. The fact is: we all failed. We were all bad! We played a game that held a mirror up to our faces. It was a performance we can't just brush aside. No, we have to learn our lessons from it. We all have to ask searching questions of ourselves and accept responsibility for the defeat. All the players, all the trainers, even the club management. Because this fiasco also represents a great opportunity!

When we lost with Real Madrid to Barcelona, José Mourinho said – and I've already mentioned this in the book – 'Forget the game… Don't think about it any more. I'm sure we're going to break Barcelona's dominance in this country. I'm sure we're going to be champions. But we won't do it if we allow this defeat to get on top of us.'

That's how we have to deal with it now too. I have thought long and hard about the match. I've visualised what went wrong. But I can't allow this game to inhibit me in the future and destroy my confidence, which is the most important thing a footballer can have on the field. This defeat mustn't get the better of any of us.

In my footballing life I've often fallen flat on my face and been knocked to the ground. But I've always got up again and won victories and titles following the defeat. In spite of the disappointments with Germany in South Africa and Poland and Ukraine, we became World Champions. In spite of the humiliation at the hands of Barcelona we won the Spanish league with Real Madrid. And this defeat by Bayern Munich will produce something good at the end too. It has left me with a little scar. But nothing more. Just like the scornful sledging I received at the start of my adventure in England and the blue marks on my shins and the bruises on my torso, it has made me tougher, harder-nosed and better able to take what's thrown at me.

And I'm going to prove it!

EPILOGUE

DANKE SCHÖN, TEŞEKKÜRLER, GRACIAS, THANK YOU

The photo of Mrs Merkel and me, which was taken in the dressing room at the Berlin Olympic stadium in 2010, still hangs in my office in Königsallee in Düsseldorf. It's where I keep the few souvenirs that are really important to me. I'm not someone who puts everything on show. My house is London isn't full of football things. In fact there's nothing on display. It was like that in Madrid too. No collection of jerseys. No cups. I don't feel the need to show my visitors how brilliant I am, all the people I know and all the places I've played football. I have an aversion to that. Quite apart from the fact that I don't own that many shirts. I've never asked a player for his shirt after the game's over. I'm not the type. I don't want to annoy anyone. It wouldn't mean much to me anyway.

I might have made an exception for Zinédine Zidane, because this man was a footballing legend and the player I most admire. If I'd ever had the fortune to play against him I'd have definitely asked for his shirt. But only his. Otherwise the jerseys I have are mostly mine. My collection includes my complete kit from my first game for Schalke, as well as those from my debuts with Bremen, Real Madrid and Arsenal. And of course a kit from each of the tournaments I've played for Germany. I've also got a shirt from Cristiano Ronaldo that he signed for me when I left Madrid, as well as one from Sergio Ramos, on which he wrote in Spanish, 'For my brother. All the best. It was great playing in a team with you. Yours, Sergio.'

In November 2010, almost exactly a month after that legendary match between Germany and Turkey, I'm on a plane from Madrid to Berlin. After ten rounds of matches Real are top of the table. I'm bursting with confidence. In our recent 2–0 victory over Atlético Madrid I scored from a free kick. In the first ten games of the season I've managed five assists and three goals. And yet, at this precise moment, I feel tiny and my confidence has vanished. I'm about to give a speech live on television.

I shift fretfully in my seat. Again and again I rehearse in my head the words I'm going to say. My hands are sweaty with nerves and so the notes on my crib sheet are smeared. I have to jot them down again halfway through the flight.

I'm not the sort of bloke to make big speeches. I've never enjoyed being the centre of attention and talking in front of others. It doesn't suit me, and it probably never will. There are people who are born orators. Who can enter a sitting room at a birthday party, open their mouth and within seconds the assembled company is hanging on their every word because they can make what they say sound so exciting. I admire these people. But I don't think it's a great tragedy that this is not one of my strengths.

Especially not on that November day in 2010. From Berlin airport it's a limousine ride to Potsdam. 'Just please listen to it again, Mutlu,' I implore my brother, who must have heard my thank-you speech at least 20 times. And now a twenty-first and twenty-second time on the 40-minute drive.

Hubert Burda Media has invited us to the Bambi awards in the Babelsberg Metropolis Halle. The event is being held for the 62nd time. This evening I'm going to be one of the prize-winners.

Sarah Jessica Parker, the *Sex and the City* actress, is presenting the evening. The fashion designer Karl Lagerfeld is one of the guests. Orlando Bloom, the English actor who played Will Turner in *Pirates of the Caribbean*, is also here. I can see the drummer, Udo Lindenberg and the actress and singer, Barbara Schöneberger. The pop star Shakira, who was on the same plane to South Africa as me and the rest of the German squad, is also here. Later she'll sing the World Cup song 'Waka Waka'.

So many interesting people. But instead of talking to them I stick to my brother and agent, who are accompanying me. Even now I'm particularly annoyed that I missed the chance of chatting to Jane Goodall, who was also at the Bambis.

Before that evening I didn't know that she was a world-famous primatologist. But since then I've seen lots of her films. As I've said, I'm a complete documentary junkie. I love them and am continually watching films about the lives of chimpanzees, crocodiles and elephants or about the journeys made by whales and penguins. I've seen Goodall's films from the ancient forests of Tanzania, where she lived with and studied chimpanzees. I'm sure it would have been fascinating to get first-hand information from her.

Hannah Herzsprung won the best actress award. Best actor went to Florian David Fitz for his film *Vincent will Meer (Vincent Wants to Sea)*. I hear 800 guests laugh at a joke from comedian Michael Mittermeier. But I don't take in what he's said. The evening is going over my head. I'm only vaguely aware when people applaud. In my mind I'm already up on the stage, giving my thanks to people. The spotlights are flickering through the hall. My tie, which I only managed to get the right length after 20 attempts, is choking me. I keep taking sips from my water glass because I feel as if my throat's drying up. How am I supposed to speak with a dry mouth? When my brother spots me reaching for the bottle again to refill my glass, he chuckles. 'Calm down,' he says. 'You'll be fine.' But instead of calming down I really need the loo.

Then Nazan Eckes gets up on the stage. Now it's serious. I have another quick glug of water. 'I was born in Cologne. My parents are Turkish,' she begins. She talks of feeling that she has arrived in Germany. Describes the country as her 'home'. The country has given her opportunities that she'd never have got elsewhere.

I don't take in the rest of what Nazan says either. My heart is thumping so loudly that I can hear every beat. I see her mouth open and close on the stage. The odd smile. And the odd thoughtful expression. I only discovered what she actually said when I watched clips from the event on YouTube.

'This summer,' Eckes continues, 'a man with German and Turkish roots has shown us how nimble and straightforward integration can be. World Cup star: Mesut Özil. The Turkish national side wanted him too. We really wanted him. But for

Mesut Özil it was always clear. He grew up in Germany, he went to school here. His friends live here. So he plays for Germany. And yet all of us – Germans and Turks – are proud of him. When Mesut Özil led the German team into the World Cup semi-final, German pubs and Turkish tea houses were cheering him on. Both Germans and Turks think it's great that he immediately became a regular at Real Madrid amongst the best in the world. And the few on either side who are still confused, and want to claim Mesut Özil for themselves alone, are pretty much out on their own. They're consistently put in the shade by the sheer joy felt by the majority. For once one of the major tabloids was right when it wrote, "We need lots more Özils." Until that day comes let's be happy that we have the one Özil!'

I think she's said my name. Or at least I imagine that she has said 'Mesut Özil'. I glance at Mutlu, who gives me a smile and a nod. While I take another couple of swigs of water they play a clip. It declares me a model of successful integration in Germany. And the voice says, 'No matter where you come from – everyone's proud of this captivating team. Mesut Özil, the exceptional sportsman. His uninhibited embracing of his Turkish roots and the German football shirt is an example to us all.'

Anybody watching on TV how I get up a few seconds later, walk towards the stage and button up my jacket, might think I'm calmness personified. I have to walk up six steps to stand beside Nazan Eckes. Six little steps, each one of which is a mini-conquest. The Özil who comes out of the players' tunnel is like a brave lion ready to chase the ball. The Özil who climbs up on this stage is no better than a timid kitten.

Thankfully Nazan, with her natural manner, immediately puts me at ease. She grabs my left arm to give me support and let me know that she's with me. Everything is fine. After she's given me the Bambi she blows me another kiss.

The people in the room get to their feet and give me a standing ovation. They applaud. All of a sudden the sound is no longer muffled; I'm hearing it as it really is. I see the happiness in people's faces. The smiles of weightlifter and Olympic gold medallist Matthias Steiner, for example. It feels similar to scoring a goal and hearing the fans cheer in the stadium.

'First of all I'd like to thank you for this special honour,' I hear myself say. The words are tumbling out of my mouth as if by themselves. 'I'm very happy. Integration means becoming part of the whole. Participating without losing your own identity. Integration means mutual respect – this is particularly important. Integration leads to something new, a more colourful Federal Republic of Germany. Danke schön. Teşekkürler. Gracias. Thank you.'

My thank-you speech lasted 32 seconds. I stalled very briefly once, but I don't think anybody noticed. Then I'd done it. It's a crazy feeling getting off the stage with this prize. I'm proud of it, even though I should say that Sami Khedira deserved the Bambi just as much as me. His mother is German and his father Tunisian. They met in Hammamet, northern Tunisia. But, like me, Sami was born in Germany and grew up in a town called Fellbach-Oeffingen, somewhere in Baden-Württemberg. He is no less integrated than me.

I didn't speak for long or say much at the Bambis. But I thought about my words very carefully. I didn't just recite some nice-sounding phrases – I chose words I believed in, and still do.

Integration is a good thing. Integration is important. I wish that integration could always be like our World Cup semi-final in 2014, when we beat Brazil 7–1. We played in perfect harmony. Each pass worked. Our game wasn't impeded by egoism, but inspired by togetherness. That's how it needs to work in society too, no matter where your fellow-citizens come from. Together it always works.

ACKNOWLEDGEMENTS

I don't think that grand words are always needed to express thanks. I know that I wouldn't have got anywhere without the help, trust and support of many people. If I had the choice and it were possible, I'd love to have a game with these 22 people in 'my' Monkey Cage. In the place where it all began. Where I fell in love with football in a fun, carefree way. On the – for me – most beautiful football pitch in the world. Even though it was just a mix of cinder and gravel, fenced in by metal bars. On this bumpy surface, 50 or 60 paces long, and perhaps 30 wide. Where the ball never went out, but just bounced back. Where we were afraid of falling in winter because you'd graze your hands on the frozen ground. Where I – and this is no exaggeration – scored at least 3,000 goals in the 12 years I played football on this pitch in Olgastrasse in Gelsenkirchen.

I don't care who's on what team. It's not important who plays in which position. Who wins is beside the point. It would be a very special friendly match. With 22 other people who are very, very important to me. Thank you for everything! I'm incredibly grateful.

Yours, Mesut.

PHOTOGRAPHIC ACKNOWLEDGEMENTS

The author and publisher would like to thank the following for permission to reproduce photographs:

Getty Images/Javier Soriano, Fabian Marun, Adidas, Getty Images/Boris Streubel, ullsteinbild/TopFoto, Getty Images/Robert Michael, Getty Images/Martin Rose, Getty Images/AFP, Getty Images/Stuart McFarlane, picture-alliance/Sven Simon, Getty Images, dpa, Horst. A. Friedrichs London, Getty Images/Stuart Franklin, Getty Images/Lars Baron, Getty Images/John MacDougall, Getty Images/David R. Anchuelo, Getty Images/Steve Haag, Getty Images/Pool, Getty Images/Dominique Faget, Getty Images/Cesar Manso, Getty Images/Angel Martinez, Getty Images/ Josep Lago, Getty Images/Lluis Gene, Getty Images/Pierre Philippe Marcou, Getty Images/David Price, Julian Baumann, Getty Images/Patrik Stollarz, Getty Images/ Lars Baron/FIFA, Dennis Brosda, ©Colorsport/Andrew Cowie, Chadwick/ANL/ REX/Shutterstock, Marc Atkins/Offside, Chadwick/ANL/REX/Shutterstock, Xinhua / Alamy Stock Photo, REUTERS / Alamy Stock Photo, Matthew Ashton/ AMA/Corbis via Getty Images, Julian Finney/Getty Images, Xinhua/Alamy Stock Photo, Marc Atkins/Offside, James Marsh/BPI/REX/Shutterstock, Adam Davy/ PA Archive/PA Images, BPI/REX/Shutterstock, Stuart MacFarlane/Arsenal FC via Getty Images, JUSTIN TALLIS/AFP/Getty Images

Other photographs are from private collections.

Every reasonable effort has been made to trace the copyright holders, but if there are any errors or omissions, Hodder & Stoughton will be pleased to insert the appropriate acknowledgement in any subsequent printings or editions.

INDEX

305

Index

Index

An invitation from the publisher

Join us at www.hodder.co.uk, or follow us
on Twitter @hodderbooks to be a part of
our community of people who love the very
best in books and reading.

Whether you want to discover more about a book
or an author, watch trailers and interviews, have the
chance to win early limited editions, or simply browse
our expert readers' selection of the very best books,
we think you'll find what you're looking for.

And if you don't, that's the place to tell us what's missing.

We love what we do, and we'd love you to be a part of it.

www.hodder.co.uk

@hodderbooks

HodderBooks

HodderBooks